It has long been asserted by Calvinists that the doctrine of *Regeneration Precedes Faith* is the linchpin of Calvinism and that it is dogmatically affirmed in the New Testament. However, *theological traditions are not to be assumed automatically or assimilated uncritically. Theological traditions must be open to inspection and if necessary, rejection.* Bob Kerrey understands what Calvinism teaches regarding regeneration precedes faith. He does an excellent job demonstrating the Scriptures teach Faith Precedes Regeneration.

—Fred Chay, PhD
Professor of Theology
Grace School of Theology

Kerrey's work is groundbreaking in that he deftly navigates the choppy theological waters and proffers something of a *via media* for our consideration. Methodologically, Kerrey engages in an exegesis of all the key texts impinging on the question. He lists and discusses all the arguments in favor of the two major positions and then seeks to construct from Scripture a better alternative that best harmonizes all the biblical data.

The topic could not be more important. This work is a significant advance in the seeming stalemate between competing views. Kudos to Dr. Kerrey for forging a well-constructed, biblical path forward.

—David L. Allen, PhD
Dean of the School of Preaching
Southwestern Baptist Theological Seminary

A passage like John 6:44 is a trigger text for a theological controversy. What does it mean that God draws people to Jesus Christ? Bob Kerrey jumps headlong into the different theological views that influence interpretation of the passage, and along the way covers a multitude of relevant verses used by those views, from strong Calvinists to Arminians. He settles on a view that is both theologically and scripturally satisfying and applies it to John 6:44 making good use of the context. The reader will find that Kerrey is thorough, fair, convincing, and humble—he is willing to admit what he does not know. It is also helpful when he shows how one's theological position impacts life and ministry. I guess I can say that when I read the Table of Contents, I was drawn in such a way that I chose to read every word of this definitive work. I think readers will agree and discover that Kerrey has done a masterful job.

—Charlie Bing, PhD
Founder and Director of GraceLife Ministries

I love this book! It has filled a lacuna in my own understanding of numerous passages related to the question of whether regeneration precedes faith or follows it. The latter view always seemed to have more credibility to me. However, by zeroing in on the question of "How does God draw all men to Himself," Bob Kerrey leads us to the core of the issue. Is this drawing achieved by regeneration or by Spirit guided illumination and God's providential guidance. The former is deterministic and applies only to the elect thus leaving millions born in sin with no recourse. They are eternally damned before they had a chance to believe. With compelling exegesis of all the relevant passages, and thoughtful and irenic interaction with those who disagree, Kerrey argues that God draws all men without exception.

—Joseph Dillow, ThD
Author of *Final Destiny: The Future Reign of the Servant Kings*

How Does God Draw People to Believe in Jesus?

A Biblical Analysis of Alternative Answers and Why It Matters

Robert J. Kerrey

How Does God Draw People to Believe in Jesus?
A Biblical Analysis of Alternative Answers and Why It Matters

Copyright © 2019 by Robert J. Kerrey

Published by Grace Theology Press.

All rights reserved. No part of this book may be reproduced in any form without permission in writing from the author, except in the case of brief quotations embodied in or reviews or in the case of using the material to teach on the subject.

Unless otherwise indicated, all Scripture quotations are from The Holy Bible, English Standard Version®, copyright © 2001 by Crossway, a publishing ministry of Good News Publishers. Used by permission. All rights reserved.

Scripture quotations marked NASB are taken from the New American Standard Bible®, copyright © 1960, 1995 by the Lockman Foundation. Used by permission. All rights reserved.

Scripture quotations marked NKJV are taken from the New King James Version®, copyright © 1982 by Thomas Nelson. Used by permission. All rights reserved.

Scripture quotations marked NLT are taken from the New Living Translation®, copyright © 1996, 2004, 2007 by Tyndale House Publishers, Inc. Used by permission. All right reserved.

ISBN:10 1-7336223-6-5 | ISBN-13: 978-1-7336223-6-3
eISBN-10: 1-6337223-8-1 | eISBN-13: 978-1-7336223-8-7

Special Sales: Most Grace Theology Press titles are available in special quantity discounts. Custom imprinting or excerpting can also be done to fit special needs. Contact Grace Theology Press at info@gracetheology.org.

Printed in the United States of America

CONTENTS

FOREWORD xiii
PREFACE xv
LIST OF FIGURES xix
LIST OF TABLES xxi
LIST OF ABBREVIATIONS xxiii
INTRODUCTION 1
  Purpose 1
    The Faith-After-Regeneration View 1
    The Faith-Before-Regeneration View 3
      The Arminian View 4
      The Modified View 5
        The Deterministic Modified View 6
        The Nondeterministic Modified View 6
  Reasons 8
  Methodology 12
  Definitions 12
    Faith 12
    Regeneration 16
    Monergism & Synergism 19
    Logical & Temporal Priority 22

CHAPTER 1: ARGUMENTS FOR THE FAITH-AFTER-REGENERATION VIEW EXPLAINED AND REBUTTED 25

Argument 1: Scripture Teaches Total Inability 26

Genesis 6:5; 8:21 29
Psalm 14:1-3; Romans 3:10-19 29
John 6:44, 65 30
John 8:36 32
John 15:5 33
Acts 9:1-4; 26:14 33
Romans 1:18 34
Romans 8:6 34
Romans 9:14-16 34
1 Corinthians 2:14 35
2 Corinthians 3:5 35
Ephesians 2:1-5 35
Philippians 1:6 36
Philippians 2:13 37
Rebuttal of Argument 1 37

From the Deterministic Modified View 38
From the Arminian View 41
From the Nondeterministic Modified View 41

Genesis 1:27; 9:6; James 3:9 43
Genesis 3:8-10 45
Genesis 4:3-7 45
Genesis 41:8; 1 Kings 21:5; 1 Chronicles 5:26; 2 Chronicles 36:22; Daniel 2:1; 5:5-6 46
Exodus 12:37-38 47
Matthew 13:10-17 48

Luke 8:4-15 49
John 7:17 50
Acts 10:1-2 51
Romans 1:18-20 52
Romans 6:17 53
Romans 16:25-27 55
2 Corinthians 4:3-6 56
Revelation 14:6-7 57

Argument 2: Scripture Teaches that Regeneration Precedes Faith 58

Scriptures about the Circumcision and Gift of a New Heart 58

Deuteronomy 30:6 59
Jeremiah 31:33; 32:39-40 59
Ezekiel 11:19-21; 36:26-27 60
Ezekiel 37:1-14 61
Rebuttal 63

Zephaniah 3:9 & Rebuttal 65
John 1:12-13 & Rebuttal 68
John 3:3-8 & Rebuttal 71
Acts 5:31; 11:18; 2 Timothy 2:24-26 & Rebuttal 76
Acts 9:1-20 & Rebuttal 79
Acts 13:48; Ephesians 2:8-9; Philippians 1:29-30; 2 Peter 1:1 & Rebuttal 81
Acts 16:13-15 & Rebuttal 86
2 Corinthians 4:3-6 & Rebuttal 88
Ephesians 2:1-7 & Rebuttal 89
Colossians 2:11-14 & Rebuttal 94
Titus 3:3-7 & Rebuttal 96

James 1:18 & Rebuttal 98

1 Peter 1:3-5 & Rebuttal 101

1 John 5:1 & Rebuttal 102

    Grammatical Argument 103

    Contextual Argument 108

Concluding Evaluation of
the Faith-After-Regeneration View 111

CHAPTER 2: ARGUMENTS FOR THE FAITH-BEFORE-REGENERATION VIEW EXPLAINED AND DEFENDED 115

Argument 1: Scripture Teaches that Faith Comes Before Eternal Life 116

    John 3:14-16 116

    John 3:36 116

    John 5:24 117

    John 5:39-40 117

    John 6:51 117

    John 6:53-54, 57 117

    John 11:25 117

    John 20:31 117

    1 John 5:1 118

    Rebuttal of Argument 1 & Rejoinder 118

Argument 2: Scripture Teaches that Faith Comes Before the Holy Spirit 120

    John 7:38-39 120

    Acts 2:38 120

    Galatians 3:13-14 120

    Galatians 4:6 121

Ephesians 1:13-14 121
Rebuttal of Argument 2 & Rejoinder 121
Argument 3: Scripture Teaches that Faith Comes Before Eternal Salvation 123
Mark 16:15-16 123
John 1:12 123
Acts 13:39 124
Acts 16:31 124
Acts 18:8 124
Romans 1:16 124
Romans 10:9-10 124
1 Corinthians 1:21 125
Hebrews 11:6 125
Rebuttal of Argument 3 & Rejoinder 125
More Evidence 128
Ezekiel 18:30-32 128
Acts 11:18 129
Acts 15:9 129
Galatians 3:26 129
John 12:36 129
Galatians 3:2, 5 129
2 Corinthians 3:14-16 130
1 Timothy 1:16 130
Colossians 2:12 130
James 1:18 131
Concluding Evaluation of the Faith-Before-Regeneration View 131

CHAPTER 3: THE NONDETERMINISTIC MODIFIED VIEW EXPLAINED AND DEFENDED 133

The Context and Meaning of John 6:44 as a Model for How God Draws 134

The Meaning and Use of the Word, "Draw" 135
The Context of John 6:44 149
The Role of the Father 156
The Role of Jesus 159
The Role of Humanity 160
The Role of Jesus Continued 162
The Meaning of John 6:44 in Context 163
Objection Answered 164

Some Other Ways God Draws 168
The Holy Spirit 168
Creation 169
The Behavior of Believers 171

More Affirmations 173

The Deterministic Modified View Explained and Rebutted 178
Explanation of the Deterministic Modified View 178
Rebuttal of the Deterministic Modified View 187
Election and Romans 8:29-30 Need Not Be Interpreted Deterministically 188
An Alternative Interpretation 188
Other Interpretations 189
The Deterministic Modified View Renders the General Call Meaningless 191
The Deterministic Modified View Calls into Question the Goodness of God 193

God's Love 193
God's Integrity 195
God's Fairness & Association with Sin 195

**The Deterministic Modified View Is Unclear about
What the Effectual Call Involves** 197

The Arminian View Explained and Rebutted 202

**Concluding Evaluation of
the Nondeterministic Modified View** 206

CHAPTER 4: PASTORAL IMPLICATIONS OF THE NONDETERMINISTIC MODIFIED VIEW 207

Implications for What God Is Like 207

Implications for the Primacy of Scripture 208

Implications for Giving an Answer 210

Implications for Humility 214

Eating Humble Pie and Crow 214

Middle Ground 215

Food for Thought from a Calvinist and a Liberal 216

Implications for Evangelism 217

Implications for Assurance 218

Implications for Further Study 223

Concluding Comment on Implications 223

CONCLUSION 225
APPENDIX: UNDERSTANDING JOHN 2:23-25 231
SCRIPTURE INDEX 239
AUTHOR INDEX 245
BIBLIOGRAPHY 249

FOREWORD

For centuries, theologians have wrangled over precisely what the Bible teaches about the role of the Holy Spirit in drawing people to faith in Christ. At issue is just what is the meaning of John 6:44: "No one can come to me unless the Father who sent me draws him." Since the time of the Reformation, theologians have posited different "logical orders," (*ordo salutis*), for repentance, faith, regeneration, conversion, justification, sanctification, etc. At the heart of this debate is whether faith precedes regeneration or whether regeneration precedes faith.

The debate breaks down roughly along the lines of a Calvinist (Reformed) view vs. an Arminian (non-Calvinist) view, with most Calvinists asserting regeneration precedes faith and all non-Calvinists, including Arminians, asserting faith precedes regeneration. Then there are issues as to the meaning of "precedes" in these debates. Are we talking about temporal order, logical order, or both?

Additionally, informing how one approaches this topic are the anthropological and hamartiological questions swirling around the nature and description of human depravity brought about by Adam's sin. Does the theological notion of "total depravity" include or exclude human ability to respond to the gospel offer? Is regeneration a purely monergistic act or synergistic in nature? Do humans possess some form of libertarian freedom or not? What is the nature of saving faith?

Kerrey's work is groundbreaking in that he deftly navigates the choppy theological waters and proffers something of a *via media* for our consideration. Methodologically, Kerrey engages in an exegesis of all the key texts impinging on the question. He lists and discusses all the arguments in favor of the two major positions and then seeks to construct from Scripture a better alternative that best harmonizes all the biblical data.

The topic could not be more important. This work is a significant advance in the seeming stalemate between competing views. Kudos to Dr. Kerrey for forging a well-constructed, biblical path forward.

—David L. Allen, PhD
Dean of the School of Preaching
Southwestern Baptist Theological Seminary

PREFACE

THIS IS A book about a question: how does God draw people to believe in Jesus? When I began my research, I confess I didn't know the answer. Oh, I had some ideas, but they felt fuzzy, flimsy, and frustrating. I had a bunch of related questions circling beneath the one big question. In coming to faith in Jesus, what is God's part and what is our part? Does God make us believe? Do we have a choice in the matter? And if we do have a choice, is that taking anything away from God? Am I a "moderate Calvinist" as I have described myself before? And what does that term really mean anyway?

So, this book is not so much about me having an axe to grind; it is more a record of my own journey to find a better answer. If this contributes in some small way to scholarship or to someone else's understanding of the issues, so much the better.

Just before this book went to press, I asked some friends and colleagues to proofread it. I deliberately chose a diverse group of readers I thought might have a good eye, some with formal theological training, others with little or none. One of them never got past the introduction and gave up. In his apology to me, he writes: "I cannot explain why I am struggling so much with the content, but I suspect it is because I have always resisted getting caught up in these types of theological debates so I have never understood them or their importance. Now, I truly find it exhausting just to try to sort through it and understand it."

I don't blame him. It can be exhausting. In the process of doing this research and writing this book, more than once I asked myself, "Is this really worth it? Does it matter?"

As Christians, we all have certain opinions about how God draws people to believe, whether we've thought through them carefully or not. I now realize more fully these opinions shape our view of some of the most important things in life: God, Scripture, salvation, evangelism, assurance, and our very nature as responders to God. Having endured the pain of sorting through and trying to understand all this, I can say with greater personal conviction than ever, it matters.

I owe so much to so many I'm bound to leave out someone in giving thanks. Hands down, first thanks goes to Fred Chay. As my encouraging advisor, Fred put the idea in my head that my doctoral dissertation could turn into something read by more than six people. As my benevolent taskmaster and promoter, Fred pushed and peppered me with good questions and suggestions on research and writing, and he introduced my work to important people who didn't know me from Adam.

Many thanks go also to David Allen. I had never met David before, but grew to admire his work in doing my research. I decided to shoot for the moon and ask him to serve as a reader for my dissertation. He agreed. What's more, he hosted my oral defense, provided valuable feedback on my work, and wrote the foreword to this book.

In addition, I'm very grateful to Earl Radmacher and Kem Oberholtzer for being my mentors during my formative years in seminary. They instilled in me a love for Scripture and a healthy fear to interpret it with care and integrity.

I also want to thank Charlie Bing and Joseph Dillow for reviewing and endorsing this book. That they would lend their time and their name to a relative unknown is a humbling testimony to their grace toward me.

To make sure more than six people would read this, I recruited eight proofreaders: Ricky and Mavis Amano, John and Linda Gemmill, Chris Lyding, David and Joy Simmons, and Mark Spencer. I am so grateful to them. They caught an embarrassing number of errors, and each person made a unique and helpful contribution to making my work better. Any remaining errors are of course all on me. Special thanks goes to the Gemmills and the Lydings, long-time friends who have faithfully supported me through thick and thin.

Last but not least, I want to thank my wife Cathy. Without her ongoing love and support, this book would not be possible. Technically, she didn't write a word. But we are so much a part of each other, and I floated so many ideas and questions by her, she should be the coauthor.

LIST OF FIGURES

1. Order of Events in Colossians 2:11-14 95
2. Grammatical Argument for the Faith-After-Regeneration View from 1 John 5:1 103
3. Grammatical Argument for the Faith-After-Regeneration View from 1 John 5:1 Contradicted by Other Scriptures 107
4. Aspects of Salvation 127
5. The Golden Chain of Salvation from Romans 8:29-30 183

LIST OF TABLES

1	Summary of Views on How God Draws People to Believe	7
2	Summary of Views on How God Draws People to Believe with the Focus of Chapter 1 Highlighted	25
3	Instances in 1 John Where the Verb or Participle "Born" (γεννάω) Is in the Perfect Tense	109
4	Summary of Views on How God Draws People to Believe with the Focus of Chapter 2 Highlighted	115
5	Summary of Views on How God Draws People to Believe with the Focus of Chapter 3 Highlighted	133
6.1	All Uses of ἕλκω in the New Testament and Septuagint	138
6.2	All Uses of ἕλκω in the New Testament and Septuagint (Continued)	139
6.3	All Uses of ἕλκω in the New Testament and Septuagint (Continued)	140
7	Willingness to be Drawn among Persons Drawn Physically	142
8	Willingness to be Drawn among Persons Drawn Non-Physically	144
9	Parallel Statements in John 6:39-40	158
10	All Instances in John 6 Where Jesus Says, "Come to Me"	166
11	Logic of the Deterministic Modified View	185
12	Concluding Summary of Views on How God Draws People to Believe	226

LIST OF ABBREVIATIONS

BDAG   Bauer, W., F. W. Danker, W. F. Arndt, and F. W. Gingrich. *A Greek-English Lexicon of the New Testament and Other Early Christian Literature.* 3rd ed. Chicago: University of Chicago Press, 2000.

ESV   The Holy Bible, English Standard Version®. Wheaton: Crossway, 2001.

LXX   Septuaginta (Old Greek Jewish Scriptures) Alfred Rahlfs ed. Stuttgart, Germany: German Bible Society, 1935.

NASB   The Holy Bible, New American Standard Bible®. La Habra: The Lockman Foundation, 1960, 1995.

NKJV   The Holy Bible, New King James Version®. Nashville: Thomas Nelson, 1982.

NLT   The Holy Bible, New Living Translation®. Carol Stream: Tyndale, 1996, 2004, 2007.

INTRODUCTION

Purpose

THE PURPOSE OF this work is to seek a better answer to the question: how does God draw people to believe in Jesus? That God does in fact draw people to believe is clear and conceded. Jesus himself makes the point in John 6:44: "No one can come to me unless the Father who sent me *draws* him" (ESV, emphasis added).[1]

What is unclear and widely contested, however, is just exactly how and when God draws us, and what our part is in the process. Arguments have traditionally boiled down to differences regarding the logical order of elements involved in salvation, otherwise known as the *ordo salutis*. Specifically, at issue is whether faith precedes or follows regeneration in which God gives new life.

The Faith-After-Regeneration View

Those who argue that faith follows regeneration are traditionally described as having a Calvinist or Reformed point of view.[2] Nevertheless,

---

[1] As evident in this first paragraph, divine pronouns will generally not be capitalized in this work, consistent with the *English Standard Version* of the Bible used throughout. Some exceptions occur when quoting authors who do use such capitalization.

[2] The terms "Calvinist" and "Reformed" will be used interchangeably.

for the sake of clarity and confining the argument, I will call this the faith-after-regeneration view. This is a more helpful label because Calvinism and Reformed theology encompass more than just the order of faith and regeneration.³ Moreover, some who identify themselves with Calvinism and Reformed theology do not agree on the order of these two elements.⁴

A summary of the faith-after-regeneration view is this: because of the total depravity of humankind, God must regenerate a person first for that person to believe. Moreover, having been regenerated, that person will certainly believe because faith itself is a gift from God tied to regeneration. As such, God's grace in drawing those he has chosen is traditionally described as irresistible. This view is deterministic in the sense that there is no genuine human freedom which permits a person to choose freely between two options—to accept or reject, to believe or disbelieve—because God determines.⁵ People play no role whatsoever

---

3   It is worth noting that Oliver Crisp, a Calvinist, contends that while the famous five points of Calvinism (total depravity, unconditional election, limited atonement, irresistible grace, and perseverance of the saints—acronym T.U.L.I.P.) summarize much of Reformed thought, the Reformed "tent" is historically bigger, including a broader spectrum of thinking than the narrower modern version may imply. See Oliver D. Crisp, *Saving Calvinism: Expanding the Reformed Tradition* (Downers Grove, IL: InterVarsity Press, 2016), 11-23.

4   An example is Bruce Demarest, who holds a faith-before-regeneration view, but describes his position as "Reformed" in Bruce Demarest, *The Cross and Salvation* (Wheaton, IL: Crossway, 1997), 289.

5   Reformed theologian, Richard A. Muller has recently argued that modern Reformed writers in the line of Jonathan Edwards who advocate determinism or compatibilism are not necessarily representative of historical Reformed orthodoxy, which he says is not philosophically or metaphysically deterministic. At the same time, he admits that *in soteriological matters* Reformed orthodox theology teaches that human beings have no power to choose or refuse the gift of saving grace. As such, *in soteriological matters*, Reformed theology remains deterministic and this is still an accurate label for the faith-after-regeneration view. See Richard

in regeneration. In effect, there is no human freedom or ability to respond to God; God does it all. A person cannot be persuaded to believe; he must be made to believe by God.[6] That's how God draws.[7]

The Faith-Before-Regeneration View

In contrast, those who argue that faith precedes regeneration are often associated with Arminianism. Nevertheless, for the sake of clarity and confining the argument, I will call this the faith-before-regeneration view. Again, this is a more helpful label because, like Calvinism, Arminianism encompasses more than just the order of faith and regeneration. Moreover, many who hold that faith precedes regeneration (including some moderate Calvinists, dispensationalists, traditionalists, and free-grace proponents) would not be comfortable wearing the "Arminian" label because it implies assent to some other Arminian doctrines to which they do not subscribe.

The faith-before-regeneration view argues that God's regeneration is logically conditioned upon a person's prior faith. In this way of thinking, people do play a role in regeneration: they must believe before God will regenerate them. Moreover, the person who comes to faith has

---

A. Muller, *Divine Will and Human Choice: Freedom, Contingency, and Necessity in Early Modern Reformed Thought* (Grand Rapids, MI: Baker Academic, 2017), 19-22, 322-323.

[6] Many faith-after-regeneration proponents would be quick to point out that the regenerate person "freely" chooses to believe and is not coerced. Nevertheless, in Reformed thinking, God creates a regenerate person who not only desires to believe, but also will believe, must believe, and could not do otherwise. So, in this view, faith is essentially manufactured.

[7] Some notable modern proponents of the faith-after-regeneration view who are cited in this work include: Matthew Barrett, D. A. Carson, Wayne Grudem, John MacArthur, J. I. Packer, John Piper, Thomas Schreiner, Mark Snoeberger, R. C. Sproul, and James White. Not everyone who holds this view may agree with every aspect of my characterization of it, but I have tried to provide a fair generalization.

some ability and responsibility to believe prior to regeneration, subject to God's initiative and help.

Within the faith-before-regeneration camp, however, there is some disagreement about the nature and extent of both our ability to believe and God's initiative in bringing us to faith.

The Arminian View

The Arminian view generally argues that, by the universally bestowed prevenient grace of God, everyone has the freedom and capacity to believe. It is through this prevenient grace that God draws everyone, and it is entirely up to the individual to accept or resist. The Arminian view is nondeterministic in the sense that a person is considered to have genuine freedom and ability to choose freely between two options, to believe or disbelieve. According to this view, the grace of God in drawing people to believe is resistible.

This Arminian view is generally accompanied by the belief that once a person is regenerated he or she can lose eternal salvation by turning away from Christ.[8] Since eternal salvation is conditioned on faith, it is believed that eternal security must likewise be conditioned on continuing faith.[9]

---

[8] Most but not all who hold the Arminian view believe that eternal salvation can be lost. Arminian Roger Olson says, "I think one can believe in 'once saved, always saved' (inamissable grace) and be a good Arminian" (Ben Witherington and Roger Olson, "Roger Olson's Arminian Theology—Part 7," Society of Evangelical Arminians, November 11, 2016, accessed November 3, 2017, http://evangelicalarminians.org/ben-witherington-and-roger-olson-roger-olsons-arminian-theology-part-7/).

[9] Some notable modern proponents of the Arminian view who are cited in this work include: Brian Abasciano, F. Leroy Forlines, Thomas Oden, Roger Olson, and W. Brian Shelton. Again, not everyone who holds this view may agree with every aspect of my characterization of it, but I have tried to provide a fair generalization. (Some may not even accept the label Arminian, but generally hold to its tenets.)

The Modified View

Others in the faith-before-regeneration camp hold a view that lies somewhere between the determinism of Calvinism, in which humans play no role whatsoever in their eternal salvation, and the nondeterminism of Arminianism, in which humans can freely check in and out of eternal salvation according to their faith decisions. This has been called a modified view or middle way because it is in some ways like Calvinism and in other ways like Arminianism.[10] It will be identified as the modified view in this work.[11]

Like Calvinism, the modified view holds that people are unable to believe in Jesus apart from some kind of enablement from God that leads to faith. The difference is in what the special enablement actually is. In the Calvinist view, the special enablement is regeneration; in the modified view, the special divine enablement is something else, such as an effectual call or divine illumination, which will be discussed later.

Like Arminianism, the modified view holds that faith precedes regeneration. Unlike Arminians, modified view proponents generally do not use the term, "prevenient grace" to describe God's enablement to believe, even though the enabling grace in the modified view seems to overlap the Arminian idea of prevenient grace in some ways. Also, those who hold a modified view generally do not hold to the Arminian idea that once regenerated, a person can lose eternal salvation.

The modified view can be further divided into two camps, deterministic and nondeterministic. I have found these designations to be helpful, although they are not commonly used in the theological literature.

---

[10] Matthew Barrett, *Salvation by Grace: The Case for Effectual Calling and Regeneration* (Phillipsburg, NJ: P&R Publishing, 2013), xxiii-xxv, 283.

[11] "Modified" was chosen instead of "middle" so as not to confuse this with the middle knowledge associated with Molinism.

How Does God Draw People to Believe in Jesus?

The Deterministic Modified View

According to the deterministic modified view, while God does extend a common grace to all, we remain unable to believe apart from a special or effectual calling of God. God effectually calls only those whom he chooses according to his sovereign will, and those whom he calls will believe. In the *ordo salutis*, there is an irresistible effectual call leading to faith and then regeneration.

Those who hold this view generally have Reformed leanings but are persuaded by biblical evidence to break ranks with most Calvinists by believing that faith comes *before* regeneration, not after. This view remains deterministic, however, in the sense that the effectual call is unilaterally and unconditionally given by God to the elect who will surely believe because the call is irresistible.[12]

The Nondeterministic Modified View

According to the nondeterministic modified view, God draws people to believe in various ways that fall under the rubric of divine illumination or divine enablement or divine persuasion. While this divine illumination is essential—no one can believe without it—it can be resisted. All have some capacity and responsibility to respond to God's illumination, and as they do, God draws by giving more light leading to faith. In response to God's illumination, people have a genuine choice between two alternatives, to believe or disbelieve.[13]

---

[12] Some notable modern proponents of the deterministic modified view who are cited in this work include: Lewis Sperry Chafer, R. Bruce Compton, Bruce Demarest, Millard Erickson, Gordon Lewis, Robert Pyne, and John Walvoord. Again, not everyone who holds this view may agree with every aspect of my characterization of it, but I have tried to provide a fair generalization.

[13] Some notable modern proponents of the nondeterministic modified view who are cited in this work include: Roy Aldrich, David Allen, David Anderson, Charles Bing, Fred Chay, Joseph Dillow, Leighton Flowers, Eric Hankins, Zane Hodges, Steve Lemke, George Meisinger, Earl Radmacher,

Introduction

All the above views are summarized in Table 1, which can be used as a guide.

Table 1. Summary of Views on How God Draws People to Believe

Faith-After-Regeneration View: (Calvinism/ Reformed Theology)	Faith-Before-Regeneration View:		
	Modified View:		Arminian View:
	Deterministic:	Nondeterministic:	
Regeneration (irresistible)	*Effectual Call* (irresistible)	*Divine Illumination* (resistible)	*Prevenient Grace* (resistible)

Much has been written in the Calvinism-versus-Arminianism debate. This work is not intended to address all points of contention, much less resolve them. It does, however, set out to investigate more fully two interrelated issues that seem central.

First, based on biblical data alone, can it be shown that the faith-before-regeneration view is more biblically consistent than the faith-after-regeneration view? If not—if the faith-after-regeneration view prevails—then the question that prompted this work has effectively been answered. The question is: how does God draw people to believe in Jesus? The answer would be: God regenerates them.

If, however, the faith-before-regeneration view prevails, then there remains an evaluation of the three alternative views within it. This work

---

and Robert Wilkin. Again, not everyone who holds this view may agree with every aspect of my characterization of it, but I have tried to provide a fair generalization.

concludes the nondeterministic modified view is the most strongly supported option and explains what divine illumination involves.

Reasons

Finding a better answer to how and when God draws people to believe in Jesus has far-reaching theological, pastoral, and personal implications.

Reformed theology has recently enjoyed a resurgence of popularity in America, and many popular evangelical authors are Calvinists. Columnist Mark Oppenheimer in the *New York Times* explains:

> Evangelicalism is in the midst of a Calvinist revival. Increasing numbers of preachers and professors teach the views of the 16th-century French reformer. Mark Driscoll, John Piper, and Tim Keller—megachurch preachers and important evangelical authors—are all Calvinist. Attendance at Calvin-influenced worship conferences and churches is up, particularly among worshipers in their 20s and 30s.[14]

---

[14] Mark Oppenheimer, "Evangelicals Find Themselves in the Midst of a Calvinist Revival," *The New York Times*, January 4, 2014. More recently, Mark Driscoll seems to renounce Calvinism, saying, "I don't hold to the five points of Calvinism; I think it's garbage . . . because it's not biblical" (Mark Driscoll, "Real Conversations: Pastor Mark Driscoll, Part 2," The Debrief Show, June 4, 2019, accessed July 18, 2019, https://www.youtube.com/watch?time_continue=3534&v=4OsQm6YU3OY). But then just weeks after making this statement, he prevaricates: "I am Reformed. I believe in monergism. . . . If I had to choose between the five points of Arminianism and the five points of Calvinism, I'd pick the five points of Calvinism 'cause they're better, but I don't quite frankly think that they're great" (Mark Driscoll, "What does the Bible say about Calvinism vs. Arminianism," Mark Driscoll Ministries, July 16, 2019, accessed July 19, 2019, https://www.youtube.com/watch?v=KU0szpsemeU).

Introduction

Calvinist Collin Hansen, author of the popular 2008 book, *Young, Restless, Reformed* looks back over the last decade since his book was published:

> Reformed theology may go down like a stiff drink, but it gives Christians backbone. This initial surge of Reformed theology came with John Piper telling us not to waste our lives. With Albert Mohler teaching worldview as a modern-day Francis Schaeffer. With Matt Chandler preaching sermons on God's beauty and love, uploaded to YouTube with viral effect. With Tim Keller writing book after book after book of cultural apologetics. With Kevin DeYoung churning out timely, clear, convicted blog posts.[15]

As Calvinism becomes more popular, it is reasonable to expect that evangelical pastors will be increasingly faced with questions from their congregants relating to Reformed theology. From a theological standpoint, the faith-after-regeneration view is integral and unique to Reformed theology. Calvinist R. C. Sproul confirms this:

> The classic issue between Augustinian [Reformed] theology and all forms of semi-Pelagianism [non-Reformed theology] focuses on one aspect of the order of salvation (*ordo salutis*): What is the relationship between regeneration and faith? . . . Must a person first exercise faith in order to be born again? Or must rebirth occur before a person is able to exercise faith?[16]

---

[15] Collin Hansen, "Still Young, Restless, and Reformed? The New Calvinists at 10," 9Marks, February 5, 2019, accessed May 6, 2019, https://www.9marks.org/article/still-young-restless-and-reformed-the-new-calvinists-at-10/.

[16] R. C. Sproul, *Willing to Believe: The Controversy Over Free Will* (Grand Rapids, MI: Baker Books, 1997), 196.

The integrity of Reformed theology depends on the soundness of the arguments for the faith-after-regeneration view. In fact, Calvinist Matthew Barrett says the faith-after-regeneration rationale "may be the very hinge of the Calvinist position."[17] As such, greater familiarity with the arguments for and against "the hinge" will put pastors in a better position to interact with their congregants.

While much has been written in the Calvinism-versus-Arminianism debate, much less has been written about the modified view. Mark Snoeberger, a Calvinist, traces the modified view back to the latter half of the eighteenth century, in which three men from within the Reformed tradition, Archibald McLean, John Glas, and Robert Sandeman developed an *ordo salutis* in which faith—defined simply as believing that the facts of salvation are true—precedes regeneration.[18] According to Snoeberger, this view was strongly opposed by other Reformed theologians and eventually faded, until it resurfaced in the nineteenth century and found its most successful voice when the early leaders of Dallas Theological Seminary began to teach the modified view as a form of moderate Calvinism.[19]

Indeed, Lewis Sperry Chafer, John Walvoord, and Roy Aldrich, three early professors of Dallas Theological Seminary, taught the modified view in the context of dispensationalism.[20] The modified view finds more recent expression in the writings of David Anderson, Bruce Demarest, Millard Erickson, Gordon Lewis, and Robert Pyne, among

---

[17] Barrett, *Salvation by Grace*, xxi.

[18] Mark A. Snoeberger, "The Logical Priority of Regeneration to Saving Faith in a Theological *Ordo Salutis*," *Detroit Baptist Seminary Journal* 7 (2002): 49-51. Whether Snoeberger traces the history of the modified view in general or the deterministic modified view in particular is not entirely clear.

[19] Ibid.

[20] Roy L. Aldrich, "The Gift of God," *Bibliotheca Sacra* 122 (July-September, 1965): 252-253; Lewis Sperry Chafer, *Systematic Theology*, 8 vols., (Grand Rapids, MI: Kregel, 1993), 3:222-224, 7:264-265; John F. Walvoord, *The Holy Spirit* (Wheaton: Van Kampen Press, 1954), 119-137.

others, not all of whom are dispensationalists (and not all of whom agree on whether God's drawing is deterministic).[21]

Snoeberger observes that, although the modified view has enjoyed considerable acceptance, it has not been widely or thoroughly defended in scholarly works, nor has it been widely or thoroughly rebutted because Calvinists have largely eschewed it out of hand, leaving a gap in the systematic analysis of both positions.[22] Recently, Barrett has taken a step toward filling the gap from the faith-after-regeneration point of view.[23] More recently, R. Bruce Compton has argued for the deterministic modified view.[24] This work undertakes to fill the gap from the nondeterministic modified point of view.[25]

---

[21] David R. Anderson, "Regeneration: A Crux Interpretum," *Journal of the Grace Evangelical Society*, 16 no. 33 (Autumn 2004), 43-65; David R. Anderson, *Free Grace Soteriology*, 3rd ed. (n.p.: Grace Theology Press, 2018), 118-124, 229-257, Kindle; Demarest, *The Cross and Salvation*, 227, 265; Millard J Erickson, *Christian Theology*, 3rd ed. (Grand Rapids: Baker, 2013), 864; Gordon R. Lewis and Bruce A. Demarest, *Integrative Theology*, 3 vols. (Grand Rapids: Zondervan, 1994), 3:56-58, 104; Robert A. Pyne, "The Role of the Holy Spirit in Conversion," *Bibliotheca Sacra*, 150 (1993): 203-218.

[22] Snoeberger, "The Logical Priority of Regeneration to Saving Faith in a Theological *Ordo Salutis*," 51.

[23] Barrett, *Salvation by Grace*, xxiii-xxv, 283-314.

[24] R. Bruce Compton, "The *Ordo Salutis* and Monergism: The Case for Faith Preceding Regeneration, Part 1," *Bibliotheca Sacra*, 175 (January-March 2018): 34-39; R. Bruce Compton, "The *Ordo Salutis* and Monergism: The Case for Faith Preceding Regeneration, Part 2," *Bibliotheca Sacra*, 175 (April-June 2018): 159-173; R. Bruce Compton, "The *Ordo Salutis* and Monergism: The Case for Faith Preceding Regeneration, Part 3," *Bibliotheca Sacra*, 175 (July-September 2018): 284-303.

[25] Recently, Veli-Matti Kärkkäinen has proposed what he describes as "a radical middle course between the Scylla of Pelagianism and the Charybdis of extreme Augustinian Calvinism," but his work is not primarily exegetical. Veli-Matti Kärkkäinen, *Spirit and Salvation*, vol. 4, A

Methodology

The primary focus of this work will be on the exegesis of pertinent biblical passages, not historical theology. In chapter 1, biblical arguments for the faith-after-regeneration view are presented first, along with rebuttals. Chapter 2 presents biblical arguments for the faith-before-regeneration view, along with rebuttals. Chapter 3 provides arguments for the nondeterministic modified view as over against alternative faith-before-regeneration views. Finally, in chapter 4, the pastoral implications of the nondeterministic modified view are considered.

Definitions

To establish some common ground for discussion, it is necessary to define a few important terms.

Faith

The faith to which I will refer again and again in this work is the faith in Jesus Christ that is inextricably linked to regeneration and eternal salvation. It is the faith of which the Apostle Paul writes in Ephesians 2:8, "For by grace you have been saved through faith" (ESV). It is the faith of the woman who anointed the feet of Jesus, to whom he says, "Your faith has saved you; go in peace" (Luke 7:50, ESV). Some call it saving faith or the faith that saves.[26]

It is *not* the faith that represents the embodiment of Christian doctrine to which Jude refers when he says, "contend for the faith that was once for all delivered to the saints" (Jude 3, ESV). Nor is it the faith of the disciples in God's ability to take care of them, as in the case of the

---

Constructive Christian Theology for the Pluralistic World (Grand Rapids, MI: Eerdmans, 2016), 208.

[26] These terms are used with recognition that it is not our faith itself that saves, but Jesus Christ in whom we have faith.

fearful, storm-tossed ones to whom Jesus says, "Why are you afraid, O you of little faith?" (Matthew 8:26, ESV).

Snoeberger suggests that evangelicals are unified in their understanding of saving faith: "The term *faith* scarcely needs defining. Nearly all evangelicals affirm that saving faith includes three elements: (1) intellectual knowledge of, (2) emotional assent to, and (3) unreserved, volitional trust in the accomplished redemptive work of Christ as revealed in the Scriptures."[27]

Snoeberger is right; most would accept the three-part definition he holds up as the standard.[28] But the apparent unity is complicated by the fact that many who do accept this definition wrongly import obedience into "volitional trust." This leads to an unbiblical blurring and conflation of faith and works.

For example, Norman Shepherd (a Calvinist) seems to conflate faith and obedience when he says, "Faith in Christ excludes the doing of self-righteousness, but it does not exclude the obedience to Christ, which is compatible with, and demonstrative of total reliance upon the righteousness of Christ for justification."[29] J. D. Greear, a pastor of a large Southern Baptist church and the 62nd president of the Southern

---

[27] Snoeberger, "The Logical Priority of Regeneration to Saving Faith in a Theological *Ordo Salutis*," 56. Noted Reformed scholar Louis Berkhof offers essentially the same three-part definition of faith in Louis Berkhof, *Systematic Theology* (Grand Rapids, MI: Wm. B. Eerdmans, 1939), 503-505.

[28] Anderson notes that most Free Grace theologians would agree with this three-part definition of faith. See David R. Anderson, "The Faith That Saves," in *A Defense of Free Grace Theology: With Respect to Saving Faith, Perseverance, and Assurance*, ed. Fred Chay (n.p.: Grace Theology Press, 2017), 67-87. This is significant because it is commonly and mistakenly assumed that all Free Grace theologians define faith as nothing more than intellectual assent.

[29] Norman Shepherd, "The Grace of Justification" (paper presented to the Board of Trustees of Westminster Theological Seminary, Philadelphia, PA, February 8, 1979), accessed July 15, 2015, http://www.hornes.org/theologia/norman-shepherd/the-grace-of-justification.

Baptist Convention who describes himself as more on the Calvinist side,[30] also seems to conflate faith and obedience when he says, "faith starts with mental assent, but if this mental assent does not lead to obedience, it is not yet 'faith.'"[31] Along the same lines, Frank Thielman argues,

> "Faith" as mere intellectual assent to various propositions, however, is worthless for salvation or justification, and saving faith is more than simply an entry point to the people of God. The command of God that we must obey, says the Elder, is not only to "believe in the name of his Son, Jesus Christ," but also "to love one another" (1 John 3:23). Even faith that can move mountains, says Paul, has no benefit without love (1 Cor. 13:2), and faith implies obedience (Rom. 1:5; 16:26). As James points out, faith without works is dead (James 2:26).[32]

Daniel Fuller seems to import not only obedience, but also perseverance into his definition of saving faith: "This faith we are to exercise comprises three essential elements. . . . These elements are (1) faith's futuristic orientation, (2) its power to motivate obedience to God, and (3), its demand for perseverance."[33]

Matthew Bates goes so far as to suggest that the original Greek word, πίστις, commonly translated, "faith," actually means allegiance, which includes, "intellectual assent to the gospel, professed loyalty to

---

[30] J. D. Greear, "What about Calvinism?" (video from The Summit Church, "Ask Any Friday"), November 5, 2010, accessed July 21, 2015, https://vimeo.com/16506952.

[31] J. D. Greear, *Stop Asking Jesus Into Your Heart: How To Know For Sure You Are Saved*, (Nashville: B&H, 2013), 41.

[32] Frank Thielman, *Theology of the New Testament: A Canonical and Synthetic Approach* (Grand Rapids, MI: Zondervan, 2005), 694-695.

[33] Daniel P. Fuller, *The Unity of the Bible: Unfolding God's Plan for Humanity* (Grand Rapids, MI: Zondervan, 1992), 270.

the Christ, and embodied fidelity [obedience]."³⁴ Bates says, "the offer of salvation is free, but it absolutely *does* come with strings attached. Obedient loyalty to the king is required as a condition of acceptance."³⁵

From these statements, it is hard to escape the implication that faith becomes saving only when it obeys, thus making obedience a condition of salvation. Whether faith inevitably and demonstrably and unreservedly leads to obedience is a debate beyond the scope of this work. I acknowledge that faith and obedience are in some ways related. Nevertheless, I do want to be careful to clearly distinguish saving faith from works.

Obedience-freighted definitions of faith have been roundly challenged by Fred Chay and John Correia (free-grace proponents in the faith-before-regeneration camp) as importing too much into the word, inviting a distortion of "the simplicity of faith alone in Christ alone."³⁶ Charles Bing (another free-grace, faith-before-regeneration proponent) defines saving faith in a simpler way that avoids confusion and conflation with obedience:

> What makes saving faith different from any other faith is its object. Therefore, saving faith is defined as trust or confidence in the Lord Jesus Christ as the Savior from sin. It is a personal acceptance of the work of the Lord Jesus Christ on the cross for the sinner.... When one believes he takes God at His word and personally appropriates the provision of Christ's free gift of salvation for himself.³⁷

---

[34] Matthew W. Bates, *Salvation by Allegiance Alone: Rethinking Faith, Works, and the Gospel of Jesus the King* (Grand Rapids, MI: Baker Academic, 2017), 100.

[35] Ibid., 104.

[36] Fred Chay and John P. Correia, *The Faith That Saves: The Nature of Faith in the New Testament: An Exegetical and Theological Analysis on the Nature of New Testament Faith* (Eugene, OR: Wipf & Stock, 2012), 149.

[37] Charles C. Bing, "Lordship Salvation: A Biblical Evaluation and Response, Grace Life Edition" (Ph.D. diss., Dallas Theological Seminary, 1991), 59.

Bing's definition of faith will be adopted for use in this work.[38] While some may argue that this definition doesn't go far enough, it would seem most can agree that faith includes at least this much. Even John Calvin himself, from whom Calvinism derives its name, would seem to agree: "Now we shall have a complete definition of faith, if we say, that it is a steady and certain knowledge of the Divine benevolence towards us, which, being founded on the truth of the gratuitous promise in Christ, is both revealed to our minds, and confirmed in our hearts, by the Holy Spirit."[39]

Regeneration

The term "regeneration" is sometimes used in different ways by different theologians. David Anderson explains:

> Regeneration is another term which is used in many different ways. Some groups want it to serve as an umbrella arching over the whole Christian experience. Others limit it to a two-tiered approach: presumptive or promissory regeneration at the water baptism of infants and full regeneration some time later in life. Still others narrow their understanding down to one instantaneous act of new birth which occurs at the moment of faith.[40]

Regeneration will be used here in the latter sense, as an instantaneous act of new birth. Jacobus Arminius, from whom Arminianism derives its name, would not agree: "this work of regeneration and illumination is not completed in one moment; but . . . it is advanced and promoted, from time to time, by daily increase."[41] Surprisingly, Calvin

---

[38] Note that Bing's definition goes beyond mere intellectual assent to include trust in the person and work of Christ. This is characteristic of Free Grace theology. See Anderson, "The Faith That Saves," 67-87.

[39] John Calvin, *Institutes of the Christian Religion*, 2 vols., transl. Henry Beveridge (Grand Rapids: Eerdmans, 1975), 3.2.7.

[40] Anderson, *Free Grace Soteriology*, 242.

[41] James Arminius, *The Public Disputations of James Arminius, D.D.*, in James

seems to join Arminius in disagreement, contending that regeneration includes virtually everything related to a believer's process of renewal, from conversion to sanctification.[42]

It is beyond the scope of this work to give a biblical defense for regeneration being an instantaneously completed act of God and not a process. For those interested, Anderson argues compellingly that the tenses of the biblical Greek verbs used for regeneration are consistent with an instantaneous act but incongruous with a process.[43] Moreover, most theologians today in both the faith-after-regeneration camp and the modified camp seem to agree that regeneration involves God instantly imparting new spiritual life to a person who was once spiritually dead, such that the person is born again.[44] Nevertheless, further clarification is in order.

Some theologians seem to incorporate into their definition of regeneration their beliefs concerning its order in relation to faith. For example, Millard Erickson, a proponent of the modified view, defines regeneration this way: "It is God's transformation of individual believers, his giving a new spiritual vitality and direction to their lives when they accept Christ."[45] Note the subtle thread woven into his definition of regeneration. The "transformation of *believers* [emphasis

---

Arminius, *The Works of James Arminius: The London Edition*, trans. James and William Nichols, 3 vols. (1825-75; repr., Grand Rapids: Baker, 1986), 2:195 (11.13).

[42] John Calvin, *Institutes of the Christian Religion*, ed. John T. McNeil, trans. Ford Lewis Battles, LCC, vols. 20-21 (Philadelphia: Westminster John Knox, 1960), 3.3.

[43] Anderson, *Free Grace Soteriology*, 245-246.

[44] Chafer, *Systematic Theology*, 7:265; Demarest, *The Cross and Salvation*, 289; Erickson, *Christian Theology*, 874; Wayne A. Grudem, *Systematic Theology*, (Grand Rapids: Zondervan, 1994), 699; Lewis and Demarest, *Integrative Theology*, 3:104; John Piper, *Finally Alive*, (Minneapolis: Desiring God, 2009), 16-42; Earl D. Radmacher, *Salvation*, (Nashville: Word, 2000), 105-111; R. C. Sproul, *What Does It Mean to Be Born Again?* (Sanford, FL: Reformation Trust Publishing, 2010), 50; Walvoord, *The Holy Spirit*, 133.

[45] Erickson, *Christian Theology*, 872.

added]" suggests that people have already become believers when they are then transformed by regeneration. Also note *when* God is described as "giving a new spiritual vitality and direction" to people: this happens "when they accept Christ."

Erickson isn't the only one to import his view of the *ordo salutis* into his definition of regeneration. Barrett is more overt, but from a different point of view:

> As to what regeneration is, I offer the following definition: Regeneration is the work of the Holy Spirit to unite the elect sinner to Christ by breathing new life into that dead and depraved sinner so as to raise him from spiritual death to spiritual life, removing his heart of stone and giving him a heart of flesh, so that he is washed, born from above and now able to repent and trust in Christ as a new creation. Moreover, regeneration is the act of God alone and therefore it is monergistic in nature, accomplished by the sovereign act of the Spirit apart from and unconditioned upon man's will to believe. In short, man's faith does not cause regeneration but regeneration causes man's faith.[46]

Clearly, to accept Barrett's definition of regeneration is to accept his faith-after-regeneration view.

In this work, a definition of regeneration that does not include assumptions regarding its place in the *ordo salutis* is needed. The long-standing definition offered by Charles Hodge (a Calvinist) is serviceable in this regard: "By a consent almost universal the word regeneration is now used to designate, not the whole work of sanctification, nor the first stages of that work comprehended in conversion, much less justification or any mere external change of state, but *the instantaneous change from spiritual death to spiritual life* (emphasis added)."[47]

Even the theologians who tend to weave their conception of the

---

[46] Barrett, *Salvation by Grace*, 127.

[47] Charles Hodge, *Systematic Theology*, vol. 3 (New York: Scribner, 1877), 5.

ordo salutis into their definitions would likely accept this as a suitable working definition.

This is not to say there aren't still things to argue about when it comes to regeneration. For example, there is some disagreement about what kind of new nature is imparted, divine or human. Chafer, who holds a modified view, contends, "Regeneration proves to be the imparting of the divine nature."[48] In rebuttal, Sproul, who holds a faith-after-regeneration view, contends, "Of course Reformed theology agrees that regeneration is creative and that it results in a fundamental change in the individual. It involves a new nature. But this new nature is the new human nature; it is not the divine nature."[49]

I will deliberately side-step the issue as to whether regeneration imparts a new nature that is divine or human, as it is not central to the question of how God draws people to believe in Jesus. Again, in this work, regeneration is considered to be the instantaneous change from spiritual death to spiritual life.

Monergism & Synergism

It may be surprising that I will generally avoid the use of the terms, "monergism" and "synergism" in the body of this work. It may be even more surprising that I would bother to include the definitions of these terms even though I am not going to use them. Some explanations are needed.

Etymologically, the term, "synergism" is a compound word made up of two Greek constituents, meaning "together" and "work"; hence, it means "to work together."[50] Likewise, "monergism" is a compound made up of two parts, meaning, "alone" and "work"; and so, it means "to work alone." When applied to regeneration, then, "synergism"

---

[48] Chafer, *Systematic Theology*, 7:265.

[49] Sproul, *Willing to Believe*, 196.

[50] Justo L. González, *Essential Theological Terms* (Louisville: Westminster John Knox Press, 2005), 168.

means that God and humans work together to effect regeneration; "monergism" means that God alone works to effect regeneration.

Calvinists typically use the term "monergism" to describe their own faith-after-regeneration view because God alone does all the work needed for regeneration. Barrett reflects this usage:

> Monergism does not merely mean that God alone is the author of redemption, but also—and significantly—that regeneration precedes faith. Throughout its history, Reformed theology has consistently understood monergism in this way.... [T]he consensus among Calvinists, both past and present, is that regeneration precedes faith in the *ordo salutis* and this is essential to monergism.[51]

Calvinists use the term "synergism" to describe the faith-before-regeneration view because they believe this view has humans doing some of the work needed for salvation, together with God. Again, Barrett is an example when he says,

> All Calvinists have agreed that regardless of the relationship between effectual calling and regeneration, Scripture teaches that conversion is always subsequent to, caused by, and conditioned upon effectual calling and/or regeneration. God does not respond to the sinner's cooperation (i.e., synergism), but rather, the sinner responds to God, who works alone to regenerate the unbelieving heart (i.e., monergism).[52]

According to Calvinists, what is the work or "cooperation" that sinners do in synergism? The human work is faith. To believe in Jesus is viewed as a meritorious work. For example, Sproul considers faith to be a good work: "Is it [faith] a good work? Certainly it is not a bad

---

[51] Barrett, *Salvation by Grace*, 311-312.
[52] Ibid., 284-285.

work. It is good for a person to trust in Christ and in Christ alone for his or her salvation. Since God commands us to trust in Christ, when we do we are obeying this command. But all Christians agree that faith is something we do. God does not do the believing for us."[53]

Calvinists J. I. Packer and O. R. Johnston also seem to conflate faith and works: "to rely on oneself for faith is no different in principle from relying on oneself for works, and the one is as un-Christian and anti-Christian as the other."[54]

The problem is that very few who hold the modified view are happy about being called synergists. The reason is that they do not believe that humans work together with God to effect their own regeneration because they believe that faith is not a meritorious work. John C. Lennox argues that viewing faith as a meritorious work confuses the nature of faith itself: "Some of the confusion arises from overlooking a simple logical point: *meriting something and having to do something to obtain that thing are not the same.*"[55]

Anderson further explains the problem(s):

> The problems here are multitudinous. The first is with the word *synergism*. Coming directly from the Greek word *sunergeō*, which means "to work together," the very definition of the word should be enough to cause any evangelical Protestant theologian to reject categorically a synergistic approach to salvation. Neither Chafer nor Walvoord would say that man and God work together to accomplish man's salvation (see Jn 1:13). How, then, can Sproul accuse them of that very thing? It is because in his understanding any *ordo salutis* which puts faith before regenera-

---

[53] Sproul, *Willing to Believe*, 25.

[54] J. I. Packer and O. R. Johnston, "Historical and Theological Introduction," in Martin Luther, *The Bondage of the Will*, trans. J. I. Packer and O. R. Johnston (Cambridge: James Clarke/Westwood, N.J.: Revell, 1957), 59.

[55] John C. Lennox, *Determined to Believe? The Sovereignty of God, Freedom, Faith, & Human Responsibility* (Grand Rapids, MI: Zondervan, 2017), 132.

tion is synergistic. How can this be, unless *faith* is understood to be a *work*? Of course, that is precisely what Sproul is suggesting, because he thinks if man can believe prior to regeneration, then man is *morally capable* of making a contribution to his own salvation. And if man is capable of making any contribution to the salvation process before regeneration, then his salvation is not all of God. Hence, it must be synergistic.

Is this biblical thinking? Absolutely not. This kind of ratiocination makes faith a work. The Scriptures contrast faith and works so often the concept hardly needs documentation. Can Ephesians 2:8-9 and Romans 4:4-6 be any clearer? If salvation is by faith, then *works are nowhere to be found* in the process. Again, to argue that faith precedes regeneration is synergistic would only be valid if faith is *equivalent* to works....

... [T]he use of the pejorative term *synergism* to describe Dispensationalism is a misnomer, since no Dispensationalist would even suggest that man "*works* together with" God to accomplish his salvation.[56]

It is precisely because the major players in this debate cannot agree on the proper use of the terms "monergism" and "synergism" that I will avoid their use altogether. Nevertheless, these terms inevitably crop up when theologians argue, and they will appear in some citations. Hopefully, this explanation of the controversy sheds some additional light on the issues at hand and gives some needful context when the terms do appear.

Logical & Temporal Priority

Sproul seems to be representative of a number of theologians who distinguish between "logical priority" and "temporal priority" in the *ordo salutis*:

---

[56] Anderson, *Free Grace Soteriology*, 250-251, 256-257.

> Remember that in Reformed theology's *ordo salutis* regeneration precedes faith. It does so with respect to *logical priority* not *temporal priority*. Reformed theology grants that God's act of regeneration and the believer's act of faith are simultaneous, not separated with respect to time. The *ordo salutis* refers to logical dependency. Faith logically depends on regeneration; regeneration does not logically depend on faith. Again, the *priority* is logical, not temporal. Regeneration is the necessary condition for faith; faith is not the necessary condition of or for regeneration.[57]

The distinction between "logical priority" and "temporal priority" is unhelpful and illogical. How can a cause (regeneration) come before its effect (faith) in logic but *not* in time? Anderson explains the problem:

> To say it takes *logical priority* without taking *temporal priority* is contradictory. The very word "priority" in this context speaks of time. It is a "temporal" word. Unless one switches the meaning of "priority" to "first in importance" (which is obviously not intended), then a statement about "logical priority" without "temporal priority" is non-sensical.[58]

This work assumes no meaningful distinction between logical priority and temporal priority. When it comes to faith and regeneration, if one comes before the other, it does so both logically and temporally. This remains so even if one follows immediately after the other.

Having set the table, consideration of the biblical arguments for each position will follow, starting with the faith-after-regeneration view.

---

[57] Sproul, *Willing to Believe*, 193-194.
[58] Anderson, *Free Grace Soteriology*, 250.

CHAPTER 1

ARGUMENTS FOR THE FAITH-AFTER-REGENERATION VIEW EXPLAINED AND REBUTTED

THIS CHAPTER WILL present arguments given in support of the faith-after-regeneration view along with rebuttals, as shown in Table 2.

Table 2. Summary of Views on How God Draws People to Believe with the Focus of Chapter 1 Highlighted

Faith-After-Regeneration View: (Calvinism/ Reformed Theology)	Faith-Before-Regeneration View:		
	Modified View:		Arminian View:
	Deterministic:	Nondeterministic:	
Regeneration (irresistible)	Effectual Call (irresistible)	Divine Illumination (resistible)	Prevenient Grace (resistible)

There are two basic arguments given in defense of the faith-after-regeneration view. The first argument is: Scripture teaches *total inability* such that the unregenerate are completely unable to respond to God in any good way, and thus are unable to believe in Jesus apart from God's help; therefore, regeneration must logically and causally precede faith. A summary of this argument in the words of some of its notable defenders will be presented first, followed by a list of biblical texts cited and interpreted in defense of the argument, and then finally, a rebuttal.

The second argument is: Scripture explicitly teaches that regeneration precedes faith. In evaluating this second argument, biblical texts cited and interpreted in support of the argument will be given along with rebuttals for each.

Argument 1: Scripture Teaches Total Inability

The Scriptures teach total inability such that the unregenerate are completely unable to respond to God in any good way, and thus are unable to believe in Jesus apart from God's help; therefore, regeneration must logically and causally precede faith.[59]

The doctrine of total inability can be traced to Augustine of Hippo.[60] According to Augustine, the human ability to choose God has been lost:

But this part of the human race to which God has promised pardon and a share in His eternal kingdom, can they be restored through the merit of their own works? God forbid. For what good work can a lost man perform, except so far as he has been delivered from perdition? Can they do anything by the free determination of their own will? Again, I say, God forbid. For it was by the evil use of his free-will that man destroyed both it and

---

[59] This is not a quote, but reflects my own understanding and summary of the argument.

[60] Ken Wilson, "A Theological and Historical Investigation," in *A Defense of Free Grace Theology*, 42.

himself. For, as a man who kills himself must, of course, be alive when he kills himself, but after he has killed himself ceases to live, and cannot restore himself to life; so, when man by his own free-will sinned, then sin being victorious over him, the freedom of his will was lost.[61]

Calvin gives an overview of the biblical case for our inability to respond to God in any good way, concluding with Augustine that we are not free to choose God on our own:

> Since the Spirit of God declares that every imagination of man's heart from infancy is evil (Gen. 6:5; 8:21); that there is none righteous, none that understandeth, none that seeketh after God (Ps. 14:3); but that all are useless, corrupt, void of the fear of God, full of fraud, bitterness, and all kinds of iniquity, and have fallen short of the glory of God (Rom. 3:10); since he proclaims that the carnal mind is enmity against God, and does not even leave us the power of thinking a good thought (Rom. 8:6; 2 Cor. 3:5), we maintain with Augustine, that man, by making a bad use of free will, lost both himself and it. Again, that the will being overcome by the corruption into which it fell, nature has no liberty. Again, that no will is free which is subject to lusts which conquer and enchain it.[62]

Sproul joins Calvin, adding the logical necessity of regeneration preceding faith because we are morally unable to believe on our own:

---

[61] J.F. Shaw, trans., *Saint Augustine of Hippo: The Enchiridion*, ed. Paul A. Böer, Sr. (n.p.: Veritatis Splendor Publications, 2012), 61, Kindle.

[62] John Calvin, "Articles Agreed upon by the Faculty of Sacred Theology of Paris, in Reference to Matters of Faith at Present Controverted; with the Antidote," ed. and trans. Henry Beveridge (1844), in John Calvin, *Selected Works of John Calvin: Tracts and Letters*, ed. Henry Beverage and Jules Bonnet, 7 vols. (Grand Rapids: Baker, 1983), 1:76.

Man is morally incapable of choosing the things of God unless or until God changes the disposition of the soul. Man's moral inability is due to a critical lack and deficiency, namely the motive or desire for the things of God. Left to himself, man will never choose Christ. He has no inclination to do so in his fallen state. Since he cannot act against his strongest inclination, he will never choose Christ unless God first changes the inclination of his soul by the immediate and supernatural work of regeneration.[63]

... in Reformed theology's *ordo salutis*, regeneration precedes faith. It does so with respect to logical priority, not temporal priority. Reformed theology grants that God's act of regeneration and the believer's act of faith are simultaneous, not separated, with respect to time. The *ordo salutis* refers to logical dependency. Faith logically depends on regeneration; regeneration does not logically depend on faith. Again the priority is logical, not temporal. Regeneration is the necessary condition of faith; faith is not the necessary condition of or for regeneration. ... The logical priority of regeneration in Reformed theology rests on the doctrine of total depravity or moral inability. Because fallen man is morally unable to incline himself by faith to Christ, regeneration is a logical necessity for faith to occur. If we were to posit that faith precedes regeneration, then we would be assuming that unregenerate people, while still in an unregenerate state, have the moral ability to exercise faith. If the unregenerate can exercise faith, then it follows clearly that they are not fallen to the degree of moral inability.[64]

Packer summarizes the case: "We have no natural ability to discern and choose God's way because we have no natural inclination Godward; our hearts are in bondage to sin, and only the grace of regeneration can

---

[63] Sproul, *Willing to Believe*, 165.
[64] Ibid., 193-194.

Arguments for the Faith-After-Regeneration View

free us from that slavery.... I am the fallen being who only have it in me to choose against God till God renews my heart."[65]

Packer and Johnston further assert, "the faith which receives Christ for justification is itself the free gift of a sovereign God, bestowed by spiritual regeneration in the acts of effectual calling."[66]

Some Scriptures commonly cited to support this argument will now be considered.

Genesis 6:5; 8:21

> The LORD saw that the wickedness of man was great in the earth, and that every intention of the thoughts of his heart was only evil continually (Genesis 6:5, ESV).

> And when the LORD smelled the pleasing aroma, the LORD said in his heart, "I will never again curse the ground because of man, for the intention of man's heart is evil from his youth. Neither will I ever again strike down every living creature as I have done" (Genesis 8:21, ESV).

These Scriptures are cited by Calvin in the quote introducing this chapter to show that our every imagination and intention is evil from our very beginning; and thus, we are unable to respond to God in any good way on our own.[67]

Psalm 14:1-3; Romans 3:10-19

> To the choirmaster. Of David. The fool says in his heart, "There is no God." They are corrupt, they do abominable deeds, there is

---

[65] J. I. Packer, *Concise Theology: A Guide to Historic Christian Beliefs* (Wheaton: Tyndale, 1993), 86.

[66] Packer and Johnston, "Historical and Theological Introduction," 58.

[67] Calvin, "Articles Agreed upon by the Faculty of Sacred Theology of Paris," 1:76.

none who does good. The LORD looks down from heaven on the children of man, to see if there are any who understand, who seek after God. They have all turned aside; together they have become corrupt; there is none who does good, not even one (Psalm 14:1-3, ESV).

[A]s it is written: "None is righteous, no, not one; no one understands; no one seeks for God. All have turned aside; together they have become worthless; no one does good, not even one." "Their throat is an open grave; they use their tongues to deceive." "The venom of asps is under their lips." "Their mouth is full of curses and bitterness." "Their feet are swift to shed blood; in their paths are ruin and misery, and the way of peace they have not known." "There is no fear of God before their eyes." Now we know that whatever the law says it speaks to those who are under the law, so that every mouth may be stopped, and the whole world may be held accountable to God (Romans 3:10-19, ESV).

Again, these passages are cited by Calvin in the quote introducing this chapter to show that no one is righteous, no one seeks after God on his own, all are hopelessly corrupt and fallen, and thus, we are not free to believe on our own.[68]

John 6:44, 65

"No one can come to me unless the Father who sent me draws him. And I will raise him up on the last day" (John 6:44, ESV).

And he said, "This is why I told you that no one can come to me unless it is granted him by the Father" (John 6:65, ESV).

---

[68] Ibid. Technically, Calvin mentions only Psalm 14:3 and Romans 3:10. I expanded these references to include some verses following that seemed pertinent.

Arguments for the Faith-After-Regeneration View

Piper interprets John 6:44 to affirm our inability to believe unless first regenerated:

> As Jesus says three times in John 6, no one can come to him unless the Father draws him. And when that drawing brings a person into living connection with Jesus, we call it the new birth.... All of these wonderful works of drawing, granting, and giving are the work of God in regeneration. Without them we do not come to Christ, because we don't prefer to come. We so strongly prefer self-reliance that we cannot come. That is what has to be changed in the new birth. A new preference, a new ability, is given.[69]

Calvin cites John 6:44 and 65 as proof that we are unable to believe apart from divine enablement:

> To "come to Christ" being here used metaphorically for "believing," the Evangelist, in order to carry out the metaphor in the apposite clause, says that those persons are "drawn" whose understandings God enlightens, and whose hearts he bends and forms to the obedience of Christ.... we ought not to wonder if many refuse to embrace the Gospel; because no man will ever of himself be able to come to Christ, but God must first approach him by his Spirit; and hence it follows that all are not "drawn," but that God bestows this grace on those whom he has elected. True, indeed, as to the kind of "drawing," it is not violent, so as to compel men by external force; but still it is a powerful impulse of the Holy Spirit, which makes men willing who formerly were unwilling and reluctant. It is a false and profane assertion, therefore, that none are drawn but those who are willing to be "drawn," as if man made himself obedient to God by his own efforts; for the willingness with which men follow God is what

---

[69] Piper, *Finally Alive*, 52-53.

they already have from himself, who has formed their hearts to obey him.[70]

[Regarding John 6:65 in light of John 6:44] He now uses the word *give* instead of the word...he formerly used, *draw*; by which he means that there is no other reason why God *draws*, than because out of free grace he loves us; for what we obtain by the gift and grace of God, no man procures for himself by his own industry.[71]

John 8:36

"So if the Son sets you free, you will be free indeed" (John 8:36, ESV).

Augustine uses the words of Jesus in John 8:36 to argue that we are powerless to free ourselves from bondage to sin by a determination of our own will to do what is right. Presumably, this would include believing in Jesus. Rather, our liberation must come from Christ:

But whence comes this liberty to do right to the man who is in bondage and sold under sin, except he be redeemed by Him who has said, "If the Son shall make you free, ye shall be free indeed" [John 8:36]? And before this redemption is wrought in a man, when he is not yet free to do what is right, how can he talk of the freedom of his will and his good works, except he be inflated by that foolish pride of boasting which the apostle restrains when he says, "By grace are ye saved, though faith" [Eph. 2:8].[72]

---

[70] John Calvin, *Commentary on the Gospel According to John*, trans. William Pringle, 2 vols. (1847-48; Grand Rapids: Baker, 1979), 1:257.

[71] Ibid., 276.

[72] Augustine, *The Enchiridion: On Faith, Hope and Love*, trans. J.F. Shaw, in Augustine, *Basic Writings of Saint Augustine*, ed. Whitney J. Oates, 2 vols. (1948; Grand Rapids: Baker, 1980), 1:675 (chap. 30).

John 15:5

"I am the vine; you are the branches. Whoever abides in me and I in him, he it is that bears much fruit, for apart from me you can do nothing" (John 15:5, ESV).

In his classic work, *The Bondage of the Will*, to which many Calvinists refer, Martin Luther uses John 15:5 to emphasize the impossibility of doing anything, including believing in Jesus, apart from divine enablement: "It is utterly unheard-of grammar and logic to say that nothing is the same as something; to logicians, the thing is an impossibility, for the two are contradictory!"[73]

Acts 9:1-4; 26:14

But Saul, still breathing threats and murder against the disciples of the Lord, went to the high priest and asked him for letters to the synagogues at Damascus, so that if he found any belonging to the Way, men or women, he might bring them bound to Jerusalem. Now as he went on his way, he approached Damascus, and suddenly a light from heaven shone around him. And falling to the ground he heard a voice saying to him, "Saul, Saul, why are you persecuting me?" (Acts 9:1-4, ESV).

"And when we had all fallen to the ground, I heard a voice saying to me in the Hebrew language, 'Saul, Saul, why are you persecuting me? It is hard for you to kick against the goads'" (Acts 26:14, ESV).

---

[73] Martin Luther, *The Bondage of the Will*, trans. J. I. Packer and O. R. Johnston (Cambridge: James Clarke/Westwood, N.J.: Revell, 1957), 262 (5.7).

In commenting on Acts 9:1-4, Sproul says, "If there is any evidence in Scripture that regeneration is a sovereign act, this is it."[74]

Romans 1:18

> For the wrath of God is revealed from heaven against all ungodliness and unrighteousness of men, who by their unrighteousness suppress the truth (Romans 1:18, ESV).

Luther draws from Romans 1:18 the inference that our will is not free to choose good and believe. In commenting on this verse, he says, "Where now is the power of 'free-will' to endeavor after some good?"[75]

Romans 8:6

> For to set the mind on the flesh is death, but to set the mind on the Spirit is life and peace (Romans 8:6, ESV).

Calvin marshals Romans 8:6 as evidence that we are, by nature, enemies of God, without the power to even think a good thought; therefore, we are not at liberty to choose to believe.[76]

Romans 9:14-16

> What shall we say then? Is there injustice on God's part? By no means! For he says to Moses, "I will have mercy on whom I have mercy, and I will have compassion on whom I have compassion." So then it depends not on human will or exertion, but on God, who has mercy (Romans 9:14-16, ESV).

---

[74] Sproul, *What Does It Mean to Be Born Again?*, 42.

[75] Luther, *The Bondage of the Will*, 59.

[76] Calvin, "Articles Agreed upon by the Faculty of Sacred Theology of Paris," 1:76.

Arguments for the Faith-After-Regeneration View

Augustine says, "the true interpretation of the saying, 'It is not of him that willeth, nor of him that runneth, but of God that showeth mercy' [Rom. 9:16], is that the whole works belongs to God, who both makes the will of man righteous, and thus prepares it for assistance, and assists it when it is prepared."[77]

1 Corinthians 2:14

> The natural person does not accept the things of the Spirit of God, for they are folly to him, and he is not able to understand them because they are spiritually discerned (1 Corinthians 2:14, ESV).

In commenting on this verse, Barrett says, "The natural person is enslaved to the foolishness of this world and the spiritual things of God he cannot even begin to understand in a saving way."[78]

2 Corinthians 3:5

> Not that we are sufficient in ourselves to claim anything as coming from us, but our sufficiency is from God (2 Corinthians 3:5, ESV).

Calvin cites 2 Corinthians 3:5 as proof of our own insufficiency to choose anything good.[79]

Ephesians 2:1-5

> And you were dead in the trespasses and sins in which you once walked, following the course of this world, following the prince of

---

[77] Augustine, *The Enchiridion: On Faith, Hope and Love*, 1:675 (chap. 30).

[78] Barrett, *Salvation by Grace*, 57.

[79] Calvin, "Articles Agreed upon by the Faculty of Sacred Theology of Paris," 1:76.

the power of the air, the spirit that is now at work in the sons of disobedience—among whom we all once lived in the passions of our flesh, carrying out the desires of the body and the mind, and were by nature children of wrath, like the rest of mankind. But God, being rich in mercy, because of the great love with which he loved us, even when we were dead in our trespasses, made us alive together with Christ—by grace you have been saved (Ephesians 2:1-5, ESV).

In commenting on this text, Sproul takes "dead" to mean that we are incapable of faith, apart from God's regeneration: "Spiritually dead people do not suddenly develop faith, causing God to regenerate them. Rather, faith is the fruit of the regeneration God performs in our hearts: 'Even when we were dead in our trespasses, [God] made us alive together with Christ' (Eph. 2:5b)."[80]

Piper concurs, equating the deadness of Ephesians 2 with the inability to respond to God or his Word to us: "The text where we take our beginning is Ephesians 2. . . . two times Paul describes us as 'dead.' . . . What does this mean? This deadness? . . . We are dead in the sense that we cannot see or savor the glory of Christ. We are spiritually dead. We are unresponsive to God and Christ and this word."[81]

Philippians 1:6

And I am sure of this, that he who began a good work in you will bring it to completion at the day of Jesus Christ (Philippians 1:6, ESV).

Calvin uses Philippians 1:6 to argue that, upon conversion, God creates our will anew, such that it is turned from evil to good. The inference is that only then are we able to believe:

---

[80] Sproul, *What Does It Mean to Be Born Again?*, 37-38.
[81] Piper, *Finally Alive*, 46-49.

Arguments for the Faith-After-Regeneration View

God, therefore, begins the good work in us by exciting in our hearts a desire, a love, and a study of righteousness, or (to speak more correctly) by turning, training, and guiding our hearts unto righteousness.... I say the will is abolished, but not in so far as it is [a] will, for in conversion everything essential to our original nature remains: I also say, that it is created anew, not because the will then begins to exist, but because it is turned from evil to good.[82]

Philippians 2:13

[F]or it is God who works in you, both to will and to work for his good pleasure (Philippians 2:13, ESV).

Calvin says of this verse,

We certainly obey God with our will, but it is with a will which he has formed in us. Those, therefore, who ascribe any proper movement to free-will, apart from the grace of God, do nothing else than rend the Holy Spirit. Paul declares, not that a faculty of willing is given to us, but that the will itself is formed in us (Phil. 2:13), so that from none else but God is the assent or obedience of a right will. He acts within, holds our hearts, moves our hearts, and draws us by the inclinations which he has produced in us.[83]

Rebuttal of Argument 1

Those who hold the faith-before-regeneration view would generally agree with the middle part of Argument 1 as I have framed it, which

---

[82] Calvin, *Institutes of the Christian Religion*, 2 vols. trans. Henry Beveridge, 1:255 (2.3.6).

[83] John Calvin, *Acts of the Council of Trent: With the Antidote*, ed. and trans. Henry Beveridge (1851), in John Calvin, *Selected Works of John Calvin: Tracts and Letters*.

asserts that the unregenerate "are unable to believe in Jesus apart from God's help." The point is conceded. The total depravity of humankind is a problem that must be overcome if anyone is to believe.

Nevertheless, while regeneration is certainly a plausible solution, it simply does not follow that regeneration *must* be the only solution. Faith-before-regeneration proponents are united in contending that, while the unregenerate do need God's help to believe, regeneration is not the help God provides; they offer other alternatives.

From the Deterministic Modified View

The deterministic modified view is characterized by the idea that God's indispensable help for believing comes in the form of an effectual call, which is also sometimes called efficacious grace or a special calling. Walvoord calls this work of the Spirit "efficacious grace," and describes it this way:

> Efficacious grace is a theological term having in view the work of the Holy Spirit in moving men to effective faith in Jesus Christ as Savior....[84]
>
> The Scriptures speak frequently of a divine call to salvation which results in certain salvation (Rom. 1:1, 6, 7; 8:28, 30; 9:11, 24; 11:29; 1 Cor. 1:1, 2, 9, 24, 26; 7:15, 17, 18, 20, 21, 22, 24; Gal. 1:6, 15; 5:8, 13; Eph. 1:18; 4:1, 4; Col. 3:15; 1 Thess. 2:12; 4:7; 5:24; 2 Thess. 2:14; 1 Tim. 6:12; 2 Tim. 1:9; Heb. 3:1; 9:15; 1 Peter1:15; 2:9, 21; 3:9; 5:10; 2 Pet. 1:3, 10))....[85]
>
> The Scriptures bear faithful testimony to the fact that efficacious grace is an act of God.... Never in the Scriptures is divine calling attributed to human choice.[86]

---

[84] Walvoord, *The Holy Spirit*, 119.

[85] Ibid., 120.

[86] Ibid., 121.

The work of efficacious grace is necessary in view of the absence of spiritual life before regeneration. Herein lies the foundation of the doctrine of efficacious grace. A man spiritually dead cannot do a spiritual work. Total depravity demands as its corollary the doctrine of efficacious grace.[87]

Walvoord is careful to distinguish efficacious grace as preceding both faith and regeneration:

Even the work of efficacious grace, though simultaneous with regeneration, and indispensable to it, does not in itself effect regeneration. Efficacious grace only makes regeneration possible and certain. . . .[88]

The normal pattern for regeneration is that it occurs at the moment of saving faith. No appeal is ever addressed to men that they should believe because they are already regenerated. It is rather that they should believe and receive eternal life.[89]

The concept of an effectual call is not unique to the deterministic modified view, but its placement before *both* faith *and* regeneration in the *ordo salutis* is a distinguishing mark. Barrett admits that there is no clear consensus among Reformed theologians as to the relationship between the effectual call and regeneration in the *ordo salutis*; some Calvinists place the effectual call before regeneration, some after, and still others say that the effectual call and regeneration are essentially the same thing and cannot be distinguished.[90] Despite these differences, the

---

[87] Ibid., 124-125.

[88] Ibid., 133.

[89] Ibid., 135.

[90] Barrett, *Salvation by Grace*, 284-285. A common Calvinistic view is summarized by Fred G. Zaspel: "[B]y means of the general call of the gospel, God issues his sovereign, efficacious call to his elect, bringing them to spiritual life by which they are enabled to see Christ rightly and believe"

consensus among Calvinists is that, regardless of how the effectual call and regeneration are ordered, they both precede and cause faith.

John Gerstner, a Calvinist, argues against dispensationalism in general and the deterministic modified view in particular by parroting the view and then labeling it: "A man cannot believe without help, but he cannot be regenerated without believing. This is precisely the evangelical Arminian order—divine help, then human faith, followed by regeneration."[91] And, of course, he's right. But painting dispensationalists with a scarlet "A" (for "Arminian") is not a compelling biblical defense for the faith-after-regeneration view. Moreover, dispensationalists are certainly not the only ones who hold the deterministic modified view. Some professing Calvinists do as well. For example, Demarest points out the distinction between the Reformed, faith-after-regeneration view and the deterministic modified view as it relates to the effectual call and its relationship to faith and regeneration in the *ordo salutis*:

> In order to safeguard the truth that holistically depraved sinners come to Christ only by the divine initiative, many Reformed theologians place regeneration before conversion in the *ordo salutis*. . . . effectual calling is conceptually distinct from regeneration. The power that brings sinners to Christ inheres in the Spirit's effectual call rather than in the new birth itself. That is, the Spirit's effectual call is a movement preliminary to regeneration; it stops short of effecting in believers a radical re-creation (2 Cor. 5:17), whereby the latter participate in the divine nature (2 Pet. 1:4). Logically speaking, the called according to God's purpose convert, and so are regenerated. Not only is this position biblical, but we avoid the difficulty of positing, logically

---

(F.G. Zaspel, "Effectual Calling" in *Lexham Survey of Theology*, eds. M. Ward, J. Parks, B. Ellis, & T. Hains (Bellingham, WA: Lexham Press, 2018).

[91] John H. Gerstner, *Wrongly Dividing the Word of Truth: A Critique of Dispensationalism*, 3rd ed. (Draper, VA: Apologetics Group Media, 2009), 137.

Arguments for the Faith-After-Regeneration View

at least, that regeneration precedes personal belief in the Gospel, repentance from sin, and wholehearted trust in Christ.[92]

From the Arminian View

Within the faith-before-regeneration camp, the Arminian view also affirms the depravity of humankind and the need for God's help to believe. But in this view, the help is not regeneration or an effectual call; it is prevenient grace. Olson explains, "classical Arminianism does say that people can choose God, but only with the help of the Holy Spirit. This is called prevenient grace. And according to Arminius and his true followers, whenever people choose God, that is proof they are not 'natural, unregenerate' people but persons already under the supernatural influence of the Holy Spirit."[93] Olson goes on to explain, "humans are totally unable to do anything good in spiritual matters apart from a special communication of grace. . . . total depravity is mitigated by universal prevenient grace stemming from the cross of Christ through the Holy Spirit, which gives a 'gracious ability' to fallen persons to hear and respond to the gospel."[94] A key distinction relative to the deterministic modified view is that Arminians believe God's enablement (prevenient grace) can be resisted. It does not inevitably lead to saving faith; people choose to accept or reject.

From the Nondeterministic Modified View

The nondeterministic modified view also affirms human depravity and the absolute need for God's help in believing. But the help is not regeneration or an effectual call or prevenient grace; rather, God draws people to believe in various ways that are collectively described as divine

---

[92] Demarest, *The Cross and Salvation*, 227.

[93] Roger E. Olson, *Arminian Theology: Myths and Realities* (Downers Grove, IL: InterVarsity Press, 2006), 138.

[94] Ibid., 156.

illumination or divine enablement or divine persuasion. Anderson says, "... we never said that the unregenerate man can come to Christ on his own, or believe on his own. We've never argued that. It's a straw-man argument to even bring this up. We've said it takes divine enablement."[95] Ken Hemphill, who argues from a nondeterministic view, says, "people do not come to Christ of their own initiative; apart from the convicting and drawing work of the Spirit, humans would remain in our sin."[96] David Allen concurs: "the free response of any sinner is not possible without God's initiation."[97]

Even though this divine illumination is indispensable, it can be resisted. All have some capacity and responsibility to respond to God's illumination, and as they do, God draws by giving more light leading to faith. In response to God's illumination, people have a genuine choice between two alternatives, to believe or disbelieve.

While affirming the total inability of the unregenerate to *believe* on their own, the nondeterministic modified view challenges the notion that the unregenerate are totally unable to respond to God *in any good way*. Anderson offers some scriptural evidence that the unregenerate are indeed able to respond to God, subject to God's initiative and help.[98] George Meisinger also provides a somewhat different and overlapping list of passages to show some ability or volition toward God among the unregenerate.[99] Leighton Flowers (a former Calvinist) more

---

[95] David R. Anderson, "Regeneration and the *Ordo Salutis*" (lecture, Annual Conference of the Free Grace Alliance, Irving, TX, October 14, 2014).

[96] Ken Hemphill, *Unlimited: God's Love, Atonement, and Mission* (Traveler's Rest, SC: Auxano Press, 2018), 68.

[97] David L. Allen, "Claims, Clarity, Charity—Why the Traditional Baptist Statement on Soteriology Is Not and Cannot Be Semipelagian," *David L. Allen*, October 1, 2018, accessed May 6, 2019, http://drdavidlallen.com/baptist/claims-clarity-charity-why-the-traditional-baptist-statement-on-soteriology-is-not-and-cannot-be-semipelagian/.

[98] Anderson, "Regeneration and the *Ordo Salutis*."

[99] George E. Meisinger, "The Issue of One's Ability to Believe: Total

Arguments for the Faith-After-Regeneration View

recently provides several more passages in support of the idea that the unregenerate can indeed respond to God's gracious initiatives.[100] And to this I will add Genesis 1:27 and related texts concerning humans being made in the image of God as a basis for some responsiveness of the unregenerate to divine initiatives. These passages will now be considered.

Genesis 1:27; 9:6; James 3:9

> So *God created man in his own image*, in the image of God he created him; male and female he created them (Genesis 1:27, ESV, emphasis added).

> "Whoever sheds the blood of man, by man shall his blood be shed, *for God made man in his own image*" (Genesis 9:6, ESV, emphasis added).

> With it we bless our Lord and Father, and with it we curse people *who are made in the likeness of God* (James 3:9, ESV, emphasis added).

Some in the nondeterministic modified camp assert that while the image of God in man has been defaced by the Fall, it has not been erased. Intrinsic to our nature as image-bearers is the ability to respond to God. Norman Geisler asserts,

> Even though they are spiritually dead, unsaved persons can perceive the truth of God. They are still in God's image (Gen. 9:6; James 3:9), which was effaced but not erased by the Fall. In Romans, Paul declares emphatically that God's truth is "clearly

---

Depravity/Inability," *Chafer Theological Seminary Journal*, vol. 11, no. 1, (Spring 2005), 66-96.

[100] Leighton Flowers, *God's Provision for All: A Defense of God's Goodness* (n.p.: Trinity Academic Press, 2019), 59-63.

seen" by them so that they are "without excuse" (1:20). Adam and Eve were spiritually dead after they ate the forbidden fruit, yet they could hear God's voice and responded to Him (Gen. 3:10).[101]

Anthony Badger concurs:

If all men possess the image of God (part of which is the ability to think logically, appreciate beauty, reason conceptually, understand abstract concepts, have self-awareness, speak and communicate in symbols or language, be conscious of cause and effect relationships, and, yes, even believe something) why is it considered erroneous to assert that a man, regenerate or not, can actually believe a message that has spiritual-oriented content? . . . Total depravity speaks of man's inability to save himself, not his inability to believe or to accept a mercifully offered gift.[102]

Bing adds:

Man was made in God's image, which includes a measure of self-determination. The image of God was not destroyed by man's fall, but marred or corrupted, with the result that man, when left to himself, is inclined toward evil and rejection of God. Self-determination, even if used to reject God, is essential to humanness and personhood. Without self-determination man would be nothing more than a robot with every decision and action determined and controlled by God.[103]

---

[101] Norman L. Geiser, *Chosen But Free: A Balanced View of God's Sovereignty and Free Will*, 3rd ed. (Minneapolis, MN: Bethany House Publishers, 2010), 63.

[102] Anthony B. Badger, *Confronting Calvinism: A Free Grace Refutation and Biblical Resolution of Radical Reformed Soteriology* (n.p.: Author), 91, 104.

[103] Charles C. Bing, "Can an Unregenerate Person Believe the Gospel?, *Grace*

Arguments for the Faith-After-Regeneration View 45

Genesis 3:8-10

> And they heard the sound of the LORD God walking in the garden in the cool of the day, and the man and his wife hid themselves from the presence of the LORD God among the trees of the garden. But the LORD God called to the man and said to him, "Where are you?" And he said, "I heard the sound of you in the garden, and I was afraid, because I was naked, and I hid myself" (Genesis 3:8-10, ESV).

In commenting on these verses, Flowers asks questions intended to point out the unreasonableness of the claim that humankind is incapable of responding to God in any good way apart from a divine effectual call:

> Are we to assume this vulnerable reply was actually brought about by some type of inner effectual work of divine grace, or was Adam simply responding freely to the loving call of a God genuinely seeking him in his brokenness? . . . When God was explaining the curse of labor pains and toiling the soil, did He forget to mention the worst of all the curses, "You now are morally incapable of responding willingly to my appeals for reconciliation?"[104]

Genesis 4:3-7

> In the course of time Cain brought to the LORD an offering of the fruit of the ground, and Abel also brought of the firstborn of his flock and of their fat portions. And the LORD had regard for Abel and his offering, but for Cain and his offering he had no regard. So Cain was very angry, and his face fell. The LORD said to Cain, "Why are you angry, and why has your face fallen? If you

---

Notes, no. 46, n.d., accessed April 15, 2017, http://gracelife.org/resources/gracenotes/?id=46.

[104] Flowers, *God's Provision for All*, 59-60.

do well, will you not be accepted? And if you do not do well, sin is crouching at the door. Its desire is contrary to you, but you must rule over it" (Genesis 4:3, ESV).

In reference to this passage, Flowers explains that the Lord clearly expresses his expectation for Cain to trust in his provision, demonstrated in a proper offering, which Cain was expected to bring and his brother did, in fact, bring. "There is no biblical indication that mankind lost their moral ability to respond willingly to God's own gracious provision due to the fall."[105]

Genesis 41:8; 1 Kings 21:5; 1 Chronicles 5:26; 2 Chronicles 36:22; Daniel 2:1; 5:5-6

So in the morning his spirit was troubled, and he sent and called for all the magicians of Egypt and all its wise men. Pharaoh told them his dreams, but there was none who could interpret them to Pharaoh (Genesis 41:8, ESV).

But Jezebel his wife came to him and said to him, "Why is your spirit so vexed that you eat no food?" (1 Kings 21:5, ESV).

So the God of Israel stirred up the spirit of Pul king of Assyria, the spirit of Tiglath-pileser king of Assyria, and he took them into exile, namely, the Reubenites, the Gadites, and the half-tribe of Manasseh, and brought them to Halah, Habor, Hara, and the river Gozan, to this day (1 Chronicles 5:26, ESV).

Now in the first year of Cyrus king of Persia, that the word of the LORD by the mouth of Jeremiah might be fulfilled, the LORD stirred up the spirit of Cyrus king of Persia, so that he made a proclamation throughout all his kingdom and also put it in writing (2 Chronicles 36:22, ESV).

---

[105] Ibid., 60-61.

In the second year of the reign of Nebuchadnezzar, Nebuchadnezzar had dreams; his spirit was troubled, and his sleep left him (Daniel 2:1, ESV).

Immediately the fingers of a human hand appeared and wrote on the plaster of the wall of the king's palace, opposite the lampstand. And the king saw the hand as it wrote. Then the king's color changed, and his thoughts alarmed him; his limbs gave way, and his knees knocked together (Daniel 5:5-6, ESV).

Anderson cites these Old Testament texts which portray the spirit of the unregenerate as active and responsive, not like a corpse. In Genesis 41:8, Pharaoh's "spirit was troubled." In 1 Kings 21:5, Ahab's spirit was "vexed." In 1 Chronicles 5:26, "the God of Israel stirred up the spirit of Pul king of Assyria, the spirit of Tiglath-pileser king of Assyria." In 2 Chronicles 36:22, the Lord "stirred up the spirit of Cyrus." In Daniel 2:1, the spirit of Nebuchadnezzar is troubled, and in Daniel 5, his spirit is hardened. These examples depict a certain spiritual responsiveness in the unregenerate. One may argue that, in the case of Cyrus for example, it was clearly the Lord who stirred his spirit; nevertheless, this does not diminish the fact that Cyrus responded to God's stirring in a positive way without being regenerated.

Exodus 12:37-38

And the people of Israel journeyed from Rameses to Succoth, about six hundred thousand men on foot, besides women and children. A mixed multitude also went up with them, and very much livestock, both flocks and herds (Exodus 12:37-38, ESV).

In the wake of the original Passover, the Israelites are released from bondage in Egypt and are headed out on foot. "A mixed multitude" is with the Israelites. Anderson argues that these are Egyptians. Keil and Delitzsch explain: "In typical fulfilment of the promise in Gen. 12:3, and no doubt induced by the signs and wonders of the Lord in Egypt to seek their good among the Israelites, a great crowd of mixed people (בַּר בָּרֶע) attached themselves to them."[106]

Anderson cites the "mixed multitude" as an example of the unregenerate responding to spiritual truth. He says, "These are Egyptians, aren't they? Why are they going with them? Why do they hitch their camel to the Israelite wagon train? They heard the truth about this God. They saw the plagues and what happened. It convinced them, they believed it, and so they went along. These are unregenerate people."[107]

Matthew 13:10-17

> Then the disciples came and said to him, "Why do you speak to them in parables?" And he answered them, "To you it has been given to know the secrets of the kingdom of heaven, but to them it has not been given. For to the one who has, more will be given, and he will have an abundance, but from the one who has not, even what he has will be taken away. This is why I speak to them in parables, because seeing they do not see, and hearing they do not hear, nor do they understand. Indeed, in their case the prophecy of Isaiah is fulfilled that says: '"You will indeed hear but never understand, and you will indeed see but never perceive." For this people's heart has grown dull, and with their ears they can barely hear, and their eyes they have closed, lest they should see with their eyes and hear with their ears and understand with their heart and turn, and I would heal them.' But blessed are your eyes, for they see, and your ears, for they hear. For truly, I say to you, many prophets and righteous people longed to see what you see, and did not see it, and to hear what you hear, and did not hear it" (Matthew 13:10-17, ESV).

---

[106] Carl Friedrich Keil and Franz Delitzsch, *Commentary on the Old Testament*, vol. 1 (Peabody, MA: Hendrickson, 1996), 339.

[107] Anderson, "Regeneration and the *Ordo Salutis*."

Anderson contends that this passage evidences a certain receptivity to the light of truth among the unregenerate. He says, "Now in Matthew 13, we have a passage that I think talks about light received brings more light; light rejected brings the night."[108]

Bing adds that the ability of the unregenerate to respond to God's initiatives is confirmed by Jesus's use of parabolic language. He says, "God's will does not preclude man's will and freedom to respond, but includes it. If man does not have this freedom, then why does God judicially blind the Jews or use parabolic language to hide His truth? It would be like putting a blindfold on a corpse."[109]

Luke 8:4-15

> And when a great crowd was gathering and people from town after town came to him, he said in a parable, "A sower went out to sow his seed. And as he sowed, some fell along the path and was trampled underfoot, and the birds of the air devoured it. And some fell on the rock, and as it grew up, it withered away, because it had no moisture. And some fell among thorns, and the thorns grew up with it and choked it. And some fell into good soil and grew and yielded a hundredfold." As he said these things, he called out, "He who has ears to hear, let him hear." And when his disciples asked him what this parable meant, he said, "To you it has been given to know the secrets of the kingdom of God, but for others they are in parables, so that 'seeing they may not see, and hearing they may not understand.' Now the parable is this: The seed is the word of God. The ones along the path are those who have heard; then the devil comes and takes away the word from their hearts, so that they may not believe and be saved. And

---

[108] Ibid.

[109] Charles C. Bing, "How God Draws People to Salvation," *Grace Notes*, no. 75, n.d., accessed April 15, 2017, http://gracelife.org/resources/gracenotes/?id=75.

the ones on the rock are those who, when they hear the word, receive it with joy. But these have no root; they believe for a while, and in time of testing fall away. And as for what fell among the thorns, they are those who hear, but as they go on their way they are choked by the cares and riches and pleasures of life, and their fruit does not mature. As for that in the good soil, they are those who, hearing the word, hold it fast in an honest and good heart, and bear fruit with patience" (Luke 8:4-15, ESV).

Meisinger argues that this parable demonstrates that the unregenerate have some ability to believe. He states the case persuasively:

> Luke 8:12 reveals that the devil works to snatch the gospel out of unbelievers' hearts *lest they should believe and be saved* (ἵνα μὴ πιστεύσαντες σωθῶσιν). The normal way to understand the "lest" (hina + negative) clause is to see the devil working to snatch the gospel out of the minds of unbelievers precisely *because* they have the ability to believe. The grammatical construction presupposes the hearers' ability to believe, which Satan comprehends. Thus, the devil labors to snatch the gospel from the hearts of non-Christians, so that they will not believe. Accordingly, it is not that the unregenerate ontologically cannot believe, but that they will not believe, so long as Satan plucks the Word from their hearts.[110]

John 7:17

> If anyone's will is to do God's will, he will know whether the teaching is from God or whether I am speaking on my own authority (John 7:17, ESV).

In John 7, Jesus is teaching in the temple during the Feast of Booths. Many Jews are seeking to kill him, and yet they marvel that Jesus seems

---

[110] Meisinger, "The Issue of One's Ability to Believe: Total Depravity/Inability," 87.

Arguments for the Faith-After-Regeneration View

to have such learning without ever having studied. Jesus's response to the unbelieving Jews in John 7:17 seems to show that the unregenerate do have an ability to seek God's truth. Meisinger explains:

> . . . the Lord makes a straightforward statement, which clarifies that if anyone wants to do God's will, he will discover it as from God. The sequence involved is uncomplicated. Steve Dolson-Andrew [in a March 1, 2005 email correspondence] lays out the chronological order this way: A person "wants" to do God's will, then he "understands" that the doctrine is from God, then he believes the doctrine. The Lord's teaching reveals human ability, not inability, to seek God's truth.[111]

Acts 10:1-2

> At Caesarea there was a man named Cornelius, a centurion of what was known as the Italian Cohort, a devout man who feared God with all his household, gave alms generously to the people, and prayed continually to God (Acts 10:1-2, ESV).

Faith-before-regeneration proponents generally argue that, at the time Cornelius is described here in Acts 10:1-2, he is unregenerate. For example, Meisinger says,

> Cornelius did not *believe* for the *remission of sins* until Peter arrived and preached the gospel (10:34-48; cf. 10:43 with 11:17). Cornelius believed *during* Peter's preaching, not before. The moment of gospel presentation became the centurion's pivot point from death to life, darkness to light. Luke clearly defines the moment of gospel hearing as the moment of the Centurion's new birth. Peter reports that Cornelius was instructed to call for

---

[111] Ibid., 85.

the apostle so that Peter might tell him the words by which he and all his household would be saved (Acts 11:14).[112]

If, indeed, Acts 10:1-2 describes an unregenerate Cornelius, then there is strong evidence here that the unregenerate do have the ability to respond to God in a positive way. Meisinger continues:

> Now, though not a believer, this Centurion was not like a cadaver, unable to respond to God. To the contrary, Cornelius the non-Christian *was a devout man and one who feared God and he gave alms and prayed to God always* (10:2). He received revelation from God, understood, and obeyed it (10:3, 22); in addition, the Lord recognized his prayers and alms (10:4, 31). Here is a man with a strong sense of God-consciousness, and the Lord worked in him to bring him to faith in Christ. His prayers and alms did not eternally save him, but his seeking postured him to believe the gospel when he heard it preached.
>
> There is nothing in this chapter to suggest that Total Inability was Cornelius' condition.[113]

Anderson concurs, saying of Cornelius, "Now, I don't know about you, but to me, that's an unregenerate person who's understanding some level of truth about God. And that's a deeper level than just general revelation."[114]

Romans 1:18-20

> For the wrath of God is revealed from heaven against all ungodliness and unrighteousness of men, who by their unrighteousness suppress the truth. For what can be known about God is

---

[112] Ibid., 86.

[113] Ibid.

[114] Anderson, "Regeneration and the *Ordo Salutis*."

Arguments for the Faith-After-Regeneration View

plain to them, because God has shown it to them. For his invisible attributes, namely, his eternal power and divine nature, have been clearly perceived, ever since the creation of the world, in the things that have been made. So they are without excuse (Romans 1:18-20, ESV).

Anderson argues from Roman 1:18-20 that the unregenerate can know spiritual things.[115] Some receptivity and understanding is clearly reflected because "what can be known about God is plain to them."[116] God has shown truth to the unregenerate and, at some level, they apprehend it. Spiritual truths about God—his attributes, power, and nature—"have been clearly perceived."[117]

Romans 6:17

But thanks be to God, that you who were once slaves of sin have become obedient from the heart to the standard of teaching to which you were committed (Romans 6:17, ESV).

Meisinger argues that Romans 6:17 describes the previously unregenerate state of Christians in which they obeyed the command to believe in Jesus. This shows that the unregenerate have an ability to obey. Meisinger explains:

A clear implication of this passage should not be ignored: It was when they were unbelievers—before the old man was crucified, before the body of sin was stripped of its tyrannical power, when they were slaves of sin, and when they were dominated by the body's lusts—it was *then* that they obeyed (6:17).

---

[115] Ibid.

[116] Ibid.

[117] Ibid.

In their unregenerate state, they obeyed from the heart. Their obedience was real and, thus, acceptable to God. The gospel had persuaded them and they obeyed it; i.e., they obeyed the command, Believe on the Lord Jesus Christ and you will be saved. . . . unbelievers have only one command to obey: to believe in Jesus Christ for eternal salvation (Romans 3:21-22).[118]

In commenting on Romans 6:17, Schreiner seems to agree that the obedience in view is the obedience of saving faith in Jesus:

God is thanked because (ὅτι) "you have become obedient from the heart" (ὑπηκούσατε ἐκ καρδίας, *hypēkousate ek kardias*). Paul is probably thinking of the conversion of the Roman Christians in which they exercised "the obedience of faith" (1:5; 16:26). The word ὑπηκούσατε emphasizes the decision to submit to God, while the words ἐκ καρδίας reflect the depth of that obedience. No superficial obedience was involved; it was a willing and glad-hearted obedience to the gospel of Christ.[119]

While Schreiner may agree with Meisinger on the type of obedience in view, he does not agree that the obedience occurs prior to regeneration. Schreiner explains:

Nonetheless, thanks are offered to God for their glad-hearted obedience because it was his work that led to their obedience. This does not deny for a moment the authenticity of human decision in submitting to God, but in typical biblical fashion Paul attributes the decision ultimately to God's grace and power. Indeed, God must be the one who causes obedience to rise in

---

[118] Meisinger, "The Issue of One's Ability to Believe: Total Depravity/Inability," 89-90.

[119] Thomas R. Schreiner, *Romans*. vol. 6. Baker Exegetical Commentary on the New Testament (Grand Rapids, MI: Baker Books, 1998), 334.

Arguments for the Faith-After-Regeneration View

human hearts because all human beings are "slaves of sin." To be a slave of sin means that one is under its lordship and dominion, and unable to extricate oneself from its tyranny. God in his grace broke the shackles of sin, so that glad-hearted obedience became a reality for the Roman Christians.[120]

The grammar and context of Romans 6:17 alone do not seem to resolve the issue of whether the obedience of faith comes from the unregenerate (according to Meisinger) or the regenerate (according to Schreiner).

Romans 16:25-27

Now to him who is able to strengthen you according to my gospel and the preaching of Jesus Christ, according to the revelation of the mystery that was kept secret for long ages but has now been disclosed and through the prophetic writings has been made known to all nations, according to the command of the eternal God, to bring about the obedience of faith—to the only wise God be glory forevermore through Jesus Christ! Amen (Romans 16:25, ESV).

Flowers interprets this passage as affirming human ability to respond in faith to the truth claims of the gospel:

The specific truth claims of the gospel (salvation is provided by means of atonement through Christ's death and resurrection) were a mystery before they were made known through the divine inspiration of Scripture.... These glorious truths were once hidden for a good redemptive purpose, but now they are clear for anyone and everyone to know and accept. No one can say,

---

[120] Ibid.

"I could not understand the truth of the gospel due to some innate moral inability beyond my control."[121]

2 Corinthians 4:3-6

> And even if our gospel is veiled, it is veiled to those who are perishing. In their case the god of this world has blinded the minds of the unbelievers, to keep them from seeing the light of the gospel of the glory of Christ, who is the image of God. For what we proclaim is not ourselves, but Jesus Christ as Lord, with ourselves as your servants for Jesus' sake. For God, who said, "Let light shine out of darkness," has shone in our hearts to give the light of the knowledge of the glory of God in the face of Jesus Christ (2 Corinthians 4:3-6 ESV).

Meisinger contends from this passage that the unregenerate have the ability to be illuminated by the light of the gospel. This ability of the unregenerate to receive light is the very reason Satan attempts to veil the truth and blind the minds of unbelievers; otherwise, no effort from Satan would be needed. Meisinger explains,

> This important passage reveals that the devil throws a veil over the minds of non-Christians, effectively blinding them to the truth. *Why? Lest the light of the gospel ... should shine on them* (εἰς τὸ μὴ αὐγάσαι τὸν φωτισμὸν τοῦ εὐαγγελίου). Why does the devil exert himself to prevent unbelievers from comprehending the gospel? Because he knows that *the gospel is the power of God unto salvation for everyone who believes ... from faith to faith* (Romans 1:16-17). He knows that people must know the gospel to believe, for one cannot believe what one does not know![122]

---

[121] Flowers, *God's Provision for All*, 62.

[122] Meisinger, "The Issue of One's Ability to Believe: Total Depravity/Inability," 88.

Revelation 14:6-7

> Then I saw another angel flying directly overhead, with an eternal gospel to proclaim to those who dwell on earth, to every nation and tribe and language and people. And he said with a loud voice, "Fear God and give him glory, because the hour of his judgment has come, and worship him who made heaven and earth, the sea and the springs of water" (Revelation 14:6-7, ESV).

Anderson explains that this passage describes a time near the end of the tribulation period, long after the crucifixion of Christ, when unbelievers hear an "eternal gospel" preached by an angel. Anderson explains that the "gospel" or good news has its highest revelation in the cross, but can also include other good news leading to it; there is "good news before the good news," and this text is an example. Anderson argues that the angel begins with some good news these unbelievers already had available to them; namely, that God is the one "who made heaven and earth, the sea and the springs of water." So, the angel gives them more good news or more light by saying, "judgment has come." The implication is that these unregenerate people are going to be held accountable for the light they have received through creation and the angelic proclamation because they are able to respond. Anderson explains:

> These are unregenerate people who are going to be held accountable for the light given in nature and for the further light that it's judgment time.... We're saying that an unregenerate man can interact with and understand certain spiritual things—that through divine enablement, which is light, he can do that. Without the light, he can't. But with light he can.[123]

In review, the first argument of the faith-after-regeneration view is: the Scriptures teach total inability such that the unregenerate are

---

[123] Anderson, "Regeneration and the *Ordo Salutis*."

completely unable to respond to God in any good way, and thus are unable to believe in Jesus apart from God's help; therefore, regeneration must logically and causally precede faith.

This argument has been shown to be weak on two fronts. First, scriptural evidence refutes total inability; the unregenerate do have some capacity to respond to God. Second, while there is general agreement that the unregenerate cannot believe without God's help, it does not necessarily follow that the help God provides must be regeneration; alternatives such as an effectual call, prevenient grace, and divine illumination are possibilities.

Argument 2: Scripture Teaches that Regeneration Precedes Faith

Barrett provides a thorough, formidable, and recent exegetical defense of the faith-after-regeneration view.[124] The biblical passages he cites will serve as the framework for summarizing and evaluating in this section with one addition: Zephaniah 3:9 is cited by others in support of the view. For easy reference, these passages have been rearranged and presented in the general order in which they appear in the Bible. This is worth mentioning only because what is widely considered to be the strongest argument (1 John 5:1) comes last.

Scriptures about the Circumcision and Gift of a New Heart

I have grouped the following Hebrew Scriptures together because, according to Barrett, they all relate to "the circumcision and gift of a new heart."[125] I will first present each text along with associated faith-after-regeneration arguments. Then I will respond to all of these arguments collectively at the end of this subsection.

---

[124] Barrett, *Salvation by Grace*, 125-206.

[125] Ibid., 135-141. Jeremiah 24:7 could be added to this list as another example of God giving his people a new heart.

Arguments for the Faith-After-Regeneration View

Deuteronomy 30:6

> And the LORD your God will circumcise your heart and the heart of your offspring, so that you will love the LORD your God with all your heart and with all your soul, that you may live (Deuteronomy 30:6, ESV).

The contention here is that the circumcision of the heart refers to God regenerating his people, and the express purpose of the regeneration is to enable those regenerated to love the Lord, which includes believing in him. Snoeberger argues that, in this verse, to love the Lord is to have saving faith in him: "This reference ... does not include the terms 'belief' and 'trust,' but there are several factors which point to this phrase being, or at least including, faith."[126] He goes on to suggest rephrasing the verse: "Yahweh will regenerate you so that you will exercise saving faith."[127] Then Snoeberger succinctly closes his case: "To conclude, then, Moses was making a clear statement of order: regeneration precedes faith."[128]

Embracing the assumption that loving God can be equated with believing in him, Barrett agrees with Snoeberger: "Nowhere in Deuteronomy 30:6 do we see any indication that Yahweh's sovereign act of circumcising the heart is conditioned upon the will of man to believe. Rather, it is quite the opposite. Yahweh must first circumcise the heart so that the sinner can exercise a will that believes.[129]

Jeremiah 31:33; 32:39-40

> "For this is the covenant that I will make with the house of Israel after those days, declares the LORD: I will put my law within

---

[126] Snoeberger, "The Logical Priority of Regeneration to Saving Faith in a Theological *Ordo Salutis*," 71.

[127] Ibid., 73.

[128] Ibid., 74.

[129] Barrett, *Salvation by Grace*, 136.

them, and I will write it on their hearts. And I will be their God, and they shall be my people" (Jeremiah 31:33, ESV).

"I will give them one heart and one way, that they may fear me forever, for their own good and the good of their children after them. I will make with them an everlasting covenant, that I will not turn away from doing good to them. And I will put the fear of me in their hearts, that they may not turn from me" (Jeremiah 32:39-40, ESV).

The interpretation here is that God writing on the hearts of his people and giving them one heart and putting fear into their hearts all refer to the act of regeneration. Moreover, the stated purpose of God regenerating his people is so that they "may not turn" from him, or stated positively, that they may have the ability to follow him. Barrett explains, "Notice, it is only when God writes his law within, on the heart, and places within a fear of himself that the sinner can follow after him."[130] Apparently, the enablement to follow includes the enablement to believe; ergo, regeneration precedes faith.

Ezekiel 11:19-21; 36:26-27

"And I will give them one heart, and a new spirit I will put within them. I will remove the heart of stone from their flesh and give them a heart of flesh, that they may walk in my statutes and keep my rules and obey them. And they shall be my people, and I will be their God. But as for those whose heart goes after their detestable things and their abominations, I will bring their deeds upon their own heads, declares the Lord GOD" (Ezekiel 11:19-21, ESV).

"And I will give you a new heart, and a new spirit I will put within you. And I will remove the heart of stone from your flesh and

---

[130] Ibid., 137.

give you a heart of flesh. And I will put my Spirit within you, and cause you to walk in my statutes and be careful to obey my rules" (Ezekiel 36:26-27, ESV).

Here, the contention is that the imagery of God replacing the heart of stone with a heart of flesh depicts regeneration. Again, the stated purpose of this regeneration is so that God's people will obey, and again, faith is inferred to be a part of obedience. Barrett says, "Once again, God does not put a new heart and spirit within in reaction to or because of the sinner's faith, but it is God's sovereign act of implanting a new heart, a new spirit, that causes the sinner to turn in faith and obedience."[131]

Augustine uses Ezekiel 11:19 to argue that, when God sovereignly regenerates us, it is not so that we are forced to believe against our will; rather, we are given a new will in place of the old: "if God were not able to remove from the human heart even its obstinacy and hardness, He would not say, through the prophet, 'I will take from them their heart of stone and will give them a heart of flesh.'"[132]

Ezekiel 37:1-14

The hand of the LORD was upon me, and he brought me out in the Spirit of the LORD and set me down in the middle of the valley; it was full of bones. And he led me around among them, and behold, there were very many on the surface of the valley, and behold, they were very dry. And he said to me, "Son of man, can these bones live?" And I answered, "O Lord GOD, you know." Then he said to me, "Prophesy over these bones, and say to them, O dry bones, hear the word of the LORD. Thus says the Lord GOD to these bones: Behold, I will cause breath to

---

[131] Ibid., 139.

[132] Augustine, *On Grace and Free Will*, in Augustine, *Basic Writings*, 1:756 (chap. 29).

enter you, and you shall live. And I will lay sinews upon you, and will cause flesh to come upon you, and cover you with skin, and put breath in you, and you shall live, and you shall know that I am the LORD." So I prophesied as I was commanded. And as I prophesied, there was a sound, and behold, a rattling, and the bones came together, bone to its bone. And I looked, and behold, there were sinews on them, and flesh had come upon them, and skin had covered them. But there was no breath in them. Then he said to me, "Prophesy to the breath; prophesy, son of man, and say to the breath, Thus says the Lord GOD: Come from the four winds, O breath, and breathe on these slain, that they may live." So I prophesied as he commanded me, and the breath came into them, and they lived and stood on their feet, an exceedingly great army. Then he said to me, "Son of man, these bones are the whole house of Israel. Behold, they say, 'Our bones are dried up, and our hope is lost; we are indeed cut off.' Therefore prophesy, and say to them, Thus says the Lord GOD: Behold, I will open your graves and raise you from your graves, O my people. And I will bring you into the land of Israel. And you shall know that I am the LORD, when I open your graves, and raise you from your graves, O my people. And I will put my Spirit within you, and you shall live, and I will place you in your own land. Then you shall know that I am the LORD; I have spoken, and I will do it, declares the LORD" (Ezekiel 37:1-14, ESV).

Barrett argues that the bones here represent the whole house of Israel, spiritually dead, and the Lord breathes new life into (regenerates) the Israelites, with the result that the Israelites come to know the Lord.[133] The point is: God must regenerate the Israelites before they can know or have faith in the Lord.

---

[133] Barrett, *Salvation by Grace*, 139-141.

Arguments for the Faith-After-Regeneration View

Rebuttal

The evaluation of these arguments as a whole will now be presented. The first question is: do these texts truly refer to the very same act of regeneration God performs today? Although some may argue that at least some of these texts prophetically refer to a time yet future, inaugurated by the second coming of Christ,[134] it is reasonable to assume that these texts do refer to regeneration. In commenting on Deuteronomy 30:6, Joseph Dillow (who is not a Calvinist) affirms, "In the clearest possible terms, *Moses speaks not only of regeneration, but of ethical behavior.*"[135]

In these passages, it is noted that the results of regeneration include a new capacity for ethical behavior, variously expressed as loving the Lord, fearing the Lord, turning to the Lord, walking in his statutes, keeping his rules, and obeying his rules.

Conspicuous by its absence is any mention of faith in these passages. Faith-after-regeneration proponents argue that this is proof that faith cannot be a condition of regeneration. But this is an argument from silence. One could just as easily argue that the absence of faith is proof that faith does *not* follow regeneration, and that would be just as fallacious.

Some argue the new capacity for ethical behavior which comes from regeneration must include faith, even though it is not mentioned. But this is a presumption, not a fact. Similarly, it is argued that having saving faith in the Lord is essentially the same as loving the Lord; therefore, faith must be a result of regeneration. The logic goes like this:

Premise 1:   Loving the Lord is a result of regeneration.

Premise 2:   Loving the Lord is the same thing as having saving faith in the Lord.

---

[134] For example. John F. Walvoord, "The Prophetic Context of the Millennium," *Bibliotheca Sacra*, 114 (1957): 97-101.

[135] Joseph C. Dillow, *Final Destiny: The Future Reign of the Servant Kings*, 4th ed. (n.p.: Grace Theology Press, 2018), 179.

> Conclusion: Having saving faith is a result of regeneration (even though it is not explicitly mentioned to be a result).

But there is no basis for equating faith and love. Compton agrees. In commenting on Deuteronomy 30:6, he says,

> It is questionable whether loving the Lord in verse 6 can legitimately be identified as a synonym for saving faith. The standard lexical sources recognize that love of the Lord in the Old Testament is often associated with expressions that reflect faith, such as fearing the Lord (e.g. Deut 10:12) or clinging to the Lord (13:4). But these sources do not expressly equate love of the Lord with repentance or saving faith.[136]

The above Old Testament passages simply do not resolve the order of faith and regeneration one way or another.

It is significant to note that when faith is presumed to follow regeneration, and when faith is conflated with other things that do follow regeneration, such as love and obedience, a common result is to read a works-based salvation into the new covenant of Jeremiah 31:31-34. For example, Bradley Green argues that works are necessary for salvation:

> In short, "works" are "necessary" for salvation because part of the "newness" of the new covenant is actual, grace-induced and grace-elicited obedience by true members of the new covenant. When the New Testament documents are read against Old Testament texts such as Jeremiah 31:31-34 and Ezekiel 36:22-29 (cf. Ezek. 11:19; 18:31), this obedience is seen as a promised component of the new covenant.[137]

---

[136] Compton, "The *Ordo Salutis* and Monergism: The Case for Faith Preceding Regeneration, Part 1," 42-43.

[137] Bradley G. Green, *Covenant and Commandment: Works, Obedience and Faithfulness in the Christian Life*, New Studies in Biblical Theology, ed.

Arguments for the Faith-After-Regeneration View

The purpose here is not to debate the relationship between faith and works in eternal salvation, but to merely show the apparent connection between the faith-after-regeneration view and the belief that eternal salvation is in one way or another predicated on works.

Zephaniah 3:9 & Rebuttal

> "For at that time I will change the speech of the peoples to a pure speech, that all of them may call upon the name of the LORD and serve him with one accord" (ESV).

The argument of faith-after-regeneration proponents from Zephaniah 3:9 is that God giving "pure speech" is the equivalent of regeneration which enables the Israelites to "call upon the name of the LORD," which is a reference to saving faith. As such regeneration ("pure speech") precedes and enables faith ("call upon the name of the LORD").

Walter C. Kaiser, Jr. and Lloyd J. Ogilvie seem to reflect this view in their interpretation of Zephaniah 3:9:

> And when God promises to restore a "pure language," He is referring to more than a type or quality of speech; human language is merely the outward indicator of the inner ego and person. Thus the promise of a radical change of language was another statement of the uniqueness of God's re-creative work [in regeneration]. . . . Now mortals with new hearts would "call on the name of the LORD" and "serve Him . . ."[138]

D. A. Carson (Nottingham, England: Apollos, 2014; Downers Grove, IL: InterVarsity Press, 2014), 17.

[138] Walter C. Kaiser, Jr. and Lloyd J. Ogilvie, *Micah, Nahum, Habakkuk, Zephaniah, Haggai, Zechariah, Malachi.* vol. 23. The Preacher's Commentary Series (Nashville, TN: Thomas Nelson, 1992), 237-238.

O. Palmer Robertson echoes much the same view of Zephaniah 3:9 in different words:

> When the prophet reports the Lord as saying, *I shall convert the nations*, he underscores the necessity of God's immediate involvement in this momentous activity. None but the Almighty could perform this kind of task on such a massive scale. The hardening of the human heart to the point that it could not find repentance [total inability] had been declared as the occasion for cosmic condemnation. Any turning of the nations must clearly be attributed to the sovereign grace of God. The Lord's special gift to these nations is that *they speak with a purified lip.* . . . [a synonym for regeneration].
>
> The significance of this phrase is found in the next statement: *that they all may call on the name of Yahweh.* . . . They shall call on the name of Yahweh for salvation. This petition of the nations implies a ready acknowledgment of sin, together with a confession that Yahweh alone is God and Savior.[139]

The claim that the divinely imparted "pure speech" of Zephaniah 3:9 is the equivalent of regeneration is an assumption with no support. In fact, it is such a stretch that even some faith-after-regeneration proponents seem reluctant to take it. For example, Snoeberger lists the "pure speech" of Zephaniah 3:9 among certain isolated biblical descriptors that are difficult to define and are interpreted to fit whatever one's theological system requires: "these descriptors, by virtue of their infrequent usage, are nearly impossible to define apart from the *analogia fide*, that is, their meanings can be determined only after one's theological position has been established."[140]

---

[139] O. Palmer Robertson, *The Books of Nahum, Habakkuk and Zephaniah,*. The New International Commentary on the Old Testament (Grand Rapids, MI: Wm. B. Eerdmans, 1990), 328.

[140] Snoeberger, "The Logical Priority of Regeneration to Saving Faith in a

Arguments for the Faith-After-Regeneration View

Compton argues that "pure speech" is not a reference to regeneration at all, but more plausibly refers to forgiveness: "the promise of Zephaniah 3:9 that the Lord will give to the peoples 'purified lips' means that the Lord will forgive their iniquity and cleanse them from their sin."[141]

Not only is regeneration not in view in Zephaniah 3:9, neither is saving faith. There is no clear biblical support for assuming the expression, "call upon the name of the Lord" is the functional equivalent of saving faith. As Compton argues, "the majority of its uses in the Old Testament refer to calling on the Lord's name in worship, generally by those who are already saved," and, "the expression in Zephaniah is found specifically in connection with worship, not salvation."[142] For example, in Genesis 21:33, Abraham calls on the name of the Lord in worship well after his belief in the Lord was credited to him as righteousness (Genesis 15:6).

Zephaniah 3:9 simply does not support the faith-after-regeneration view.

While the Old Testament passages offered by Barrett and others do not inform the order of faith and regeneration, there is an Old Testament text that does shed some light. As recorded in Numbers 21, a text not cited or commented on by Barrett, the Lord sent fiery serpents among his rebellious people and many died. The people acknowledged their sin to Moses and asked him to pray to God for their salvation from these deadly snakes. The Lord's solution is recorded in Numbers 21:8-9: "And the LORD said to Moses, 'Make a fiery serpent and set it on a pole, and everyone who is bitten, when he sees it, shall live.' So Moses made a bronze serpent and set it on a pole. And if a serpent bit anyone, he would look at the bronze serpent and live" (ESV).

The order is clear: the people had to look at the bronze serpent to live. First look, then live. Jesus uses this event in history to explain how

---

Theological *Ordo Salutis*," 54 ft. 22.

[141] Compton, "The *Ordo Salutis* and Monergism: The Case for Faith Preceding Regeneration, Part 1," 48.

[142] Ibid., 48-49.

one receives eternal life in John 3:14-15: "And as Moses lifted up the serpent in the wilderness, so must the Son of Man be lifted up, that whoever believes in him may have eternal life" (ESV).

The comparison is clear: just as looking at the lifted-up serpent was a prerequisite for receiving *physical* life back then, so believing in the lifted-up Christ is a prerequisite for receiving *spiritual* life now. First believe, then live. The life in view is clearly the new life of regeneration. This is strong evidence that controverts the faith-after-regeneration view.

John 1:12-13 & Rebuttal

> But to all who did receive him, who believed in his name, he gave the right to become children of God, who were born, not of blood nor of the will of the flesh nor of the will of man, but of God (John 1:12-13, ESV).

Luther uses John 1:13 to argue that regeneration is not in response to our will, but God's. Luther says, "free will avails nothing here."[143] Similarly, Snoeberger contends the part of this passage which deals explicitly with regeneration is verse 13 describing, "those who were born."[144] Snoeberger offers two "strands of evidence" from John 1:13 that prove that regeneration is logically prior to faith.[145]

The first strand of evidence is a logical syllogism purported to represent the point of John 1:13:

Premise 1: No act of the human will can inaugurate regeneration.

Premise 2: Faith is an act of human will.

Conclusion: Faith cannot inaugurate regeneration.

---

[143] Luther, *The Bondage of the Will*, 59.

[144] Snoeberger, "The Logical Priority of Regeneration to Saving Faith," 77-81.

[145] Ibid., 80-81.

Arguments for the Faith-After-Regeneration View 69

The second strand is found in the word, ἐγεννήθησαν, translated "were born." It is argued that, because the verb is in the passive voice, any human initiative in regeneration is precluded. Moreover, the meaning of the word itself is said to preclude prior human initiative because one does not choose to be born.

These arguments are not persuasive in proving faith follows regeneration for several reasons. First, the three-part negation of John 1:13 ("not of blood, nor of the will of the flesh nor of the will of man") does not have saving faith in view, and does not support the all-encompassing claim of Premise 1. As D. A. Carson points out, John's point in the three-part negation is simply that "being born into the family of God is quite different from being born into a human family."[146] Specifically, being born again is "not of blood," which means it is not by means of natural descent, blood relations, or human ancestry.[147] Nor is it "of the will of the flesh," which means it is not a result of natural human desire (presumably for children or for the act that produces them).[148] Nor is it "of the will of man," which means it is not the patriarchal decision of a human father ("man" is a translation of ἀνδρὸς meaning "male" as opposed to female). Collectively, these three limited negations do not preclude faith in Jesus. The overly broad claim of Premise 1 that "no act of the human will can inaugurate regeneration" is not the point of the text. As such, Snoeberger's syllogism is fallacious.

---

[146] D. A. Carson, *The Gospel According to John*. The Pillar New Testament Commentary (Leicester, England; Grand Rapids, MI: Inter-Varsity Press; W.B. Eerdmans, 1991), 125.

[147] Andreas J. Köstenberger, *John*, Baker Exegetical Commentary on the New Testament (Grand Rapids, MI: Baker Academic, 2004), 39.

[148] Gerald L. Borchert, *John 1–11*. vol. 25a. The New American Commentary (Nashville: Broadman & Holman Publishers, 1996), 118; Robert N. Wilkin, "The Gospel According to John," *The Grace New Testament Commentary*, ed. Robert N. Wilkin (Denton, TX: Grace Evangelical Society, 2010), 363.

Second, I agree that both the lexical meaning and passive form of the word, ἐγεννήθησαν ("were born") emphasize that God does the regenerating, but this is not determinative. Of course we can't regenerate ourselves; God must do it. But this does not rule out human faith as a necessary antecedent to God's work. God responding to faith by regenerating does not make human belief the source of the regeneration.

Third, taken together, the verses in John 1:12-13 provide some evidence which actually controverts the faith-after-regeneration view. In John 1:12, being given "the right to become children of God" can be taken as the result of "believing in his name." Admittedly, the grammar of John 1:12 does not dictate a specific causal order, but it is quite natural to take faith in Jesus as the instrumental means by which God gives us the right to become children of God. Indeed, Snoeberger seems to take it this way, but side-steps the obvious contradiction of his faith-after-regeneration view by asserting that becoming children of God does not refer to regeneration, but to adoption, saying, "We conclude, then, that the sonship of John 1:12 refers explicitly to adoption, and not to regeneration. As such, John 1:12 merely serves to place adoption after faith in the *ordo salutis*, a placement which all concede."[149]

Nevertheless, there are some good reasons to believe that becoming children of God in John 1:12 is synonymous with being born of God in John 1:13. Brian Abasciano points out in this text, "to become children of God" and to be "born" are "parallel expressions referring to the same phenomenon;" namely, regeneration.[150] Abasciano argues that, "the Johannine literature makes no distinction whatsoever between adoption and regeneration."[151] Furthermore, he points to several other Johannine texts (1 John 2:29-3:2; 3:9-10; 5:1-2) where the concepts of

---

[149] Snoeberger, "The Logical Priority of Regeneration to Saving Faith," 77-78.

[150] Brian J. Abasciano, "Does Regeneration Precede Faith? The Use of 1 John 5:1 As a Proof Text," *Evangelical Quarterly* 84, no. 4 (2012): 318.

[151] Ibid., 318-319.

becoming children of God and being born of God are used in parallel to refer to the same phenomenon.

Carson seems to confirm Abasciano's conclusion. In his commentary on John 1:12-13, Carson does not draw any conclusions about the order of faith and new birth.[152] Nevertheless, in commenting on John 3:3 in connection with John 1:12-13, he says, "'to be born again' or 'to be born from above' must mean the same thing as 'to become children of God,' to be 'born of God,' by believing in the name of the incarnate Word."[153] Compton agrees: "the lexical evidence for 'children of God' within the Johannine corpus supports taking the expression as designating regeneration, not adoption."[154]

If becoming children of God and being born of God are indeed synonymous, then the logic of John 1:12-13 makes perfect sense. According to John 1:12, those who believe in Jesus are, as a result, given the right to become children of God. John 1:13 explains that this process of becoming children of God is the *supernatural* process of birth as distinguished from the *natural* process.

In conclusion, not only does John 1:12-13 fail to support the faith-after-regeneration view, it supports faith *before* regeneration.

John 3:3-8 & Rebuttal

> Jesus answered him, "Truly, truly, I say to you, unless one is born again he cannot see the kingdom of God." Nicodemus said to him, "How can a man be born when he is old? Can he enter a second time into his mother's womb and be born?" Jesus answered, "Truly, truly, I say to you, unless one is born of water and the Spirit, he cannot enter the kingdom of God. That which is born of the flesh is flesh, and that which is born of the Spirit

---

[152] Carson, *The Gospel According to John*, 126.

[153] Ibid., 189.

[154] Compton, "The *Ordo Salutis* and Monergism: The Case for Faith Preceding Regeneration, Part 2," 162.

is spirit. Do not marvel that I said to you, 'You must be born again.' The wind blows where it wishes, and you hear its sound, but you do not know where it comes from or where it goes. So it is with everyone who is born of the Spirit" (John 3:3-8, ESV).[155]

Barrett contends it is necessary to understand John 2:23-25 as a context for properly interpreting John 3:3-8. According to Barrett, John 2:23-25 shows that Jesus is "troubled" by a lack of regeneration among some who believed in his name, but were counterfeits.[156] The Appendix provides an explanation of how Barrett and many others have likely misinterpreted John 2:23-25. This argument concerning John 2:23-25 is appended because it does not relate directly to the order of faith and regeneration, and the following evaluation of John 3:3-8 does not depend on it.

In commenting on Jesus's response to Nicodemus in John 3:3-8, Barrett says,

> The miracle of human birth is a unilateral activity. There is nothing the infant does to be born. The infant does not birth itself. Nor is it the case that birth is conditioned upon the infant's will to accept it or not.
>
> Likewise, the same is true with spiritual birth. Man is dead in his sins and spiritually in bondage to sin. His only hope is the new birth, and yet such a birth is a unilateral, monergistic act of God. Man plays no role whatsoever in the spiritual birthing event. Rather, God acts alone to awaken new life . . .[157]
>
> Therefore, to conclude that man in some way cooperates with God in regeneration . . . so that conversion causally precedes

---

[155] I am aware that the original Greek phrase translated "born again" in John 3:3 (γεννηθῇ ἄνωθεν) is different than the word translated "regeneration" in Titus 3:5 (παλιγγενεσίας), but submit that the ideas are synonymous.

[156] Barret, *Salvation by Grace*, 145.

[157] Ibid., 151.

regeneration, is an assault on the sovereignty of the Holy Spirit and furthermore denies the proper meaning of the biblical images used to speak of the Spirit's work in regeneration.[158]

John Murray (a Calvinist) concurs: "It should be specially noted that even faith that Jesus is the Christ is the effect of regeneration. This is, of course, a clear implication of John 3:3-8. . . . We are not born again by faith or repentance or conversion; we repent and believe because we have been regenerated."[159]

I would argue that in John 3:3-8 Jesus is not trying to prove that regeneration precedes faith; rather, he's saying that one cannot make himself a new creature by good works; God must do it. This is a needful dismantling of Nicodemus's works-based salvation paradigm in preparation for an entirely new construct: faith alone in Christ alone, which is explained in John 3:9-21.[160] Oddly, Barrett and others focus on the preparation in John 3:3-8 and ignore the new construct to which it points in John 3:9-21. In doing so, they shift the focus away from the need for faith. But the culminating emphasis of John 3:3-21 is unmistakably the need for faith in Jesus for eternal life: "For God so loved the world, that he gave his only Son, that whoever believes in him should not perish but have eternal life" (John 3:16, ESV).

In John 3:3, it says "Jesus answered him," which is curious because, to this point in the text, there is no record of Nicodemus asking a question. We're left to determine what the unspoken question must have been. Barrett assumes Nicodemus's question was about the identity of Jesus and whether he is from God. Barrett explains:

---

[158] Ibid., 156.

[159] John Murray, "Redemption Accomplished and Applied," *Collected Writings of John Murray* (Edinburgh: Banner of Truth, 1976), 103.

[160] I am aware that some proponents of the so-called "New Perspective on Paul" would argue that first-century Palestinian Judaism was not oriented to salvation by works, but debating this point is beyond the scope of this work.

Nicodemus seems to ask his question wanting an answer, namely, who are you Jesus? The answer Jesus gives shows that the only way one can truly know who God is (and therefore who Jesus is) is by being born again. In other words, Nicodemus will never believe that Jesus is from God (let alone that Jesus is the Son of God) unless he first receives the new birth from the Spirit. Therefore, rather than Jesus telling Nicodemus, "Yes, I am from God," he responds by saying that unless one is born by the Spirit he will never understand who Jesus is in a saving way.[161]

While we cannot be certain about Nicodemus's unspoken question, there is evidence to suggest that Barrett's assumption is wrong. While it is likely true Nicodemus is not entirely clear about Jesus's identity, he knows Jesus is from God and that God is likely with him. His own words in John 3:2 confirm it: "Rabbi, we know that you are a teacher *come from God*, for no one can do these signs that you do *unless God is with him*" (ESV, emphasis added). The way Nicodemus phrases "unless God is with him" is a third-class condition suggesting some uncertainty.[162]

Also, if Nicodemus were really asking, "who are you, Jesus?" then Jesus's answer amounts to something like, "you can't know unless you're born again," which would seem to be an odd evangelistic approach.

It seems more reasonable to assume that Nicodemus's unspoken question would fit Jesus's answer. So, if Jesus's answer in John 3:3 is "Truly, truly, I say to you, unless one is born again he cannot see the kingdom of God" (ESV), then the unspoken question was probably something like, "When will we see the kingdom of God?" This makes much more sense because, as "the teacher of Israel," Nicodemus surely knew that, according to 2 Samuel 7:12-16, God had promised that a

---

[161] Barrett, *Salvation by Grace*, 146-147.

[162] Daniel Wallace, *Greek Grammar Beyond the Basics* (Grand Rapids, MI: Zondervan, 1996), 696.

Messiah would be raised up who would come as a descendant of David to save the Jews and become the King forever.

Nicodemus was inquiring when this was going to happen. "When will we see God's kingdom?" He understood that if Jesus was sent from God as a prophet, maybe he knew. In response, Jesus is saying, "unless you are born again, you're not going to see the fulfillment of God's promise. You're going to miss it. You will not experience it."

The point of John 3:3-8 is that no one can be religious enough or good enough to be a part of God's kingdom; regeneration is required. And this is disconcerting to Nicodemus because he had dedicated his whole life to being religious enough and being good enough to be a part of God's kingdom. Understandably, this raises another question in his mind, and this time he speaks it: "How can these things be?" (John 3:9, ESV). "These things" refers to being born again in its various aspects explained by Jesus in the immediately preceding context. And the word "be" is a translation of the Greek verb, γίνομαι, and can be properly translated, "happen." So, in effect, Nicodemus is asking: how can regeneration happen?

Jesus's answer to the question indicates that faith is required for regeneration. Jesus says in John 3:14-15: "And as Moses lifted up the serpent in the wilderness, so must the Son of Man be lifted up, that whoever believes in him may have eternal life" (ESV). Jesus is referring to the historical account of the Jewish people recorded in Numbers 21:4-9. The people of Israel had sinned against God, so God sent fiery, poisonous serpents among them and they bit the people so that many were dying. But, God provided a way of salvation. He told Moses to make a bronze serpent to be lifted up high on a pole so that anyone who looked upon it in faith would be healed.

Because of their sin, the people were dying and there was absolutely nothing they themselves could do about it. They couldn't cure themselves by resolving to be better or more religious. They were not in control; they were at God's mercy.

But God provided a way of salvation. God arranged it. All the people had to do was look up in faith to the serpent who had been lifted up, and they would be healed physically. Looking up in faith was a necessary prior condition of being saved. Jesus is saying that, in the same way, the Son of Man, is going to have to somehow be lifted up, just like the serpent, so that "whoever believes in him may have eternal life." So, Jesus's answer to the question, "how can regeneration happen?" is simply, "believe in me."

In conclusion, John 3:3-8, does not support the faith-after-regeneration view. On the contrary, it is a part of a broader argument that supports faith as a necessary prior condition of regeneration.

Acts 5:31; 11:18; 2 Timothy 2:24-26 & Rebuttal

> "God exalted him at his right hand as Leader and Savior, to give repentance to Israel and forgiveness of sins" (Acts 5:31, ESV).

> When they heard these things they fell silent. And they glorified God, saying, "Then to the Gentiles also God has granted repentance that leads to life" (Acts 11:18, ESV).

> And the Lord's servant must not be quarrelsome but kind to everyone, able to teach, patiently enduring evil, correcting his opponents with gentleness. God may perhaps grant them repentance leading to a knowledge of the truth, and they may come to their senses and escape from the snare of the devil, after being captured by him to do his will (2 Timothy 2:24-26, ESV).

These three passages are offered by Barrett in support of the faith-after-regeneration view, according to the following logic[163]:

> Premise 1: Repentance is a gift from God that only comes after regeneration.

---

[163] Barrett, *Salvation by Grace*, 202-204. This particular logical syllogism is not expressly presented by Barrett or others; it merely reflects my own understanding of their faith-after-regeneration argument.

Premise 2: Repentance and faith are always inseparable.

Conclusion: Faith must come after regeneration.

The first part of Premise 1 that asserts that repentance is a gift from God is not a primary point of contention. Roger Olson explains, "Both Reformed and Arminian evangelicals equally regard repentance as a work of God."[164] The question at hand is: does repentance necessarily follow regeneration? Of course, faith-after-regeneration proponents argue that it does. For example, Herman Bavinck states unequivocally, "True repentance according to Scripture, does not arise from the natural 'man' but from the new life that was planted in a person by regeneration."[165] But do the given passages prove it?

Granted, God is definitely the giver of repentance in Acts 5:31, Acts 11:18, and 2 Timothy 2:24-26. But these verses provide no evidence that repentance comes after regeneration. In fact, there is some evidence to the contrary. For example, in Acts 11:18, Jewish believers in the Jerusalem church respond to Peter's report of God's inclusion of Gentiles by saying: "Then to the Gentiles also God has granted repentance that leads to life" (ESV). Here, repentance comes before "life." If this "life" is describing the new life of regeneration, then it can be argued that this is evidence for repentance actually preceding regeneration instead of following it.

Regarding 2 Timothy 2:24-26, Barrett argues, "The opponents Paul refers to are unbelievers, as is evident by the fact that they are opposing the Lord's servant (2 Tim. 2:24), are in need of repentance and knowledge of the truth (2 Tim. 2:25), and are in 'the snare of the devil.'"[166]

---

[164] Roger E. Olson, "Repentance," in *The Westminster Handbook to Evangelical Theology* (Louisville: Westminster John Knox, 2004), 251.

[165] Herman Bavinck, *Reformed Dogmatics*, ed. John Bolt, trans. John Vriend, vol. 4 (Grand Rapids, MI: Baker, 2008), 163.

[166] Barrett, *Salvation by Grace*, 204.

The assumption that Paul is referring to unbelievers is debatable; for example, Dillow, Wilkin, and Litfin take the opponents to be believers.[167] But, for the sake of argument, if we concede that the opponents are unbelievers, we are once again left with the idea of repentance "leading to" and thus preceding some important things: "a knowledge of the truth," "coming to their senses," and "escaping from the snare of the devil." Gordon Fee takes "a knowledge of the truth" to be synonymous with eternal salvation, saying, "Such a change of heart has as its goal that they will come to a knowledge of the truth, a term that in the PE [Pauline Epistles] is nearly synonymous for 'getting saved' (1 Tim. 2:4) or belonging to God's true people (1 Tim. 4:3)."[168] If this is true, then it is more evidence controverting Premise 1: repentance does not come after salvation and regeneration; if anything, the evidence here is that repentance comes before.

Not only is Premise 1 unsupported by the given biblical texts, it is also contradicted by the ministry of John the Baptist—a ministry that called people to repentance before being regenerated. Anderson explains:

> Much of John the Baptist's ministry was to unbelievers. We know this from John 1:7 where we are told that John came as a testimony concerning the Light (Jesus) that through Him all men might *believe*. It could be argued that many of the OT saints had already exercised faith in God's promises seen through the shadow of the Law, and now these "believers" needed to believe in God's highest revelation, His Son. Even so, they needed to

---

[167] Dillow, *Final Destiny*, 542-543; Robert N. Wilkin, "The Second Epistle of Paul the Apostle to Timothy" in *The Grace New Testament Commentary*, ed. Robert N. Wilkin (Denton, TX: Grace Evangelical Society, 2010), 1003; A. Duane Litfin, "2 Timothy," in *The Bible Knowledge Commentary: An Exposition of the Scriptures*, ed. J. F. Walvoord and R. B. Zuck, vol. 2 (Wheaton, IL: Victor Books, 1985), 756.

[168] Gordon D. Fee, *1 and 2 Timothy, Titus*, New International Biblical Commentary, (Peabody, MA: Hendrickson Publishers, 1988), 265.

believe after repentance. And most of these more than likely had not believed the first time, for John 5:35 implies that many Jews responded to the message of John and rejoiced in his light, but when the Messiah came on the scene, they did not believe in Him (John 5:36-47), nor were they saved (John 5:34). The point is that for most of John's listeners, repentance came before regenerating faith.[169]

Anderson's argument not only discredits Premise 1, but also Premise 2. Repentance and faith are not always inseparable. More arguments could be made for distinguishing repentance and faith, but they are simply unnecessary here; the logic of the faith-after-regeneration view cannot be sustained by the three passages offered as proof.

Acts 9:1-20 & Rebuttal

But Saul, still breathing threats and murder against the disciples of the Lord, went to the high priest and asked him for letters to the synagogues at Damascus, so that if he found any belonging to the Way, men or women, he might bring them bound to Jerusalem. Now as he went on his way, he approached Damascus, and suddenly a light from heaven shone around him. And falling to the ground he heard a voice saying to him, "Saul, Saul, why are you persecuting me?" And he said, "Who are you, Lord?" And he said, "I am Jesus, whom you are persecuting. But rise and enter the city, and you will be told what you are to do." The men who were traveling with him stood speechless, hearing the voice but seeing no one. Saul rose from the ground, and although his eyes were opened, he saw nothing. So they led him by the hand and brought him into Damascus. And for three days he was without sight, and neither ate nor drank. Now there was a disciple at Damascus named Ananias. The Lord said to him in a vision, "Ananias." And

---

[169] Anderson, *Free Grace Soteriology*, 134.

he said, "Here I am, Lord." And the Lord said to him, "Rise and go to the street called Straight, and at the house of Judas look for a man of Tarsus named Saul, for behold, he is praying, and he has seen in a vision a man named Ananias come in and lay his hands on him so that he might regain his sight." But Ananias answered, "Lord, I have heard from many about this man, how much evil he has done to your saints at Jerusalem. And here he has authority from the chief priests to bind all who call on your name." But the Lord said to him, "Go, for he is a chosen instrument of mine to carry my name before the Gentiles and kings and the children of Israel. For I will show him how much he must suffer for the sake of my name." So Ananias departed and entered the house. And laying his hands on him he said, "Brother Saul, the Lord Jesus who appeared to you on the road by which you came has sent me so that you may regain your sight and be filled with the Holy Spirit." And immediately something like scales fell from his eyes, and he regained his sight. Then he rose and was baptized; and taking food, he was strengthened. For some days he was with the disciples at Damascus. And immediately he proclaimed Jesus in the synagogues, saying, "He is the Son of God" (Acts 9:1-20, ESV).

Barrett echoes Hodge in asserting, "there is perhaps no text which more demonstrates how erroneous the Arminian view is than Acts 9."[170] Barrett goes on to explain: "God's sovereign choice resulted in Saul's regeneration to new life. Saul was determined by God to believe, and when it came time, God struck Saul down violently, radically changing his understanding of Christ."[171]

God took the initiative in a dramatic way in Saul's conversion. It was indeed the work of God. What is not clear in this biblical narrative is the exact point at which faith and regeneration occurred. As such,

---

[170] Barrett, *Salvation by Grace*, 185; Hodge, *Systematic Theology*, 2:707-8.

[171] Barrett, *Salvation by Grace*, 185.

while this passage gives us reason to marvel at God's sovereignty, it gives us no solid clues concerning the relative positions of faith and regeneration in the *ordo salutis*.

Moreover, the nondeterministic modified view is in no way challenged by Saul's conversion account. God's dramatic initiatives in striking down Saul can be viewed as God's illumination leading to faith then regeneration. And this certainly fits Paul's description of his own conversion: "But when he who had set me apart before I was born, and who called me by his grace, was pleased to reveal his Son to me, in order that I might preach him among the Gentiles, I did not immediately consult with anyone" (Galatians 1:15-16, ESV). From Paul's point of view, Acts 9:1-20 is simply a description of how God "called me by his grace" and "was pleased to reveal his Son to me." Such calling and revealing seem to fit nicely within the nondeterministic modified view.

Acts 13:48; Ephesians 2:8-9; Philippians 1:29-30; 2 Peter 1:1 & Rebuttal

> And when the Gentiles heard this, they began rejoicing and glorifying the word of the Lord, and as many as were appointed to eternal life believed (Acts 13:48, ESV).

> For by grace you have been saved through faith. And this is not your own doing; it is the gift of God, not a result of works, so that no one may boast (Ephesians 2:8-9, ESV).

> For it has been granted to you that for the sake of Christ you should not only believe in him but also suffer for his sake, engaged in the same conflict that you saw I had and now hear that I still have (Philippians 1:29-30, ESV).

> Simeon Peter, a servant and apostle of Jesus Christ, To those who have obtained a faith of equal standing with ours by the righteousness of our God and Savior Jesus Christ (2 Peter 1:1, ESV).

Barrett presents this group of four passages as proof that saving faith is a gift from God.[172] According to the faith-after-regeneration view, faith is not a human response to a divine initiative; instead, as stated by Sproul, "God himself creates the faith in the believer's heart."[173] And the creation or gift of faith arises from regeneration.

Most proponents of the faith-before-regeneration view would likely agree that saving faith is a gift in the sense that, apart from God's gracious enablement, no one would believe. But these four passages do not prove that regeneration, in particular, must be the divine enablement that makes faith possible.

When Luke says in Acts 13:48, "as many as were appointed to eternal life believed," this may say something about the sovereignty of God, but it says nothing about the necessity of regeneration preceding faith. The very same language could be used to describe a football game: "as many as were appointed to attend the game received tickets." We can say that the person appointing apparently had a gracious desire and plan for the "many" to attend the game. But we cannot say that this is proof that they received the tickets only *after* they attended.

In Ephesians 2:8-9, some argue that the gift is actually faith.[174] As such, they say that God gives us faith, thereby making us believe in him. The argument revolves around the demonstrative pronoun "this" in the clause, "and this is not your own doing." To what does "this" refer? According to the clause that immediately follows, "it is the gift of God," but what is the gift?

Four possible interpretations have typically been given: 1) "grace" is the antecedent gift, 2) "faith" is the antecedent gift, 3) the whole

---

[172] Ibid., 191-202.

[173] R. C. Sproul, *What Is Reformed Theology: Understanding the Basics* (Grand Rapids, MI: Baker, 1997), 156.

[174] For example, R. C. Sproul, *Chosen by God* (Wheaton, IL: Tyndale House Publishers, 1986), 119; John F. MacArthur, Jr., *Faith Works: The Gospel According to the Apostles* (Dallas, TX: Word Publishing, 1993), 68-69, 149; Robert H. Countess, "Thank God for the Genitive!," *Journal of the Evangelical Theological Society*, vol. 12 (1969), 121.

concept of being saved by grace through faith is the antecedent gift, and 4) the phrase, "and this" is interpreted adverbially to mean something like "and especially" with no antecedent.[175] The first two options have generally been dismissed because of a gender mismatch: "this" is neuter, while "grace" and "faith" are feminine. The third option seems to be the prevailing view of modern biblical scholarship.[176] Faith is not the gift.

Some faith-after-regeneration proponents concede this prevailing view of Ephesians 2:8-9, but insist that faith is still a gift because faith is a part of the total salvation package. Barrett explains: "While the 'gift' refers to salvation in its totality, salvation is all of grace and, as Paul says in Ephesians 2:8, it is 'by grace you have been saved through faith.' Therefore, if salvation is 'not your own doing' but is a 'gift of God,' so also must it be the case that faith is also by grace and a gift of God."[177]

This argument seems to prove nothing more than what has already been conceded: saving faith is graciously enabled by God. This does not prove that regeneration precedes faith. Chafer sums it up well, saying,

> The point in the verse is that salvation is by grace in its totality... Though it is true that faith on the part of an unsaved person would be impossible apart from divine help, it nevertheless, is a human decision... The problem with making faith a particular gift from God is that it removes from man any responsibility to

---

[175] Wallace, *Greek Grammar Beyond the Basics*, 334.

[176] For example, Andrew T. Lincoln, *Ephesians*, Word Biblical Commentary, vol. 42, ed. Bruce M. Metzger (Dallas: Word Books, 1990), 111-112; Gregory P. Sapaugh, "Is Faith A Gift?," *Journal of the Grace Evangelical Society*, vol. 7 (1994; 2002), 39; Aldrich, "The Gift of God"; Norman Geisler, *Chosen But Free*, 181-183; Harold Hoehner, *Ephesians: An Exegetical Commentary* (Grand Rapids, MI: Baker Academic, 2002), 342-344; Peter T. O'Brien, *The Letter to the Ephesians*, The Pillar New Testament Commentary, ed. D. A. Carson (Grand Rapids, MI: Wm B. Eerdmans Publishing and Leicester, England: APOLLOS, 1999), 175; Jim Townsend, "Saved by Grace Alone—This is All My Plea," *Emmaus Journal*, 7 (1998), 235-236.

[177] Barrett, *Salvation by Grace*, 199.

believe and leaves it entirely in the hands of God. If this were true it would be useless to exhort men to believe inasmuch as they could not do so.[178]

It is ironic that Ephesians 2:8-9 is used unsuccessfully as a proof text for faith as a gift that comes with regeneration, because it is actually supportive of the faith-before-regeneration view. This text explains how God "made us alive." In Ephesians 2:5, Paul says, "by grace you have been saved." So, grace is the principal cause of being "made alive."

Then Paul expands on this in Ephesians 2:8: "For by grace you have been saved through faith." The phrase "through faith" (διὰ πίστεως) can be taken as causal, such that faith is the means by which God "made us alive." Indeed, Lukaszewski and Dubis take it as a preposition of means.[179] Hoehner affirms, "the addition of the words, 'through faith,' denote the subjective means by which one is saved."[180] So, while God's grace is the principal cause of being made alive, man's faith is the instrumental cause. Allen explains how this supports the faith-before-regeneration view:

> When it comes to salvation in Ephesians 2:8-9, the Scripture indicates that grace is the principal cause and faith is the instrumental cause of salvation. One might illustrate this from the following syllogism:
>
> 1. "Through faith" is the instrumental cause of "made alive."
> 2. An instrumental cause necessarily precedes its effect.
> 3. Therefore, faith precedes regeneration.
>
> The only place an effect can precede its cause is in Star Trek.[181]

---

[178] Chafer, *Systematic Theology*, vol. 2, 129.

[179] Albert L. Lukaszewski, and Mark Dubis. *The Lexham Syntactic Greek New Testament: Expansions and Annotations*, s.v. Eph 2:8.

[180] Hoehner, *Ephesians: An Exegetical Commentary*, 340.

[181] David L. Allen, "Does Regeneration Precede Faith?," *Journal for Baptist*

Arguments for the Faith-After-Regeneration View 85

Compton concurs. In commenting on Ephesians 2:8, he says, "The prepositional phrase 'through faith' signifies the means by which the readers 'have been saved.' In short, faith conditioned and therefore preceded the actions God performed on their behalf—as expressed in the phrase, 'you have been saved.'"[182]

Similarly, Philippians 1:29 does not make the case for the faith-after-regeneration view. Faith has indeed been "granted" by God. "Granted" comes from χαρίζομαι, which means to give freely or graciously.[183] For faith to be "granted" does not necessarily mean it is given by God as a result of regeneration. "Granted" can simply mean that God's gracious and indispensable enablement was given.

Moreover, the context of Philippians 1:29 is suffering. As such, the word "granted" can be understood as granting a privilege. Lopez explains,

> In fact the word "granted" (from χαρίζομαι, "give graciously") should be understood here as conveying a privilege. It is a graciously granted privilege that God allows a person to believe in Christ and suffer for Him. Since "to believe" and "to suffer" are parallel, it follows that if faith is a gift then so is suffering. But the Bible nowhere speaks of suffering as a divine gift.[184]

In 2 Peter 1:1, there are "those who have obtained a faith." The term, "obtained" is from, λαγχάνω, which describes, "what comes to someone always apart from his own efforts," or "what comes by

---

Theology and Ministry, 11, no. 2 (Fall 2014): 45.

[182] Compton, "The *Ordo Salutis* and Monergism: The Case for Faith Preceding Regeneration, Part 3," 286.

[183] Timothy Friberg, Barbara Friberg, and Neva Miller, *Analytical Lexicon of the Greek New Testament*, s.v. "χαρίζομαι," (Grand Rapids, MI: Baker Academic, 2000).

[184] Réne A. López, "Is Faith a Gift from God or a Human Exercise?," *Bibliotheca Sacra*, vol. 164 (July-Sep. 2007): 270.

divine will."[185] Storms makes much of this word, saying: "What is of paramount importance here is the word translated, 'have obtained' or 'have received.' ... Thus, faith is removed from the realm of human free will and placed in its proper perspective as having originated in the sovereign and altogether gracious will of God."[186]

Nevertheless, several factors blunt the force of Storms' logic. First, the use of the term, "obtained" (from λαγχάνω) may simply convey that God's help to believe comes quite apart from human effort. This in no way contradicts a modified view. Second, if the point of this verse is to emphasize God's work, then the use of the passive voice for λαγχάνω would be expected; instead the active voice is used. Third, the same word, λαγχάνω, is used in Acts 1:17 where Peter says that Judas, "was allotted [from λαγχάνω] his share in this ministry." While it may be argued that Judas had no part in determining his allotment, he still had a part in accepting it.

Acts 16:13-15 & Rebuttal

> And on the Sabbath day we went outside the gate to the riverside, where we supposed there was a place of prayer, and we sat down and spoke to the women who had come together. One who heard us was a woman named Lydia, from the city of Thyatira, a seller of purple goods, who was a worshiper of God. The Lord opened her heart to pay attention to what was said by Paul. And after she was baptized, and her household as well, she urged us, saying, "If you have judged me to be faithful to the Lord, come to my house and stay." And she prevailed upon us (Acts 16:13-15, ESV).

In arguing for the faith-after-regeneration view based on this passage, Barrett explains: "Why is it that Lydia believed and was

---

[185] Friberg, *Analytical Lexicon of the Greek New Testament*, s.v. "λαγχάνω."

[186] C. Samuel Storms, *Chosen for Life: The Case for Divine Election* (Wheaton, IL: Crossway, 2007), 72.

Arguments for the Faith-After-Regeneration View

baptized? Answer: The Lord opened her heart. Again, the order in the text is telling. The Lord does not open Lydia's heart because she believed, as the Arminian view must have it. Rather, the text says the exact opposite: Lydia believed the gospel message because the Lord opened her heart."[187]

For this to be a legitimate proof for the faith-after-regeneration view, it must be shown that the opening of Lydia's heart is synonymous with regeneration—an idea Barrett seems to assume but does not defend. Nevertheless, there is nothing in the text that requires the opening of Lydia's heart to be regeneration. It could just as easily be God's illumination preceding both faith and regeneration, which would fit perfectly within the nondeterministic modified view. Alberto Valdés explains simply: "The opening of the heart does not equate with believing, which occurs as a result of this opening, nor with regeneration, which occurs at the moment of faith, not before."[188]

In commenting on this passage, Wilkin affirms the sovereignty of God in Lydia's conversion, saying, "God was drawing Lydia to Himself. He sent someone to bring the Gospel to her. And He opened her eyes so that she could believe the Gospel and be saved. If any of those things had not occurred, Lydia would not have been born again."[189] Wilkin also acknowledges Lydia's involvement in the process: "Lydia was not totally uninvolved in the matter of coming to faith. She was not like a rock which has no spiritual sensitivity whatsoever. She had been responding to the light which God gave her. She was seeking God and

---

[187] Barrett, *Salvation by Grace*, 188.

[188] Alberto S. Valdés, "The Acts of the Apostles," in *The Grace New Testament Commentary*, ed. Robert N. Wilkin (Denton, TX: Grace Evangelical Society, 2010), 566.

[189] Robert N. Wilkin, "The Lord Opened Her Heart," *Grace in Focus*, Sep.-Oct. 1995, accessed March 15, 2017, http://faithalone.org/magazine/y1995/95E2.html.

was worshiping Him. And when He opened her heart, she believed the Gospel and was born again."[190]

2 Corinthians 4:3-6 & Rebuttal

> And even if our gospel is veiled, it is veiled to those who are perishing. In their case the god of this world has blinded the minds of the unbelievers, to keep them from seeing the light of the gospel of the glory of Christ, who is the image of God. For what we proclaim is not ourselves, but Jesus Christ as Lord, with ourselves as your servants for Jesus' sake. For God, who said, "Let light shine out of darkness," has shone in our hearts to give the light of the knowledge of the glory of God in the face of Jesus Christ (2 Corinthians 4:3-6, ESV).

In commenting on this text Barrett explains,

> Notice that Paul does not say here that, while man is blinded and veiled, he is not so blinded and veiled that he cannot see or come to the light of Christ (Semi-Pelagianism). . . . Nor is it the case that man was blinded and veiled but that God provided a prevenient grace so that every man can, if he wills to, cooperate and come to the light (classic Arminianism). Neither of these options is present in the text. To the contrary, God acts in a direct, unilateral, unconditional, monergistic manner, creating light where there was *only* blindness.[191]

While these may be good arguments against semi-Pelagianism, they are not good arguments against the faith-before-regeneration view in general or the modified view in particular, unless it can be shown that the "light" that God shines in the heart is, in fact, regeneration. Barrett

---

[190] Ibid.

[191] Barrett, *Salvation by Grace*, 183.

tries to equate the "light" with regeneration, saying, "The language of calling light out of darkness resembles the biblical language of regeneration as an act that brings about a new creation (2 Cor. 5:17; Gal. 6:15). But this is a stretch.

The text itself is the better source of information regarding the nature of calling forth light, and 2 Corinthians 4:6 indicates that it is a light characterized by a revealed "knowledge" of the truth about God in Jesus, not regeneration. Indeed, Jesus describes himself as the "light of the world" (John 8:12). And this fits well with the nondeterministic modified view. Hodges explains:

> What then is God's role in the conversion of sinner blinded by Satan? The obvious answer is that God's role is revelatory—which is to say, He allows His truth to break through to man's heart in the same way light penetrates darkness. This divine action is beautifully stated by the Apostle in 2 Cor. 4:6. . . . God is in the business of penetrating satanically-induced darkness. Whenever that happens, faith is awakened in man's heart and he is instantly born again.[192]

Ephesians 2:1-7 & Rebuttal

> And you were dead in the trespasses and sins in which you once walked, following the course of this world, following the prince of the power of the air, the spirit that is now at work in the sons of disobedience—among whom we all once lived in the passions of our flesh, carrying out the desires of the body and the mind, and were by nature children of wrath, like the rest of mankind. But God, being rich in mercy, because of the great love with which he loved us, even when we were dead in our trespasses, made us alive together with Christ— by grace you have been saved—and

---

[192] Zane C. Hodges, "God's Role in Conversion," *Grace in Focus*, Sep.-Oct. 1993, accessed March 20, 2017, http://faithalone.org/magazine/y1993/93sep1.html.

raised us up with him and seated us with him in the heavenly places in Christ Jesus, so that in the coming ages he might show the immeasurable riches of his grace in kindness toward us in Christ Jesus (Ephesians 2:1-7, ESV).

Those in the faith-after-regeneration camp cite Ephesians 2:1-7 as proof that the unregenerate are simply unable to respond to God in any positive way. "Dead" is interpreted to mean completely unresponsive; ergo, God "made us alive" through regeneration in order for us be able to respond to Jesus in faith. The spiritually dead cannot believe.

The ESV Study Bible reflects this view, noting the spiritually dead in Ephesians 2:1 "have no inclination or responsiveness toward God and no ability to please God."[193] Hoehner agrees, saying, "as those who are physically dead cannot communicate with the living, so also those who are spiritually dead cannot communicate with the eternal living God..."[194] Stott says, "... they are as unresponsive to him as a corpse."[195] MacArthur joins the corpse chorus: "Dead people have no ability to respond to any stimulus. A corpse can't feel pain and doesn't hear the pleading of a loved one.... That is exactly the case with those who are spiritually dead. They have no capacity on their own to perceive (much less respond to) the truth of God's Word or the generous overtures of the gospel call."[196]

James White adds: "Once we understand the condition of man in sin, that he is dead, enslaved to a corrupt nature, incapable of doing

---

[193] Crossway Bibles, *The ESV Study Bible* (Wheaton, IL: Crossway Bibles, 2008), 2264.

[194] Hoehner, *Ephesians*, 308.

[195] John R. W. Stott, *Message of Ephesians: God's New Society*, ed. John R. W. Stott (Downers Grove, IL: InterVarsity Press, 1979), 72.

[196] John MacArthur, *The Gospel According to Paul* (Nashville: Nelson Books, 2017), 99.

what is pleasing to God, we can fully understand the simple assertion that God must raise the dead sinner to life."[197]

There does seem to be at least some lexical support for this position. Friberg lists three figurative definitions of "dead" (νεκρός) as it relates to persons: "(i) of persons unable to respond to God because of moral badness or spiritual alienation *dead, powerless* (EP 2.1, 5); (ii) of persons regarded as dead because of separation *dead* (LU 15.24, 32); (iii) of persons no longer under the control of something *dead to* (RO 6.11)."[198] Clearly, the first definition relates to the inability of persons to respond to God and Ephesians 2:1 is given as an example of such usage.

But does "dead" really mean that the unregenerate cannot respond to God? Anderson argues that "dead" in Ephesians 2 refers to the unregenerate's position of spiritual separation from God, not the unregenerate's condition of total unresponsiveness to God.[199] He seems to argue for Friberg's second definition as opposed to the first. The preposition "in" as in "dead in the trespasses and sins" provides a clue that Paul is talking about our former position. Believers were once dead in sins, separated from God; we are now alive in Christ, together with him. The emphasis is on being separated from God, not on being an unresponsive spiritual corpse.

Along the same lines, Hodges argues that using the metaphor of deadness to prove the total inability of the unregenerate to believe presses the metaphor too far:

> The answer to the jailor's classic question, "Sirs, what must I do to be saved?" is still the same, "*Believe* on the Lord Jesus Christ, and you will be saved" (Acts 16:30-31; italics added).
>
> What must man *do*? He must *believe*.

---

[197] James R. White, *The Potter's Freedom: A Defense of the Reformation and a Rebuttal of Norman Geisler's Chosen But Free* (Merrick, NY: Calvary Press Publishing, 2000), 283.

[198] Friberg, *Analytical Lexicon of the Greek New Testament*, s.v. "νεκρός."

[199] Anderson, "Regeneration and the *Ordo Salutis*."

But *can* he believe? Today, many give a negative answer to this question. Man, they say, is constitutionally incapable of faith since he is totally dead in sins. This answer, however, overplays the metaphor of deadness.

In addressing the Ephesian Christians, Paul reminds them that they were once "dead in trespasses and sins" (Eph 2:1). But Paul pushes beyond the limits of the metaphor in the very next verse. He writes: "in which you once *walked*" (Eph 2:2; italics added). Can a dead man *walk*? On a literal level, obviously not! On a literal level, if I say, "That man is *dead* in the mud and filth of his own back yard," I cannot go on to say, "He is *walking* in the mud and filth of his own back yard." That would be a transparent contradiction.

The expression "dead in trespasses and sins" can be explained by a parallel statement in Eph 4:18 where Paul describes unsaved people as "alienated from the life of God, because of the ignorance that is in them, because of the blindness of their heart." Unsaved men are dead in the sense that they do not have God's kind of life (eternal life) and thus do not know God on a personal level. This is certainly confirmed by John 17:3, "and this is eternal life; that they may *know* You, the only true God, and Jesus Christ whom You have sent" (NKJV, italics added). Eternal life brings the *knowledge* of God . . . Those who have never *known* God at all are *dead* toward God.

But it is wrong to push this metaphor to an unbiblical extent. Deadness towards God signals one's need of God's life (eternal life). But, like all figures of speech, this figure cannot be pressed beyond its basic biblical application. In other words, the fact that man is "dead in trespasses and sins" tells us nothing about such issues as "free will" or man's "capacity to believe." Those who think that it does, are guilty of forcing the metaphor into a framework it was never intended to fit.

In fact, God holds man responsible for *not believing*. The Lord Jesus said, "He who believes in Him [the Son] is not condemned; but he who does not believe is condemned already, *because he has not believed* in the name of the only begotten Son of God" (John 3:18, NKJV, italics added).

If God condemns men for *not believing*, and men have *no capacity* whatsoever to believe, then the justice of God is called into question. How can a man be held responsible for what he is incapable of doing? On that basis, why could not God cast babies who die in infancy into hell? Why not also the mentally impaired? When man's capacity to believe is totally denied, what is left behind is a horrible, even monstrous, conception of God.

Such is the penalty for wrongly pressing a metaphor beyond its proper parameters![200]

David Allen argues from Romans 6:1-14 that the concept of deadness cannot be understood to mean total inability.

In the context of Rom 6, to be "dead to sin" does not have anything to do with one's sin nature. . . . What has been changed at conversion that causes believers to be "dead to sin" is not their sin nature, but their relationship to sin. Sin no longer has authority over the Christian. Because of what Christ has done on the cross and our union with Him, we are now dead to sin's authority. But our "deadness" does not preclude our ability to choose to sin as believers, as Rom 6:12–14 makes perfectly clear.

Now the point is this: the metaphorical concept of "dead" in Romans 6 simply cannot be understood to mean total inability. To counter that the context of Romans 6 is about the life of the believer while the context of Eph 2:1 is the state of the unbeliever changes nothing. The point still remains: the metaphorical use of "dead" in Scripture simply does not inculcate all the nuances that a literal use of "dead" conveys. . . .

---

[200] Hodges, "Man's Role in Conversion."

> To be "dead in trespasses and sins" (Eph 2:1) need not be understood that the unsaved are so depraved that they have no capacity to understand and/or respond to God.[201]

Beyond the above arguments, Laurence Vance adds that pressing the analogy of deadness too far leads to absolving the dead person of any responsibility for unbelief: "if you make an exact parallel between a physically dead man and a spiritually dead man and say that neither one can believe on Jesus Christ, then you likewise have to say that neither one can *not* believe. If a dead man can't accept Christ because he is dead then he can't reject him either."[202]

Nevertheless, even if it is conceded that the unregenerate are unable to believe, it does not necessarily follow that regeneration must be the means by which God enables belief. God's illumination preceding both faith and regeneration could be the answer.

Colossians 2:11-14 & Rebuttal

> In him also you were circumcised with a circumcision made without hands, by putting off the body of the flesh, by the circumcision of Christ, having been buried with him in baptism, in which you were also raised with him through faith in the powerful working of God, who raised him from the dead. And you, who were dead in your trespasses and the uncircumcision of your flesh, God made alive together with him, having forgiven us all our trespasses, by canceling the record of debt that stood against us with its legal demands. This he set aside, nailing it to the cross (Colossians 2:11-14, ESV).

On this text, Barrett contends, "Spiritual circumcision is an act per-

---

[201] Allen, "Does Regeneration Precede Faith?", 42.

[202] Laurence M. Vance, *The Other Side of Calvinism*, rev. ed. (Orlando, FL: Vance Publications, 2014), 222.

Arguments for the Faith-After-Regeneration View

formed upon the recipient by God, apart from the sinner's cooperation. God and God alone circumcises the heart and then and only then can the sinner trust in Christ."[203]

That God is the one who circumcises the heart is conceded. But it's hard to see how this passage provides any support at all for the notion that such circumcision precedes faith. In fact, if anything, the syntax of the passage argues against it.

The main clause in verse 11 is "you were circumcised," which is a translation of the aorist verb, περιετμήθητε. This is modified by "having been buried with him in baptism," which includes the aorist passive participle, συνταφέντες ("having been buried with"). Aorist participles modifying aorist main verbs normally describe action that is antecedent to or contemporaneous with the main verb.[204] As such, the burial of baptism would normally be taken as occurring before the circumcision, or perhaps at the same time, but not after.

This is relevant because having been "raised with him through faith" is also part of the baptism both syntactically and logically. And faith is presented here as the means by which the raising occurs and it is therefore antecedent.[205] As such, the most natural order of events in the text is shown in Figure 1.

Figure 1: Order of Events in Colossians 2:11-14

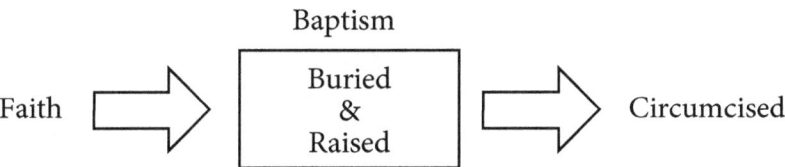

Faith leads to the burial and rising of baptism, which leads in turn to

---

[203] Barrett, *Salvation by Grace*, 179.

[204] Wallace, *Greek Grammar Beyond the Basics*, 614.

[205] Lukaszewski and Dubis, *The Lexham Syntactic Greek New Testament: Expansions and Annotations*, s.v. Col 2:11-14.

circumcision of the heart. Even if one argues that the burial and rising of baptism are contemporaneous with circumcision, faith remains antecedent. Compton confirms this understanding of the order of events:

> The readers' circumcision was accomplished (2:11) by their "being buried" with Christ and "being raised up" with him in baptism (2:12).... That being the case, Paul specifically stated in 2:12 that the readers' being raised up with Christ was accomplished "through faith," that is, by means of their faith.... since Paul stated that the readers were "raised up" by faith, then the conclusion must be that faith logically precedes regeneration and not the reverse.[206]

The faith-after-regeneration view is not supported by Colossians 2:11-14; if anything, it is controverted. Indeed, Allen affirms, "Col 2:12-13 indicates even though unbelievers are spiritually dead, they can still exercise faith in God."[207]

Titus 3:3-7 & Rebuttal

> For we ourselves were once foolish, disobedient, led astray, slaves to various passions and pleasures, passing our days in malice and envy, hated by others and hating one another. But when the goodness and loving kindness of God our Savior appeared, he saved us, not because of works done by us in righteousness, but according to his own mercy, by the washing of regeneration and renewal of the Holy Spirit, whom he poured out on us richly through Jesus Christ our Savior, so that being justified by his

---

[206] Compton, "The *Ordo Salutis* and Monergism: The Case for Faith Preceding Regeneration, Part 3," 290-291.

[207] Allen, "Does Regeneration Precede Faith?," 42.

Arguments for the Faith-After-Regeneration View

grace we might become heirs according to the hope of eternal life (Titus 3:3-7, ESV).

Barrett claims that this passage supports the unconditional nature of God's salvation, saying, "... out of his love and goodness, 'God our Savior' saved us. How exactly did he save us? Not by our own works of righteousness but purely according to his 'own mercy.' Therefore, according to Paul, salvation is unconditional."[208] Barrett goes on to argue that the two prepositional phrases in Titus 3:5 which provide the basis for God's redemption—"not because of works done by us" and "according to his own mercy"—prove that "Paul clearly eliminates works righteousness, or works plus faith."[209]

I would certainly agree that Paul eliminates works as a condition for eternal salvation. But I don't see how this eliminates faith. Requiring faith as a prior condition for regeneration would also fit perfectly well with the two bases for God's redemption cited from Titus 3:5. Faith is not a work done by us. And the basis of our salvation would still be God's mercy. Can anyone argue that offering eternal life conditioned on faith alone is not merciful?

The concept of mercy (ἔλεος) does not intrinsically require unconditionality. In Hebrews 4:16, for example, receiving mercy is conditioned on drawing near to the throne of grace. As such, saying God's salvation must be unconditional because it's according to God's mercy is an unsupported assumption.

Barrett persists in saying that "man is passive in the washing of regeneration," and that this proves regeneration is not conditioned on faith. I agree that we do not and cannot regenerate ourselves: God does it, and therefore, we are indeed passive in regeneration. But it does not follow that faith must not be required. Our passivity in regeneration does not rule out faith as a condition. If I were to undergo a heart transplant, I would be entirely passive for the surgical procedure. But

---

[208] Barrett, *Salvation by Grace*, 180.
[209] Ibid.

that doesn't mean that I had no role whatsoever in saying yes to the transplant beforehand when it was offered by the physician.

For the above reasons, Titus 3:3-7 does not support the faith-after-regeneration view.

James 1:18 & Rebuttal

> Of his own will he brought us forth by the word of truth, that we should be a kind of firstfruits of his creatures (James 1:18, ESV).

Barrett argues that "brought us forth" (ἀποκυέω) is referring to regeneration.[210] Literally, the term means to give birth to a child; figuratively, it means to bring forth something or to bring it into being.[211] Peter Davids agrees with Barrett and says that most recent commentators take James 1:18 to be a reference to regeneration and not a reference to the creation of human beings in general or to the birth of Israel.[212] I also understand James to be referring to the new birth of regeneration.

Barrett further argues that because regeneration happens "of his own will" it cannot be conditioned on human faith. He says, "no mention is made of man's cooperation with God's grace, nor is there any hint by James that God's work of bringing us forth is conditioned upon man's will to believe."[213] But this argument has problems.

First, this is an argument from silence. The context is not

---

[210] Barrett, *Salvation by Grace*, 171-172.

[211] W. Bauer, F. W. Danker, W. F. Arndt, and F. W. Gingrich, *A Greek-English Lexicon of the New Testament and Other Early Christian Literature*, 3d ed., s.v. "ἀποκυέω" (Chicago: University of Chicago Press, 2000), hereinafter abbreviated BDAG.

[212] Peter H. Davids, *The Epistle of James: A Commentary on the Greek Text*, New International Greek Testament Commentary (Grand Rapids, MI: Eerdmans, 1982), p 89.

[213] Barrett, *Salvation by Grace*, 173.

Arguments for the Faith-After-Regeneration View

soteriological, and the primary audience already believes; therefore, it is not surprising that James doesn't mention saving faith because it's not material to his point. James is encouraging his readers to remember some things about God the Father in the midst of trials. The focus is on the Father. In James 1:17, we're reminded that the Father is the creator of the universe ("the Father of lights"), so he's powerful enough to protect us in trials. In James 1:17, we're reminded that the Father is unchanging ("there is no shifting shadow"), so his ongoing care is assured in trials. In James 1:17, we're reminded that the Father is the giver of "every good thing" and "every perfect gift," so we have every reason to embrace our trials as God's perfect gift of refinement. In James 1:18, new life is presented as the supreme example of a perfect gift. James doesn't mention saving faith because it's not germane to his argument.

Second, Barrett seems to conflate human will and human faith in saying that regeneration is according to God's will and not according to "man's will to believe."[214] But is saving faith an act of the will? Hodges argues that it is not:

> God's role in conversion may be described as revelatory. As an act of *His own will* He commands the light of the Gospel to shine into a person's heart so that he can perceive that light in faith, as Jesus said to Peter after his great confession (Matt 16:17). This of course in no way diminishes man's responsibility to seek God and the illumination He alone can give (Acts 17:26–27; Heb 11:6). . . . By insisting that saving faith is an act of the will, it demolishes the Biblical concept of faith as a reception of God's truth. Biblical saving faith is a conviction or persuasion about what God says in the gospel (Rom 4:21). There is no place here for man's will—even as influenced by God's Spirit. God commands the light of His Word to shine into one's heart and, like blind men suddenly able to see, he perceives it as truth (2 Cor 4:6). Once received

---

[214] Ibid.

as truth, that is, believed, there is no room for man's will to act. Faith and regeneration have already occurred.[215]

If saving faith is not an act of the will, then James 1:18 has nothing to say in support of the faith-after-regeneration view.

Third, even if believing can be considered an act of human will, it does not necessarily mean that faith must follow regeneration. James affirms the will of God as the principal cause of regeneration, but this does not rule out human faith as an instrumental cause. Philosophically, as Allen points out, a principal cause (God's will) produces an effect (regeneration) by virtue of its own power. An instrumental cause (human faith) produces an effect (regeneration) by virtue of the power of another cause (God's will). And both the principal and instrumental causes precede the effect; they do not follow it.[216]

Fourth, the role of "the word of truth" seems to not only undermine Barrett's argument, but also to support the faith-before-regeneration view. Most scholars take "the word of truth" to mean the gospel.[217] Moreover, when James says that the Father "brought us forth by the word of truth," he is saying that "the word of truth" or the gospel is the instrument through which regeneration occurs. Moo explains: "The syntax suggests that this 'word' is the instrument through which God brings people to life. All four of the other occurrences of the phrase in the NT refer to the gospel as the agent of salvation (2 Cor. 6:7; Eph. 1:13; Col. 1:5; 2 Tim. 2:15)."[218] Hodges concurs: "Let us note carefully,

---

[215] Zane C. Hodges, "The Epistle of James," in *The Grace New Testament Commentary*, ed. Robert N. Wilkin (Denton, TX: Grace Evangelical Society, 2010), 1106-1107.

[216] Allen, "Does Regeneration Precede Faith?," 44-45.

[217] For example, Davids, *The Epistle of James: A Commentary on the Greek Text*, 89; Douglas J. Moo, *The Letter of James*, The Pillar New Testament Commentary (Grand Rapids, MI: Eerdmans, 2000; Leicester, England: Apollos, 2000), 79.

[218] Moo, *The Letter of James*, 79.

then, that God has 'brought us forth' using as His instrument 'the word of truth.' People are saved at the very moment they believe any of the promises God makes in His Word about giving eternal life to the believer in Jesus."[219]

If the gospel is indeed the agent of regeneration, then it seems that the role of the gospel must come before regeneration in the *ordo salutis*. And what would the prior role of the gospel be? Wouldn't the gospel be the thing that must be believed as a condition for receiving new life? This argues for the faith-before-regeneration view.

1 Peter 1:3-5 & Rebuttal

> Blessed be the God and Father of our Lord Jesus Christ! According to his great mercy, he has caused us to be born again to a living hope through the resurrection of Jesus Christ from the dead, to an inheritance that is imperishable, undefiled, and unfading, kept in heaven for you, who by God's power are being guarded through faith for a salvation ready to be revealed in the last time (1 Peter 1:3-5, ESV).

Concerning this passage Barrett argues that, "Peter shows that God the Father takes the initiative in producing spiritual children by his Word," and that "Peter says that this new birth is according to God's great mercy." I agree. But Barrett goes further, saying, "By definition mercy precludes any possibility of human works or contribution."[220]

By what definition does mercy preclude any human contribution, including receiving something by faith? In the parable of the Good Samaritan in Luke 10:25-37, the Samaritan is described as showing mercy (ἔλεος, the same word Peter uses for mercy) to a man who desperately needed help. Does the Samaritan's mercy preclude the

---

[219] Zane C. Hodges, *Six Secrets of the Christian Life* (Corinth, TX: Grace Evangelical Society, 2016), 41-42.

[220] Barrett, *Salvation by Grace*, 173.

possibility that the man he helped could have cooperated in some way, say by asking for his assistance or by being willing to receive the aid being offered? Of course not.

Barrett further argues that, in using the image of birth, Peter precludes any human contribution to the process leading to regeneration.[221] On this passage, Schreiner concurs, saying, "The focus therefore is on God's initiative in producing new life. No one takes any credit for being born. It is something that happens to us."[222]

I agree the birth imagery focuses on God's initiative and we can take no credit for being born. But that doesn't mean we play no role whatsoever. Even the birth imagery cannot sustain such a categorical conclusion. In a recent *Parents* magazine article, Donna Christiano explains to the pregnant woman: "as your labor progresses, your infant will be doing the best he can to push the process along." She goes on to explain, "[i]nfants usually twist and turn during labor to find the easiest way to squeeze through."[223] This sounds like some degree of participation.[224]

And so, this passage fails to make the case for the faith-after-regeneration view.

1 John 5:1 & Rebuttal

> Everyone who believes that Jesus is the Christ has been born of God, and everyone who loves the Father loves whoever has been born of him (1 John 5:1, ESV).

---

[221] Barrett, *Salvation by Grace*, 174.

[222] Thomas R. Schreiner, *1, 2, Peter, Jude*, The New American Commentary (Nashville: Broadman & Holman Publishers, 2003), 61.

[223] Donna Christiano, "A Baby's View of Birth," *Parents*, January 2008, accessed April 15, 2017, http://www.parents.com/pregnancy/giving-birth/labor-and-delivery/a-babys-view-of-birth/.

[224] I am not suggesting we must somehow twist and turn to find the way to new life, only that the birth imagery does not preclude human involvement.

Arguments for the Faith-After-Regeneration View

This seems to be a flagship verse for faith-after-regeneration proponents. Piper says of this verse, "This is the clearest text in the New Testament on the relationship between faith and the new birth [regeneration]."[225] There are two basic arguments based on 1 John 5:1, one grammatical and one contextual. These will be considered in order.

Grammatical Argument

The grammatical argument is based on the relationship between the participle, ὁ πιστεύων, "the one who believes," (my translation) and the verb, γεγέννηται, "has been born," as shown in Figure 2.

Figure 2: Grammatical Argument for the Faith-After-Regeneration View from 1 John 5:1

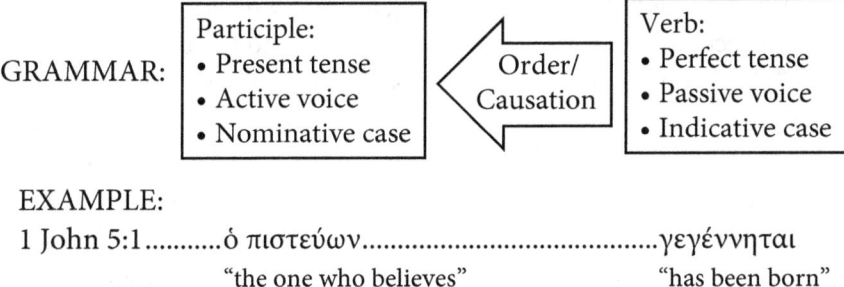

It is argued that because "has been born" is a past event, as indicated by the perfect tense, it must therefore precede and cause the faith of "the one who believes" which is present and ongoing, as indicated by the present tense. John Stott explains it this way:

> The combination of the present tense (believes) and perfect tense (has been born) is important. It shows clearly that believing is the consequence, not the cause, of the new birth. Our present, continuing activity of believing is the result, and therefore, the

---

[225] Piper, *Finally Alive*, 118.

evidence, of our past experience of new birth by which we became and remain God's children.[226]

Piper cites John Stott's analysis of this verse, saying, "I agree totally," and adds, "watch the verbs closely as we read 1 John 5:1 'Everyone who *believes* that Jesus is the Christ *has been born of God.*'"[227] Elsewhere, Piper says of 1 John 5:1, "Faith is the evidence that we have been born of God. We do not make ourselves born again by deciding to believe. God makes us willing to believe by causing us to be born again."[228] Schreiner concurs: "Those who believe that Jesus is the Christ exercise such belief because they are born of God (1 John 5:1)."[229]

G. K. Beale agrees:

> Verse 1 affirms that "whoever believes that Jesus is the Christ" is someone who already "has been born of God." The present born-again condition results from a begetting action in the past that also precedes and thus is likely foundational to the believing. . . .
>
> "Has been born" (*gegennētai*) is a perfect passive verb, which typically highlights the present or resulting condition produced by a past action and likely stands in the background, esp. in light of v. 4. Therefore, the one characterized in the present as a "believing one" (*pisteuōn*, a present substantival participle) possesses an ongoing born-again condition as a result of a begetting action in the past.[230]

---

[226] John R. W. Stott, *The Letters of John* (Grand Rapids: Eerdmans, 1988), 175.

[227] Piper, *Finally Alive*, 118.

[228] John Piper, *Future Grace: The Purifying Power of the Promises of God*, rev. ed. (New York: Multnomah, 2012), 158.

[229] Thomas R. Schreiner, *New Testament Theology: Magnifying God in Christ* (Grand Rapids, MI: Baker Academic, 2008), 161.

[230] G. K. Beale, *A New Testament Biblical Theology: The Unfolding of the Old Testament in the New* (Grand Rapids, MI: Baker Academic, 2011), 855, 855 ft. 51.

Arguments for the Faith-After-Regeneration View 105

Robert Culver casts essentially the same interpretation of 1 John 5:1 in a broader Reformed or Augustinian framework:

> The principal effect [of regeneration], perhaps an accompaniment, in any case not possible without new life, is participation (as all the first Reformers insisted) in repentance, faith, conversion, and sanctification. Arminian and semi-Pelagian theology puts faith ahead of regeneration in the order of salvation. But this supposes that men in the state of nature can initiate repentance and faith or at least co-operate with the Spirit in creating faith. Augustinians interpret 1 John 5:1 to say, "whoever believeth that Jesus is the Christ *has been already* born of God".[231]

Barrett also explains, "The grammar . . . is absolutely essential. . . . In 1 John 5:1, the action in the perfect passive indicative (regeneration) precedes and causes the action in the present active participle (faith). The result is clear: God's act of regeneration precedes belief."[232] And then Barrett cites fellow Calvinists, Bruce Ware, James White, Robert Peterson, Michael Williams, Anthony Hoekema, and Robert Yarbrough in further support for this interpretation of the verse.[233]

As impressive as this grammatical argument and its adherents may seem, recent scholarly arguments invalidate it. For example, Brian Abasciano argues persuasively that the grammatical argument is fallacious.[234] The present-tense participle, ὁ πιστεύων ("the one who believes") is an adjectival participle describing the subject of the sentence, "everyone" (πᾶς); as such, it does not necessarily say anything about the logical or temporal relationship between believing and being born. Grammar alone does not inform the order or the

---

[231] Robert Duncan Culver, *Systematic Theology: Biblical & Historical* (Geanies House, Fearn, Ross-shire, Great Britain: Mentor Imprint, 2005), 698.

[232] Barrett, *Salvation by Grace*, 158-159.

[233] Ibid., 159.

[234] Abasciano, "Does Regeneration Precede Faith? The Use of 1 John 5:1 As a Proof Text," 307-322.

causal relationship between faith and regeneration. Abasciano asserts: "... the grammar of the text leaves the order of faith and regeneration unaddressed..."[235] And he states unequivocally, "... one thing is certain: the grammar gives no positive support to the claim that the verse teaches that regeneration precedes faith."[236]

Anderson agrees. He says,

> ... believing is not an adverbial participle describing the main verb (is born); it is an adjectival participle describing the subject of the sentence (Whoever). How do we know? Because of the Greek letter ὁ right before πιστεύων. That one letter makes their interpretation [Piper, Stott, Barrett, et al.] grammatically impossible. It would be like my saying, "My barber, who cuts hair five days a week, completed his first full marathon last month," and then claiming that completing a marathon is the cause of his cutting hair or that cutting hair is the result of his completing a marathon. The present tense, "cuts" simply tells you something currently true about my barber. "Cuts" is not related to the completed past action of running the marathon in any way."[237]

The arguments of Abasciano and Anderson are supported by Greek grammarians. Faith-After-Regeneration proponents have wrongly assumed that the participle, ὁ πιστεύων ("the one who believes") is an *adverbial* participle modifying the verb, γεγέννηται, "has been born." This assumption is simply a mistake. The participle, ὁ πιστεύων, is articular as evidenced by the article, ὁ. As such, it is *certainly* an attributive adjectival participle and *not* an adverbial one. Wallace removes all doubt: "Note the article: If it stands before the participle

---

[235] Ibid., 313.

[236] Ibid., 315.

[237] Anderson, "Regeneration and the *Ordo Salutis*." See also, David R. Anderson, "Fellowship with the Father," in *A Defense of Free Grace Theology*, 604-607, and Anderson, *Free Grace Soteriology*, 246-249.

and functions as a modifying article (normal use) then that participle *must* be adjectival."[238] A. T. Robertson is just as emphatic: "When the article is used there is no doubt about the participle being attributive [adjectival]. . . . All articular participles are, of course, attributive [adjectival]."[239] It is indeed ironic that Barrett would say that the grammar "is absolutely essential" because the grammar absolutely eviscerates the faith-after-regeneration argument.

One verse not cited by Anderson or Abasciano that makes their point is Mark 6:14. It describes a time after John the Baptist was beheaded when people were wondering who Jesus was: "Some said, 'John the Baptist has been raised from the dead'" (Mark 6:14, ESV). Here is the very same grammatical construction as in 1 John 5:1, as shown in Figure 3.

Figure 3: Grammatical Argument for the Faith-After-Regeneration View from 1 John 5:1 Contradicted by Other Scriptures

GRAMMAR:	Participle: • Present tense • Active voice • Nominative case	⊘ Order/Causation	Verb: • Perfect tense • Passive voice • Indicative case
1 John 5:1	ὁ πιστεύων "the one who believes"		γεγέννηται "has been born"
Mark 6:14	ὁ βαπτίζων "the one who baptizes"		ἐγήγερται "has been raised"
John 3:18	ὁ μὴ πιστεύων "the one who does not believe"		κέκριται "has been condemned"

---

[238] Wallace, *Greek Grammar Beyond the Basics*, 617.

[239] A. T. Robertson, *A Grammar of the Greek New Testament in the Light of Historical Research* (Nashville, TN: Broadman Press, 1934), 1105-1106.

In Mark 6:14, there is a present-tense participle, ὁ βαπτίζων; it is commonly translated "the Baptist," but could also be rendered, "the one who baptizes." It is an adjectival participle that describes the subject of the sentence, "John." It would be nonsense to conclude, based on grammar, that the prospect of John being raised precedes and causes him to baptize. And if that is indeed nonsense, then in 1 John 5:1, it is just as nonsensical to conclude, based on grammar alone, that the one who believes does so because he has been born of God. Moreover, in complete contradiction to the arguments of faith-after-regeneration proponents, we know that the prospect of John being raised actually *follows* his baptizing chronologically; it does not precede it. We know this, not from grammar, but from biblical history.

Other contradictory Scriptures could be cited in which present participles are logically antecedent to their main verbs.[240] For example, one comes from the writings of John and has to do with believing in Jesus. John 3:18 says, "Whoever believes in him is not condemned, but whoever does not believe is condemned already, because he has not believed in the name of the only Son of God" (ESV). The clause, "whoever does not believe is condemned" follows that same grammatical pattern as 1 John 5:1, as shown in Figure 3. Are we to conclude, based on grammar, that the cause of people's unbelief is God's condemnation such that God is responsible for their unbelief? If not, then neither can we say that the grammar of 1 John 5:1 teaches us that regeneration causes faith.

Contextual Argument

Some in the faith-after-regeneration camp point to the parallel uses of the verb "born" (γεννάω) in the perfect tense in 1 John which

---

[240] Abasciano lists Exodus 3:14; Numbers 14:14; 24:9; 1 Samuel 14:22; Proverbs 28:18; Isaiah 14:14, 22:3; Ezekiel 7:4; Mark 14:42; John 3:18; Romans 13:2; Hebrews 7:6; 1 John 5:10b. Abasciano, "Does Regeneration Precede Faith? The Use of 1 John 5:1 As a Proof Text," 315.

consistently show the present results of a past regeneration (See Table 3 below). The one who has been born again (perfect tense) evidences certain ongoing behaviors (present tense): practices righteousness (1 John 2:29), does not practice sin (1 John 3:9), loves (1 John 4:7), overcomes the world (1 John 5:4), and does not sin (1 John 5:18).[241] Therefore, consistent with this pattern, the faith of 1 John 5:1 must be yet another result of regeneration.

Table 3. Instances in 1 John Where the Verb or Participle "Born" (γεννάω) Is in the Perfect Tense

Verse	Participle/Phrase	Verb/Phrase
1 John 2:29	ὁ ποιῶν τὴν δικαιοσύνην "the one who practices righteousness" (present participle)	γεγέννηται "has been born" (perfect verb)
1 John 3:9	ὁ γεγεννημένος "the one who has been born" (perfect participle)	ἁμαρτίαν οὐ ποιεῖ "does not practice sin" (present verb)
1 John 4:7	ὁ ἀγαπῶν "the one who loves" (present participle)	γεγέννηται "has been born" (perfect verb)
1 John 5:1	ὁ πιστεύων "the one who believes" (present participle)	γεγέννηται "has been born" (perfect verb)
1 John 5:4	τὸ γεγεννημένον "the one who has been born" (perfect participle)	νικᾷ τὸν κόσμον "overcomes the world" (present verb)
1 John 5:18	ὁ γεγεννημένος "the one who has been born" (perfect participle)	οὐχ ἁμαρτάνει "does not sin" (present verb)

---

[241] Barrett lists all these verses, Barrett, *Salvation by Grace*, 157f.

In commenting on the first four texts in Table 3, Thomas Schreiner (a Calvinist) explains,

> We can make two observations from these texts. First, in every instance the verb "born" (*gennao*) is in the perfect tense, denoting an action that precedes the human actions of practicing righteousness, avoiding sin, loving, or believing.
>
> Second, no evangelical would say that before we are born again we must practice righteousness for such a view would teach works-righteousness. Nor would we say that first we avoid sinning, and then are born of God, for such a view would suggest that human works cause us to be born of God. Nor would we say that first we show great love for God, and then he causes us to be born again. No, it is clear that practicing righteousness, avoiding sin, and loving are all the consequences or results of the new birth. But if this is the case, then we must interpret 1 John 5:1 in the same way, for the structure of the verse is the same . . . It follows, then, that 1 John 5:1 teaches that first God grants us new life and then we believe Jesus is the Christ.[242]

While this contextual argument may be stronger than the grammatical one, it also fails to save 1 John 5:1 as the flagship proof text for the faith-after-regeneration view. Abasciano presents a number of reasons.[243]

First, even if every other verse of similar construction in context describes the results of regeneration, this does not prove that the faith of 1 John 5:1 is also a result.

Second, it appears that 1 John 5:1 is indeed an exception. All the other verses, shown in Table 3, seem to describe communicable attributes

---

[242] Thomas R. Schreiner, "Does Regeneration Necessarily Precede Conversion?" 9Marks, March 1, 2010, accessed July 24, 2015, http://www.9marks.org/journal/does-regeneration-necessarily-precede-conversion.

[243] Abasciano, "Does Regeneration Precede Faith? The Use of 1 John 5:1 As a Proof Text," 316-318.

of the Father that are or should be reflected in his children: practices righteousness, does not practice sin, loves, overcomes the world, and does not sin. But the faith of 1 John 5:1 is an exception. The Father does not believe in Jesus for eternal life the same way we do.

Third, it can be argued that a primary purpose of all these parallel, "has-been-born" verses is to provide evidence of regeneration as a basis for assurance. If that is true, then both a result of regeneration and a cause of regeneration can serve the very same evidentiary function because both are inextricably tied to the reality of regeneration. To illustrate, if an ignition key is turned off and the internal combustion engine it operates is silent, then both these facts provide assurance that the engine is not running, even though the key is a cause and the silence is a result. As such, even if every other parallel verse depicts a result of regeneration, that doesn't mean that the faith of 1 John 5:1 must also be a result. It can be a cause and serve the same purpose in the context.

Fourth, faith is unique among the other phenomena connected to regeneration in that it is elsewhere described as instrumental to receiving eternal life (e.g. John 3:15-16, 36; 4:14; 5:24, 40; 6:47, 51-54; 20:31). If faith is instrumental to receiving eternal life, and if regeneration describes that moment when eternal life is first received, then faith must come before regeneration, not after.

In summary, the arguments of faith-after-regeneration proponents in connection with 1 John 5:1 are unpersuasive. There is no clear evidence that 1 John 5:1 teaches that regeneration precedes faith. If, as some faith-after-regeneration proponents claim, 1 John 5:1 is the clearest biblical text in support of their view, then their case is weak indeed.

Concluding Evaluation of the Faith-After-Regeneration View

Faith-after-regeneration proponents have offered a considerable list of Scriptures in support of their view, but not one of them is convincing. And the sheer number of texts offered does not make up for the lack of substance. If every bucket leaks, stringing them together still doesn't hold water.

Shawn D. Wright has recently synthesized and consolidated faith-after-regeneration arguments into "four lines of biblical evidence for monergistic regeneration;" nevertheless, there are no new arguments presented, just a rearrangement of those already shown to be wanting.[244]

These results support the conclusion of Allen:

> There is no Biblical text that connects faith and regeneration in a grammatical structure that prescribes an order that supports regeneration preceding faith. Nor is there any statement in Scripture which precludes faith preceding regeneration....
>
> There is no Scripture anywhere that directly says regeneration precedes faith. That is a theological deduction made by some Calvinists that is driven more by their system than it is by Scripture....
>
> Regeneration does not precede faith.[245]

Not only do the Scriptures cited by faith-after-regeneration proponents fail to make their case, it is surprising how many of these Scriptures boomerang. For example, the following passages turn against their view: John 1:12-13, John 3:3-8 (cf. Numbers 21:8-9); Acts

---

[244] Shawn D. Wright, *40 Questions about Calvinism*, ed. Benjamin L. Merkle (Grand Rapids, MI: Kregel Academic, 2019), 219-221. Wright's four lines of evidence include: "First, although people are completely responsible to repent and believe, the Bible is clear that they will not do so unless God in his grace gives them the ability to do what they can't do themselves due to their rebellion.... Second, God is the author of regeneration according to various New Testament texts that show the two conditions of salvation—repentance and faith—are gifts of God to his people.... Third, the language of the New Testament demonstrates that God is the actor in a person's salvation and that the individual is passive until the Lord has regenerated him or her.... Fourth, the syntax and grammar of 1 John proves that regeneration precedes faith."

[245] Allen, "Does Regeneration Precede Faith?," 51-52.

11:18; 2 Corinthians 4:3-6; Ephesians 2:5, 8; Colossians 12:11-14; 2 Timothy 2:24-26, and James 1:18. If, as Barrett suggests, the faith-after-regeneration view is, "the very hinge of the Calvinist position,"[246] then it seems that the position is unhinged.

In the next chapter, biblical evidence in support of the faith-before-regeneration view will be examined.

---

[246] Barrett, *Salvation by Grace*, xxi.

CHAPTER 2

ARGUMENTS FOR THE FAITH-BEFORE-REGENERATION VIEW EXPLAINED AND DEFENDED

Having evaluated the case for the faith-after-regeneration view, arguments given in support of the faith-before-regeneration view will now be considered, as shown in Table 4.

Table 4. Summary of Views on How God Draws People to Believe with the Focus of Chapter 2 Highlighted

Faith-After-Regeneration View: (Calvinism/ Reformed Theology)	Faith-Before-Regeneration View:		Arminian View:
	Modified View:		
	Deterministic:	Nondeterministic:	
Regeneration (irresistible)	*Effectual Call (irresistible)*	*Divine Illumination (resistible)*	*Prevenient Grace (resistible)*

The purpose of this chapter is to present arguments for the faith-before-regeneration view without regard for various distinctive beliefs within the category. These variations will be considered in chapter 3. The arguments here are those with which most faith-before-regeneration adherents would likely agree.

Steve Lemke provides a helpful list of three types of biblical passages to show that faith precedes the believer's receipt of 1) eternal life, 2) the Holy Spirit, and 3) eternal salvation.[247] I will use Lemke's types to frame the first three arguments for the faith-before-regeneration view. Lemke basically lists the verses as evidence with little or no comment on each one.

Argument 1: Scripture Teaches that Faith Comes Before Eternal Life

The Scriptures repeatedly present faith as a necessary prior condition to receiving *eternal life*; therefore, faith must precede regeneration.

John 3:14-16

> "And as Moses lifted up the serpent in the wilderness, so must the Son of Man be lifted up, that whoever believes in him may have eternal life. For God so loved the world, that he gave his only Son, that whoever believes in him should not perish but have eternal life" (John 3:14-16, ESV).

John 3:36

> Whoever believes in the Son has eternal life; whoever does not obey the Son shall not see life, but the wrath of God remains on him (John 3:36, ESV).

---

[247] Steve W. Lemke, "A Biblical and Theological Critique of Irresistible Grace," in *Whosoever Will: A Biblical-Theological Critique of Five-Point Calvinism*, ed. David L. Allen and Steve W. Lemke (Nashville: B&H Publishing, 2010), 136-139.

John 5:24

"Truly, truly, I say to you, whoever hears my word and believes him who sent me has eternal life. He does not come into judgment, but has passed from death to life" (John 5:24, ESV).

John 5:39-40

"You search the Scriptures because you think that in them you have eternal life; and it is they that bear witness about me, yet you refuse to come to me that you may have life" (John 5:39-40, ESV).

John 6:51

"I am the living bread that came down from heaven. If anyone eats of this bread, he will live forever. And the bread that I will give for the life of the world is my flesh" (John 6:51, ESV).

John 6:53-54, 57

So Jesus said to them, "Truly, truly, I say to you, unless you eat the flesh of the Son of Man and drink his blood, you have no life in you. Whoever feeds on my flesh and drinks my blood has eternal life, and I will raise him up on the last day . . . As the living Father sent me, and I live because of the Father, so whoever feeds on me, he also will live because of me" (John 6:53-54, 57, ESV).

John 11:25

Jesus said to her, "I am the resurrection and the life. Whoever believes in me, though he die, yet shall he live" (John 11:25, ESV).

John 20:31

but these are written so that you may believe that Jesus is the Christ, the Son of God, and that by believing you may have life in his name (John 20:31, ESV).

1 John 5:1

Everyone who believes that Jesus is the Christ has been born of God, and everyone who loves the Father loves whoever has been born of him (1 John 5:1, ESV).

Rebuttal of Argument 1 & Rejoinder

In response to the above passages listed by Lemke to argue that faith precedes receiving eternal life, Barrett argues that the eternal life in view does not refer to regeneration; rather, it refers to a believer's experience in the age to come.[248] According to Barrett, "... equating eternal life with regeneration is a case of eisegesis."[249] Here is how Barrett defends his contention that the eternal life in view is to be received in the life to come:

> ... eternal life is an eschatological concept.[250]

> ... unlike regeneration, which is a one-time instantaneous act that occurs at initiation, eternal life is an eschatological hope that pervades into the present but ultimately is received in the life to come.[251]

> The point is made clear when one examines other passages ... that use the phrase eternal life to refer to a gift to be received in the age to come (Mark 10:17, 29-30; Rom. 2:6-7, 23: Gal. 6:8; 1 Tim. 6:19; Titus 1:2; 3:7; James 1:12; Rev. 2:10). Notice how peculiar it sounds if we equate eternal life in these passages with regeneration.[252]

---

[248] Barrett, *Salvation by Grace*, 298-300.

[249] Ibid., 298.

[250] Ibid.

[251] Ibid., 298-299.

[252] Ibid., 299.

Arguments for the Faith-Before-Regeneration View

> ... the flaw of equating regeneration with eternal life is most evident in Titus 3:5-7 ... How can regeneration be equated with eternal life when in Titus 3:5 it is regeneration that is said to lead to the hope of eternal life?[253]

When Barrett says, "... equating eternal life with regeneration is a case of eisegesis," he seems to be attacking a straw man. No one I know argues that eternal life is the same thing as regeneration. The point is: eternal life *begins with* regeneration. New birth *starts* new life. As such, the argument is this:

Premise 1: Faith is a necessary prior condition to receiving eternal life.

Premise 2: Eternal life begins with regeneration.

Conclusion: Faith must precede regeneration.

Barrett seems to concede the first premise but tries to invalidate the second by arguing that "eternal life is an eschatological concept." To be sure, eternal life does include the future, and in some texts (such as Titus 3:5-7) the emphasis does seem to be on the future aspect of eternal life. But it is also a present and ongoing reality from the moment of regeneration, when the believer passes from death to life.

In John 5:24, for example, Jesus says the one who hears and believes "has eternal life." The verb translated "has" is in the present tense (ἔχει), suggesting the possession of eternal life is a present reality. This is confirmed when Jesus says the believer "has passed from death to life." The verb for "passed" is in the perfect tense (μεταβέβηκεν), suggesting that the transition to new life was completed at a past point in time and has abiding results in the present. Clearly, the life in view here cannot be dismissed as merely an "eschatological concept."

In commenting on Johannine passages such as John 5:24 where an offer of life is made, Compton says, "taking these passages together,

---

[253] Ibid., 299-300.

they speak with one voice in placing saving faith as conditioning and, therefore, as logically preceding regeneration."[254]

Argument 2: Scripture Teaches that Faith Comes Before the Holy Spirit

The Scriptures repeatedly present faith as a necessary prior condition to receiving *the Holy Spirit*; therefore, faith must precede regeneration.

John 7:38-39

> "Whoever believes in me, as the Scripture has said, 'Out of his heart will flow rivers of living water.'" Now this he said about the Spirit, whom those who believed in him were to receive, for as yet the Spirit had not been given, because Jesus was not yet glorified (John 7:38-39, ESV).

Acts 2:38

> And Peter said to them, "Repent and be baptized every one of you in the name of Jesus Christ for the forgiveness of your sins, and you will receive the gift of the Holy Spirit" (Acts 2:38, ESV).

Galatians 3:13-14

> Christ redeemed us from the curse of the law by becoming a curse for us—for it is written, "Cursed is everyone who is hanged on a tree"—so that in Christ Jesus the blessing of Abraham might come to the Gentiles, so that we might receive the promised Spirit through faith (Galatians 3:13-14, ESV).

---

[254] Compton, "The *Ordo Salutis* and Monergism: The Case for Faith Preceding Regeneration, Part 2," 169.

Arguments for the Faith-Before-Regeneration View

Galatians 4:6

> And because you are sons, God has sent the Spirit of his Son into our hearts, crying, "Abba! Father!" (Galatians 4:6, ESV).

Ephesians 1:13-14

> In him you also, when you heard the word of truth, the gospel of your salvation, and believed in him, were sealed with the promised Holy Spirit, who is the guarantee of our inheritance until we acquire possession of it, to the praise of his glory (Ephesians 1:13-14, ESV).

Rebuttal of Argument 2 & Rejoinder

In response to the above passages listed by Lemke to argue that faith precedes receiving the Holy Spirit, Barrett argues that the reception of the Holy Spirit does not refer to regeneration, but to conversion, which occurs after regeneration.[255] Barrett's reasoning is this:

> No reason or explanation is given as to why one should equate the reception of the Spirit with regeneration. Why not interpret the reception of the Spirit as the result of regeneration? Or why should it refer to regeneration at all? Why not to conversion, adoption, justification, indwelling, or union with Christ? Or why not interpret the reception of the Spirit as distinct from all of them?[256]

> To the contrary, these passages are best interpreted as meaning that one receives the indwelling of the Spirit at conversion.[257]

---

[255] Barrett, *Salvation by Grace*, 300-304.
[256] Ibid., 300-301.
[257] Ibid., 301.

> ... since regeneration precedes conversion in the *ordo salutis*, and since after Jesus is glorified, it is at conversion that the sinner is indwelt by the Spirit (John 7:38-39; Acts 2:38; Gal. 3:13; 4:6; Eph. 1:13), the passages where belief is said to bring about reception of the Spirit present no problem for the Calvinist.[258]

Lemke's use of the above texts in support of the faith-before-regeneration view seems to rest on the following logic:

Premise 1: Faith is a necessary prior condition to receiving the Holy Spirit.

Premise 2: The Holy Spirit is received upon regeneration.

Conclusion: Faith must precede regeneration.

Again, it seems that Barrett is taking aim at the second premise, arguing that the indwelling of the Spirit is received at conversion, which follows regeneration in the *ordo salutis*. Admittedly, it seems faith-before-regeneration proponents assume the second premise rather than prove it. (Similarly, Barrett seems to merely assume that the Holy Spirit is received at conversion.)

Barrett argues that regeneration and the indwelling of the Spirit are distinct events and not synonymous, as evidenced by John 7:38-39.[259] His point is well taken. Actually, the second premise of the above syllogism does not require that regeneration and the reception of the Spirit be the exact same event, only that they happen at the same time. Even so, to my knowledge, such concurrency has not been argued persuasively, at least not through the exegesis of specific biblical texts. Unless and until it is, the above texts do not present a strong argument for the faith-before-regeneration view.

Nevertheless, if the reception of the Spirit does indeed follow regeneration, it does raise some difficult questions. For example,

---

[258] Ibid., 303-304.

[259] Ibid., 301-304.

Romans 8:9 tells us that anyone who does not have the Spirit does not belong to Christ. Does this mean that a person can temporarily be regenerate and not belong to Christ? Similarly, Ephesians 1:13-14 tells us that believers are sealed with the Spirit who is "the guarantee of our inheritance." Does this mean that a person can temporarily be regenerate and have no such guarantee? Likewise, 1 Corinthians 12:12-13 tells us that believers are baptized into the body of Christ through the Spirit. Does this mean that a person can temporarily be regenerate and not be a member of the body of Christ?

Perhaps it is questions like these that prompt faith-after-regeneration proponents such as Sproul to say that, "regeneration precedes faith," but only, "with respect to logical priority, not temporal priority."[260] But, as pointed out in the introduction, this seems unhelpful and illogical.

Argument 3: Scripture Teaches that Faith Comes Before Eternal Salvation

The Scriptures repeatedly present faith as a necessary prior condition to receiving *eternal salvation*; therefore, faith must precede regeneration.

Mark 16:15-16

> And he said to them, "Go into all the world and proclaim the gospel to the whole creation. Whoever believes and is baptized will be saved, but whoever does not believe will be condemned" (Mark 16:15-16, ESV).

John 1:12

> But to all who did receive him, who believed in his name, he gave the right to become children of God (John 1:12, ESV).

---

[260] Sproul, *Willing to Believe*, 193.

Acts 13:39

and by him everyone who believes is freed from everything from which you could not be freed by the law of Moses (Acts 13:39, ESV).

Acts 16:31

And they said, "Believe in the Lord Jesus, and you will be saved, you and your household" (Acts 16:31, ESV).

Acts 18:8

Crispus, the ruler of the synagogue, believed in the Lord, together with his entire household. And many of the Corinthians hearing Paul believed and were baptized (Acts 18:8, ESV).

Romans 1:16

For I am not ashamed of the gospel, for it is the power of God for salvation to everyone who believes, to the Jew first and also to the Greek (Romans 1:16, ESV).

Romans 10:9-10

because, if you confess with your mouth that Jesus is Lord and believe in your heart that God raised him from the dead, you will be saved. For with the heart one believes and is justified, and with the mouth one confesses and is saved (Romans 10:9-10, ESV).[261]

---

[261] One could argue that this passage is not talking about being saved from the penalty of sin (justification), but from the power of it (sanctification) and/or the wrath of God. For example, see Dillow, *Final Destiny*,192-193; Zane C. Hodges, *Romans: Deliverance from Wrath*, ed. Robert N. Wilkin (Corinth, TX: Grace Evangelical Society, 2013), 298-301; *Rene A. Lopez,*

1 Corinthians 1:21

For since, in the wisdom of God, the world did not know God through wisdom, it pleased God through the folly of what we preach to save those who believe (1 Corinthians 1:21, ESV).

Hebrews 11:6

And without faith it is impossible to please him, for whoever would draw near to God must believe that he exists and that he rewards those who seek him (Hebrews 11:6, ESV).

Rebuttal of Argument 3 & Rejoinder

In response to the above passages listed by Lemke to argue that faith precedes receiving eternal salvation, Barrett argues that the salvation in view does not refer to regeneration. His rationale is this:

> ...why should one interpret being saved in such a narrow manner? Why not interpret it as referring to adoption or justification? Or why not interpret it in a much broader sense as referring to the sinner's escape from hell and wrath in the age to come? Or, better yet, why not interpret being saved as a distinct metaphor in and of itself? To interpret it as synonymous with regeneration is fallacious....[262]

> It is obvious that Arminians who equate "saved" with "regeneration" in their appeal to such passages have succumbed to a reductionistic interpretation.[263]

Romans Unlocked: Power to Deliver (Springfield, MO: 21st Century Press, 2005), 210-214. But such an interpretation would not materially affect the weight of Argument 3.

[262] Barrett, *Salvation by Grace*, 305.

[263] Ibid., 308.

In each of the first three arguments for the faith-before-regeneration view, Barrett seems to concede that faith is a necessary prior condition to eternal life, the indwelling of the Spirit, and eternal salvation. In each case, Barrett's counter argument is basically the same: these results of faith—eternal life, the indwelling Holy Spirit, and eternal salvation—are not the same thing as regeneration; therefore, it cannot be said that faith precedes regeneration. Barrett's logic seems to be as follows:

Premise 1: Faith is a necessary prior condition to receiving eternal life, the Holy Spirit, and eternal salvation.

Premise 2: Regeneration is not the same as eternal life, the indwelling of the Holy Spirit, and salvation.

Conclusion: It cannot be said that faith is a necessary prior condition to regeneration.

The problem with Barrett's rebuttal is that no one is arguing that regeneration is the same thing as eternal life, the indwelling of the Holy Spirit, and salvation. Once again, premise 2 is a straw man. Of course these are all distinct concepts—interrelated, but distinct.

The argument of the faith-before-regeneration view is not that regeneration is equated with these other events, but that they are all received together as a tight salvific package that the Scriptures do not unpack for us in any kind of tidy chronological order. Allen asserts, "The Scripture itself does not set forth a clear *ordo salutis* ("order of salvation") with respect to all of the terms that are used to describe salvation."[264] If regeneration, eternal life, Spirit indwelling, and salvation are all a part of the tight salvific package that is received together all at once, then what is true for one part of the package is true for all parts with respect to their temporal relationship to faith. For example, if faith is a necessary prior condition for eternal life, it must also be so for regeneration.[265]

---

[264] Allen, "Does Regeneration Precede Faith?," 38.

[265] It should be noted that the indwelling of the Holy Spirit became a part of the salvific package in the church age after Christ's ascension.

Barrett argues that salvation is a multifaceted concept that includes future aspects that cannot possibly be equated with regeneration.[266] He is right. Salvation can refer to salvation from the penalty of sin (justification), salvation from the power of sin (sanctification), and salvation from the presence of sin (glorification), as shown in Figure 4 below.[267] Although these aspects of salvation are realized at different points in time—past, present, and future—the ability to realize them comes all at once as part of the salvific package. So, while it is in one sense true that glorification salvation comes well after regeneration; it is equally true that the ability to realize these gifts is received at the same time in the salvific package.

Figure 4: Aspects of Salvation

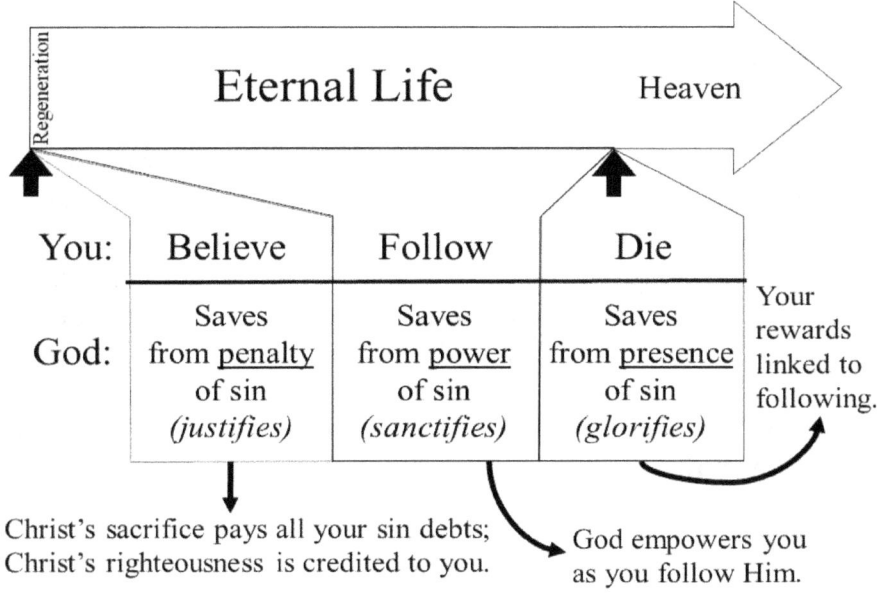

---

[266] Barrett, *Salvation by Grace*, 304-308.

[267] It can also refer to salvation from earthly trouble.

Barrett also argues that salvation can be taken more broadly to mean "salvation in its totality."[268] Again, I think he is right, but this actually leads to an argument against him. Surely, salvation in its totality includes regeneration. And as Allen points out: "If regeneration is a part of salvation and if faith logically precedes salvation, it also logically precedes regeneration."[269]

More Evidence

In addition to the biblical passages cited by Lemke which have framed the arguments for the faith-before-regeneration view and their rebuttals by Barrett, Flowers provides more scriptural evidence for faith preceding regeneration.[270] I will list the passages here (excluding those already cited by Lemke) with a brief comment on each.

Ezekiel 18:30-32

> "Therefore I will judge you, O house of Israel, every one according to his ways, declares the Lord GOD. Repent and turn from all your transgressions, lest iniquity be your ruin. Cast away from you all the transgressions that you have committed, and make yourselves a new heart and a new spirit! Why will you die, O house of Israel? For I have no pleasure in the death of anyone, declares the Lord GOD; so turn, and live" (Ezekiel 18:30-32, ESV).

The order is clear: first "repent and turn," then receive "a new heart and a new spirit." First "turn," then "live."

---

[268] Barrett, *Salvation by Grace*, 306.

[269] Allen, "Does Regeneration Precede Faith?," 43.

[270] Leighton Flowers, "Does Regeneration Precede Faith?" *Soteriology 101,* June 27, 2018, accessed May 6, 2019. https://soteriology101.com/2018/06/27/does-regeneration-precede-faith-2/ .

Acts 11:18

When they heard these things they fell silent. And they glorified God, saying, "Then to the Gentiles also God has granted repentance that leads to life" (Acts 11:18, ESV).

The order is clear: first "repentance," then "life."

Acts 15:9

and he made no distinction between us and them, having cleansed their hearts by faith (Acts 15:9, ESV).

The order is clear: first "faith," then "cleansed."

Galatians 3:26

for in Christ Jesus you are all sons of God, through faith (Galatians 3:26, ESV).

The order is clear: first "faith," then become "sons of God."

John 12:36

"While you have the light, believe in the light, that you may become sons of light." When Jesus had said these things, he departed and hid himself from them (John 12:36, ESV).

The order is clear: first "believe," then "become sons."

Galatians 3:2, 5

Let me ask you only this: Did you receive the Spirit by works of the law or by hearing with faith? ... Does he who supplies the

Spirit to you and works miracles among you do so by works of the law, or by hearing with faith— (Galatians 3:2, 5, ESV).

The order is clear: first "faith," then "receive the Spirit."

2 Corinthians 3:14-16

But their minds were hardened. For to this day, when they read the old covenant, that same veil remains unlifted, because only through Christ is it taken away. Yes, to this day whenever Moses is read a veil lies over their hearts. But when one turns to the Lord, the veil is removed (2 Corinthians 3:14-16, ESV).

The order is clear: first "turn," then "the veil is removed."

1 Timothy 1:16

But I received mercy for this reason, that in me, as the foremost, Jesus Christ might display his perfect patience as an example to those who were to believe in him for eternal life (1 Timothy 1:16, ESV).

The order is clear: first "believe," then "eternal life."

Colossians 2:12

having been buried with him in baptism, in which you were also raised with him through faith in the powerful working of God, who raised him from the dead (Colossians 2:12, ESV).

The order is clear: first "faith," then "raised."

James 1:18

> Of his own will he brought us forth by the word of truth, that we should be a kind of firstfruits of his creatures (James 1:18, ESV).

The order is clear: first "the word of truth (received by faith)," then he "brought us forth (regenerated)."

Concluding Evaluation of the Faith-Before-Regeneration View

The scriptural evidence presented in this section clearly supports the faith-before-regeneration view. The plain and repeated teaching of Scripture is that faith is a prior condition to receiving salvation from God in all its aspects, including regeneration.

CHAPTER 3

THE NONDETERMINISTIC MODIFIED VIEW EXPLAINED AND DEFENDED

IN THIS CHAPTER, the nondeterministic modified view will be distinguished and defended as the best option among the alternative faith-before-regeneration views, as shown in Table 5.

Table 5. Summary of Views on How God Draws People to Believe with the Focus of Chapter 3 Highlighted

Faith-After-Regeneration View: (Calvinism/ Reformed Theology)	Faith-Before-Regeneration View:		Arminian View:
	Modified View:		
	Deterministic:	Nondeterministic:	
Regeneration *(irresistible)*	*Effectual Call* *(irresistible)*	*Divine Illumination* *(resistible)*	*Prevenient Grace* *(resistible)*

The Context and Meaning of John 6:44 as a Model for How God Draws

Foundational to the discussion of how God draws people to believe in Jesus are the words of Jesus himself in John 6:44: "No one can come to me unless the Father who sent me draws him" (ESV).

First, I want to show that when Jesus says, "come to me" in this verse, it is the equivalent of "believe in me." In the context, Jesus uses the terms "comes to me" (ἐρχόμενος πρὸς ἐμε) and "believes in me" (πιστεύων εἰς ἐμὲ) interchangeably. For example, in John 6:35, Jesus says, "I am the bread of life; whoever *comes to me* shall not hunger, and whoever *believes in me* shall never thirst" (ESV, emphasis added). The metaphorical results, "shall not hunger" and "shall not thirst" both describe essentially the same idea: the security and everlasting satisfaction of the one who has received eternal life.[271] And so, in John 6:35, Jesus is not describing two different means for two different results; he's describing the very same process in two different ways. As such, "comes to me" (with the verb, ἔρχομαι) means the same thing as "believes in me." Barclay Newman and Eugene Nida agree. In commenting on John 6:35, they say, "*Comes to me* and *believes in me* are placed together here and at 7:37-38; the phrases are parallel in meaning."[272]

So, back in John 6:44, Jesus is essentially saying that no one can believe in him unless the Father draws him. Clearly, the Father's drawing is a prerequisite to faith in Jesus, but what does it mean to draw? First, the meaning and use of the word, "draw" will be considered; then, the context of its use in John 6:44.

---

[271] Jesus corroborates this in John 6:37 when he says, ". . . whoever comes to me I will never cast out" (ESV).

[272] Barclay Moon Newman and Eugene Albert Nida, *A Handbook on the Gospel of John*, UBS Handbook Series (New York: United Bible Societies, 1993), 198.

The Meaning and Use of the Word, "Draw"

The original Greek term behind the English translation, "draw" is ἕλκω.[273] It is used only eight times in the New Testament. One prominent lexicon (BDAG) lists three possible definitions.[274]

The first definition is: "**to move an object from one area to another in a pulling motion,** *draw*, with implication that the object being moved is incapable of propelling itself or in the case of pers. is unwilling to do so voluntarily, in either case with implication of exertion on the part of the mover."[275] Six of the eight occurrences of ἕλκω in the New Testament are listed by BDAG as examples reflecting this meaning. In John 18:10, Peter "drew" a sword. In John 21:6, fishermen try to "haul" a fishing net into a boat, and then in John 21:11, Peter "hauled" the net ashore. In Acts 21:30, Paul was "dragged" out of the temple by the people. In Acts 16:19, Paul and Silas were "dragged" before the rulers by business owners. In James 2:6, the rich "drag" the oppressed into court. Under this definition, the act of drawing is said to be physical and forcible.

The second definition is: "**to draw a pers. in the direction of values for inner life,** *draw, attract*, an extended fig. use of mng. 1."[276] The other two instances of ἕλκω in the New Testament are listed by BDAG as examples carrying this second meaning. One is John 12:32, where Jesus says, "And I, when I am lifted up from the earth, will *draw* all people to myself" (ESV, emphasis added). The other example is our text, John 6:44, where the Father "draws" people to believe. Under this definition, the act of drawing is figurative, non-physical, and attractional.

The third definition is: "**to appear to be pulled in a certain direction,** *flow* an ext. fig. use intr. *flow along*."[277] Under this definition, the act of

---

[273] Or ἑλκύω. The forms are used interchangeably.

[274] BDAG, s.v. "ἕλκω."

[275] Ibid.

[276] Ibid.

[277] Ibid.

drawing or flowing is figurative, but the verb is intransitive; it is not linked to an object that is drawn. As such, these uses of the verb—and there are only a few—are not likely to help much in understanding how one entity draws another.

Based on these definitions, the nature of one entity drawing another is either physical and forcible according to the first definition, or non-physical and attractional according to the second. The authors of this lexicon cast their vote for John 6:44 as an example of a non-physical, attractional drawing. I agree. But the question remains: to what extent are the persons drawn willing to be drawn?

It is interesting to note that in the prior, second edition of this lexicon, the first definition does not include, "with implication that the object being moved is incapable of propelling itself or in the case of pers. is unwilling to do so voluntarily."[278] The more recent third edition adds the idea that the person being drawn could not or would not choose to be drawn voluntarily; in effect, he is being drawn against his will. Ken Wilson characterizes this addition as "totally gratuitous."[279] Is he right? Does it matter?

It matters because if the first meaning does indeed carry an inherent unwillingness without exception, and if the second meaning is simply a figurative extension of the first, then the unwillingness would seem to pass to the second meaning as well. And in the case of John 6:44, that would suggest that the Father drags unwilling people. And this is essentially what Sproul argues to defend the faith-after-regeneration view.[280] It is understandable that Reformed thinkers would argue this way because, in their way of thinking, the unregenerate have no

---

[278] Walter Bauer, William F. Arndt, F. Wilbur Gingrich, and Frederick W. Danker, *A Greek-English Lexicon of the New Testament and Other Early Christian Literature*, 2nd ed., s.v. "ἕλκω" (Chicago: University of Chicago Press, 1979).

[279] Ken Wilson, "How Does God 'Draw' a Person Unto Belief for Justification?" Lecture at the Annual Conference of the Free Grace Alliance, Irving, TX, October 13-15, 2014.

[280] Sproul, *Chosen by God*, 69-71.

capacity to respond to God's attraction, so the drawing in John 6:44 cannot be purely attractional.

I will argue that unwillingness is not a necessary part of either definition, the first or the second. In some cases, the persons drawn, whether physically or non-physically, are perfectly willing and even happy to be drawn. Let's consider the evidence.

Besides the eight occurrences of ἕλκω in the New Testament, there are another thirty-four occurrences in the Septuagint,[281] bringing the total to forty-two. I have cataloged these in Tables 6.1, 6.2, and 6.3.[282]

---

[281] The Septuagint is a Greek translation of ancient Hebrew writings, both canonical and extracanonical. LXX Septuaginta (Old Greek Jewish Scriptures) Alfred Rahlfs ed. (Stuttgart, Germany: German Bible Society, 1935).

[282] In these tables, canonicity refers to whether a writing is considered to be a divinely-inspired part of the Bible (canon).

Table 6.1. All Uses of ἕλκω in the New Testament and Septuagint

Reference	Canonicity	Verbal Sense of ἕλκω	Entities Drawing	Entities Drawn	Definition (BDAG)	Willing?
Deut 21:3	Canonical	A heifer draws a yoke.	Impersonal	Impersonal	1. Physical	Does not apply
Judg 5:14	Canonical	People draw a staff.	Personal	Impersonal	1. Physical	Does not apply
Judg 20:2	Canonical	Men draw a sword.	Personal	Impersonal	1. Physical	Does not apply
Judg 20:15	Canonical	Men draw a sword.	Personal	Impersonal	1. Physical	Does not apply
Judg 20:17	Canonical	Men draw a sword.	Personal	Impersonal	1. Physical	Does not apply
Judg 20:25	Canonical	Men draw a sword.	Personal	Impersonal	1. Physical	Does not apply
Judg 20:35	Canonical	Men draw a sword.	Personal	Impersonal	1. Physical	Does not apply
Judg 20:46	Canonical	Men draw a sword.	Personal	Impersonal	1. Physical	Does not apply
2 Sam 22:17	Canonical	The Lord draws David.	Personal	Personal	1. Physical	Willing
Neh 9:30	Canonical	The Lord draws along with Israel.	Personal	None	3. Intransitive	Does not apply
Job 20:28	Canonical	Destruction draws a house.	Impersonal	Impersonal	1. Physical	Does not apply
Job 28:18	Canonical	You draw wisdom.	Personal	Impersonal	2. Non-physical	Does not apply
Job 39:10	Canonical	An ox draws furrows.	Impersonal	Impersonal	1. Physical	Does not apply
Ps 10:9 (9:30 LXX)	Canonical	The wicked draw the poor.	Personal	Personal	1. Physical or 2. Non-physical	Willing

List continued in Table 6.2.

Table 6.2. All Uses of ἕλκω in the New Testament and Septuagint (Continued)

Reference	Canonicity	Verbal Sense of ἕλκω	Entities Drawing	Entities Drawn	Definition (BDAG)	Willing?
Ps 118:131	Canonical	The psalmist draws a breath.	Personal	Impersonal	1. Physical	Does not apply
Prov 25:20	Canonical	Vinegar draws a sore or soda.	Impersonal	Impersonal	1. Physical	Does not apply
Eccl 1:5	Canonical	The sun draws along to its place.	Impersonal	None	3. Intransitive	Does not apply
Eccl 2:3	Canonical	Qoheleth draws his body with wine.	Personal	Impersonal	1. Physical	Does not apply
Song 1:4	Canonical	Women (or the bride) draw(s) the groom.	Personal	Personal	1. Physical or 2. Non-physical	Willing
Hab 1:15	Canonical	The wicked draw the righteous.	Personal	Personal	1. Physical or 2. Non-physical	Unwilling
Isa 10:15	Canonical	A person draws a saw.	Personal	Impersonal	1. Physical	Does not apply
Jer 14:6	Canonical	Donkeys draw wind.	Impersonal	Impersonal	1. Physical	Does not apply
Jer 31:3 (38:3 LXX)	Canonical	The Lord draws Israel.	Personal	Personal	2. Non-physical	Willing
Jer 38:13 (45:13 LXX)	Canonical	Men draw Jeremiah.	Personal	Personal	1. Physical	Willing
Dan 4:14 (4:17 LXX)	Canonical	Nebuchadnezzar draws leaves from a tree.	Personal	Impersonal	1. Physical	Does not apply
Dan 7:10	Canonical	A stream of fire draws along from the throne.	Impersonal	None	3. Intransitive	Does not apply
John 6:44	Canonical	The Father draws the one who comes.	Personal	Personal	2. Non-physical	Willing
John 12:32	Canonical	Jesus draws all people.	Personal	Personal	2. Non-physical	Willing

List continued in Table 6.3.

Table 6.3. All Uses of ἕλκω in the New Testament and Septuagint (Continued)

Reference	Canonicity	Verbal Sense of ἕλκω	Entities Drawing	Entities Drawn	Definition (BDAG)	Willing?
John 18:10	Canonical	Peter draws a sword.	Personal	Impersonal	1. Physical	Does not apply
John 21:6	Canonical	Fishermen draw a net.	Personal	Impersonal	1. Physical	Does not apply
John 21:11	Canonical	Peter draws a net.	Personal	Impersonal	1. Physical	Does not apply
Acts 16:19	Canonical	Business owners draw Paul and Silas.	Personal	Personal	1. Physical	Unwilling
Acts 21:30	Canonical	People draw Paul.	Personal	Personal	1. Physical	Unwilling
Jas 2:6	Canonical	The rich draw the oppressed.	Personal	Personal	1. Physical	Unwilling
1 Macc 10:82	Extra-canonical	Simon draws his troops.	Personal	Personal	1. Physical	Willing
3 Macc 4:7	Extra-canonical	Captors draw captives.	Personal	Personal	1. Physical	Unwilling
3 Macc 5:49	Extra-canonical	Infants draw milk.	Personal	Impersonal	1. Physical	Does not apply
4 Macc 11:9	Extra-canonical	Guards draw a brother.	Personal	Personal	1. Physical	Unwilling
4 Macc 14:13	Extra-canonical	Parental love draws everyone.	Personal	Personal	2. Non-physical	Willing
4 Macc 15:11	Extra-canonical	Love draws a mother.	Personal	Personal	2. Non-physical	Willing
Wis 19:4	Extra-canonical	Fate draws enemies.	Impersonal	Personal	2. Non-physical	Willing
Sir 28:19	Extra-canonical	A person draws the tongue's yoke.	Personal	Impersonal	2. Non-physical	Does not apply

For each occurrence of ἕλκω, I have shown the definition from BDAG that applies. For all the New Testament references, BDAG provides the suggested meaning. For the other references, I have used contextual judgment in assigning a meaning. In cases where the entity drawn is personal, I relied upon context to determine whether the person is willing to be drawn voluntarily.

There are up to thirty-one cases where ἕλκω describes a *physical* drawing consistent with the first definition.[283] In eleven of these cases, a person is being drawn, as shown in Table 7.

The eleven instances where a person is being drawn physically show no clear pattern of unwillingness; nearly as many cases are willing (5) as unwilling (6). Below is a summary of each case of *physical* drawing where those being drawn are willing, in the order in which they appear in Table 7.

In 2 Samuel 22:17, David says of the Lord, "he *drew* me out of many waters" (ESV, emphasis added). The context makes it clear that "many waters" is a metaphor for many life-threatening troubles. In 2 Samuel 22:5, David says, "For the *waves* of death encompassed me, the *torrents* of destruction assailed me" (ESV, emphasis added). It is also clear that David was willingly drawn out of those troubles. In fact, he prayed to be drawn out of them. In 2 Samuel 22:7, David says, "In my distress I called upon the Lord" (ESV).

---

[283] Three of these cases may be considered physical or non-physical.

Table 7. Willingness to be Drawn among Persons Drawn Physically

Reference	Canonicity	Verbal Sense of ἕλκω	Entities Drawing	Entities Drawn	Definition (BDAG)	Willing?
2 Sam 22:17	Canonical	The Lord draws David.	Personal	Personal	1. Physical	Willing
Ps 10:9 (9:30 LXX)	Canonical	The wicked draw the poor.	Personal	Personal	1. Physical or 2. Non-physical	Willing
Song 1:4	Canonical	Women (or bride) draw(s) groom.	Personal	Personal	1. Physical or 2. Non-physical	Willing
Jer 38:13 (45:13 LXX)	Canonical	Men draw Jeremiah.	Personal	Personal	1. Physical	Willing
1 Macc 10:82	Extra-canonical.	Simon draws troops.	Personal	Personal	1. Physical	Willing
Hab 1:15	Canonical	The wicked draw the righteous.	Personal	Personal	1. Physical or 2. Non-physical	Unwilling
Acts 16:19	Canonical	Business owners draw Paul and Silas.	Personal	Personal	1. Physical	Unwilling
Acts 21:30	Canonical	People draw Paul.	Personal	Personal	1. Physical	Unwilling
Jas 2:6	Canonical	The rich draw the oppressed.	Personal	Personal	1. Physical	Unwilling
3 Macc 4:7	Extra-canonical.	Captors draw captives.	Personal	Personal	1. Physical	Unwilling
4 Macc 11:9	Extra-canonical.	Guards draw a brother.	Personal	Personal	1. Physical	Unwilling

Psalm 10:9 describes a wicked person oppressing the poor: "he seizes the poor when he *draws* them into his net" (ESV, emphasis added). There is some question as to which definition is in view here. On one hand, the language of the metaphor describes a physical drawing into a net; on the other hand, the metaphor probably stands for a non-physical drawing of the poor by some deception, perhaps by some financial scam, for example. It is likely that the poor are willing, but unwitting. If the poor knew about the presence and danger of the net, they would probably not be so willing.

In Song of Solomon 1:4, the bride says to her groom, "*Draw* me after you; let us run" (ESV, emphasis added). This could be a physical drawing in which the groom may take the bride by the hand so they can run together. It also could be a non-physical drawing in which the bride is drawn by the love of her groom. In either case, it's hard to see how the bride could be any more willing. This is certainly not an invitation to be dragged against her will.[284]

In Jeremiah 38:13, it says, "Then they *drew* Jeremiah up with ropes and lifted him out of the cistern" (ESV, emphasis added). Clearly, Jeremiah was drawn willingly; in fact, he could not have been drawn out without his cooperation.

In 1 Maccabees 10:82, it says, "Simon *led* [drew] his force forward and engaged the foreign enemy in battle" (*Common English Bible*, emphasis added). I would argue that the troops are described as going forward willingly. Simon is not pictured as dragging them against their will.

Based on these examples, it is quite clear that physical drawing does not necessarily involve an unwillingness on the part of the persons being drawn. In fact, in five of eleven cases considered, there is a willingness. So, it seems that Wilson's charge that unwillingness is a "totally gratuitous" addition to the first definition of ἕλκω has merit. More

---

[284] The Septuagint does not exactly match the Hebrew text here. In the Hebrew text, as in the English translation, the bride directs the groom to draw her. In the Septuagint, it seems that some young women draw the groom. In either case, there is a willingness to be drawn.

importantly, this means that the second definition does not necessarily carry any baggage of unwillingness from the first definition. Therefore, the nature of drawing is not necessarily coercive or involuntary.

The usages of ἕλκω that are most relevant to the study of John 6:44 involve a person who is drawn in a *non-physical* way, according to the second definition. As shown in Table 8, there are up to nine such cases, including John 6:44.

Table 8. Willingness to be Drawn among Persons Drawn Non-Physically

Reference	Canonicity	Verbal Sense of ἕλκω	Entities Drawing	Entities Drawn	Definition (BDAG)	Willing?
Ps 10:9 (9:30 LXX)	Canonical	The wicked draw the poor.	Personal	Personal	1. Physical or 2. Non-physical	Willing
Song 1:4	Canonical	Women (or bride) draw(s) groom. ♥	Personal	Personal	1. Physical or 2. Non-physical	Willing
Jer 31:3 (38:3 LXX)	Canonical	The Lord draws Israel. ♥	Personal	Personal	2. Non-physical	Willing
John 6:44	Canonical	The Father draws one who comes. ♥	Personal	Personal	2. Non-physical	Willing
John 12:32	Canonical	Jesus draws all people. ♥	Personal	Personal	2. Non-physical	Willing
4 Macc 14:13	Extra-canonical	Parental love draws everyone. ♥	Personal	Personal	2. Non-physical	Willing
4 Macc 15:11	Extra-canonical	Love draws a mother. ♥	Personal	Personal	2. Non-physical	Willing
Wis 19:4	Extra-canonical	Fate draws enemies.	Impersonal	Personal	2. Non-physical	Willing
Hab 1:15	Canonical	The wicked draw the righteous.	Personal	Personal	1. Physical or 2. Non-physical	Unwilling

Of these nine, there is only one case where the person drawn is clearly unwilling. It's in Habakkuk 1:15, where it is said of the wicked concerning the ones he oppresses, "he drags them out with his net" (ESV). And it can be argued that this case may not even belong in the non-physical category because the metaphor is clearly physical even though the idea it conveys is probably non-physical.

I will summarize the remaining cases to demonstrate the rationale for classifying each of them as willing, in the order in which they appear in Table 8, with the exception that John 6:44 will come last. Along the way, I will highlight the prevalent theme of love as an attractional force that draws, indicated in Table 8 by the heart symbol appearing in the "verbal sense" column of each verse to which it applies.

As shown in Table 7 and the accompanying comments, both Psalm 10:9 and Song of Solomon 1:4 may include a non-physical drawing and the ones drawn are willing. It is clear in Song of Solomon 1:4 the drawing force is love. It is equally clear that Psalm 10:9 is *not* about love.

Jeremiah 31:3 is an important reference because it is one of the few that describes God as the one who draws. As such, it can give us more direct insight to the nature of God's drawing in John 6:44. Jeremiah 31:3 says, "The LORD appeared to him from afar, saying, 'I have loved you with an everlasting love; Therefore I have drawn you with lovingkindness'" (*NASB*[285]). In this verse, the object of God's love and the object of his drawing are the same: it is "you," a feminine singular pronoun referring to Israel. And, as *The ESV Study Bible* points out, this is "referring to the whole people,"[286] not just a subset. So, God loves and draws all of Israel. Some Israelites were willing to be drawn, and so I have counted them as willing in Table 8. Nevertheless, not all were so willing; many were rebellious. This reflects a significant principle: the

---

[285] I used the *New American Standard Bible* here because it more clearly shows the use of the word, "draw."

[286] *The ESV Study Bible*, 1428.

people God loves and draws can receive or reject his overture, at least as Jeremiah 31:3 describes it.

The closest, most direct comparison to John 6:44 is John 12:32, where in reference to his own crucifixion Jesus says, "And I, when I am lifted up from the earth, will draw all people to myself" (ESV). John 12:32 does not explicitly present love as a drawing influence, but the biblical connection between the cross and love is undeniable, and the love of Jesus is the most plausible attractional force. What other aspect of such a gruesome death would be attractive? Jesus says in John 15:13, "Greater love has no one than this, that someone lay down his life for his friends" (ESV).

But are the ones Jesus draws willing? The most plausible answer is that some are and some are not. The parallel is Jeremiah 31:3, where God draws *all* of Israel, and some are willing and some are not. Here in John 12:32, Jesus is said to "draw all people." Wilkin contends that the "all" is most naturally taken to mean all without exception; Jesus draws all people, inviting all to believe in him.[287] This is consistent with the parallel in Jeremiah 31:3. Jesus draws all persons, demonstrating his love for all and inviting all to believe. But not all will believe.

Of course, this idea is incompatible with the concept of total inability in Reformed theology because the unregenerate are spiritual corpses that cannot be drawn. It also contradicts the Reformed idea that God's drawing is irresistible. As such, the "all" in John 12:32 is generally interpreted not as all without *exception*, but all without *distinction*.[288] The idea is that Jesus draws all kinds of people, not just Jews. This interpretation is certainly possible and may be correct.[289] Nevertheless,

---

[287] Wilkin, "The Gospel According to John," 434-435.

[288] For example, Carson, *The Gospel According to John*, 444.

[289] Allen argues that the concept of "all without distinction" is not always as limiting as it may seem: "the use of this language is not meant to denote 'some of all kinds.' Merely appealing to the notion of 'all people without distinction' does not preclude the idea of all people without limitation. 'All people' often means everyone without any ethnic distinction" See David L. Allen, *The Extent of the Atonement: A Historical Critical Review* (Nashville,

whether the correct interpretation is all without exception or all without distinction, there is no basis to conclude from John 12:32 that the drawing is always efficacious or that the "all people" is restricted to mean "all the elect." But that's precisely what Paul Williamson (a Calvinist) argues: "the 'all people' mentioned in John 12:32 are in fact drawn to Jesus."[290] The fact remains, the Jeremiah 31:3 parallel suggests that the drawing does not always work. The most natural and plausible reading of John 12:32 is that the person and work of Jesus on the cross draw every person (or every kind of person) out of love, and the drawing can be received or rejected.

In 4 Maccabees 14:13, the general context is the parental love of a mother who endures the martyrdom of her seven sons. Parental love is described as drawing everyone to sympathy. Similarly, in 4 Maccabees 15:11, the love of children is described as drawing a mother to sympathy. While it can be argued that parental love is an emotion that is in some sense involuntary, it is the norm for mothers to be willing to be drawn by it.

In Wisdom 19:4, it is said that enemies are drawn by fate to their demise. The context here is certainly not love. But inasmuch as the drawing involves a change of mind on the part of the ones drawn, they seem willing.

Finally, the primary text remains to be considered. In John 6:44, Jesus does not directly explain the specific nature of the Father's drawing, but

---

TN: B&H Academic, 2016), 636. More recently, Allen says, "with respect to the NT atonement texts that use universal language, the bifurcation of 'all without distinction' and 'all without exception' is ultimately a distinction without a difference." See David L. Allen, *The Atonement: A Biblical, Theological, and Historical Study of the Cross of Christ* (Nashville, TN: B&H Academic, 2019), 226.

[290] Paul R. Williamson, "Because He Loved Your Forefathers: Election, Atonement, and Intercession in the Pentateuch," in *From Heaven He Came and Sought Her: Definite Atonement in Historical, Biblical, Theological, and Practical Perspective*, ed. D. Gibson and J. Gibson (Wheaton, IL: Crossway, 2013), 241.

it can also be tied to God's love indirectly. In John 6:45, Jesus connects the drawing to teaching, saying, "It is written in the Prophets, 'And they will all be taught by God.' Everyone who has heard and learned from the Father comes to me" (ESV). Back in John 6:44 *the ones whom the Father draws* come to Jesus; likewise, here in John 6:45, *the ones whom the Father teaches* come to Jesus. So, both the drawn and the taught come, suggesting that the Father's teaching is intrinsic to his drawing.

Traditionally, the quotation of the prophets in John 6:45, "and they will all be taught by God," has been taken to be a paraphrase of Isaiah 54:13. The context of Isaiah 54:13 is God wooing the people of Israel as a wife is wooed in the context of a loving relationship with her husband. Isaiah 54:6-8 says,

> "For the LORD has called you like a wife deserted and grieved in spirit, like a wife of youth when she is cast off, says your God. For a brief moment I deserted you, but *with great compassion I will gather you*. In overflowing anger for a moment I hid my face from you, but *with everlasting love I will have compassion on you*," says the LORD, your Redeemer (ESV, emphasis added).

That John 6:45 apparently paraphrases Isaiah 53:14 does not rule out a broader reference to the writings of other prophets along the same line. In commenting on John 6:45, Köstenberger explains, "the expression 'the prophets' could refer to the general tenor of prophetic OT teaching or to the prophetic writings as a division of the OT. In Judaism, it was held that to learn the Torah was to be taught by God himself."[291] Another prophet to whom Jesus may refer is Hosea, who speaks from God's perspective in Hosea 11:1-4, and once again God's drawing and teaching are characterized by love as the attractional force:

> When Israel was a child, *I loved him*, and out of Egypt I called my son. The more they were called, the more they went away; they

---

[291] Köstenberger, *John*, 214.

kept sacrificing to the Baals and burning offerings to idols. Yet *it was I who taught* Ephraim to walk; *I took them up* by their arms, but they did not know that I healed them. *I led them* with cords of *kindness*, with the bands of *love*, and I became to them as one who eases the yoke on their jaws, and *I bent down to them* and fed them (ESV, emphasis added).

Once again God's love is evident behind and through his drawing in John 6:44-45, reflected in Old Testament referents. And the ones drawn may justifiably be counted as willing to be drawn, or at least able to be willing, according to the same logic discussed for John 12:32. Moreover, in Table 8, the preponderance of willingness among people drawn in a non-physical way suggests that, in the absence of evidence to the contrary, John 6:44 is probably not an exception; the Father draws those who have the capacity for willingness, whether or not they exercise it.[292]

In sum, the word study for ἕλκω suggests that its meaning in John 6:44 describes God drawing all people, not just the elect, in a non-physical, attractional, non-coercive, didactic way based on his great love, and that this divine overture can be received or rejected. In the next section, the context of John 6:44 will be considered to shed further light on the nature of drawing.

The Context of John 6:44

It is important to understand John 6:44 in its proper context. To that end, what follows is a summary of the Bread of Life discourse in John 6:22-59. I will argue that the entire discourse is characteristic of the way God draws people to believe in Jesus. It's not just a biblical text that happens to mention the Father drawing in passing. It's a story *about* the Father drawing. And so, the following summary has a story-telling,

---

[292] Reformed thinkers may argue there *is* evidence to the contrary based on the total inability of the unregenerate to be willing. Nevertheless, as shown in the first chapter, this idea is not supported from Scripture.

homiletical aspect. This is a good way to enter the story and see and feel the drawing unfold.

John 6:22 begins by giving a time reference, "on the next day" (ESV). A lot had happened the day before. Jesus had miraculously fed a very large crowd with just five loaves and two fishes. Everybody was amazed, and the crowd wanted to make Jesus their political king. Later that day in the afternoon, Jesus sent his disciples by boat back across the Sea of Galilee to the town of Capernaum on the northwest side. Jesus himself remained with the crowd near the northeast shore. But Jesus soon left the crowd to go up into some nearby hills by himself to pray.

As night fell, the disciples found themselves in the middle of a life-threatening storm on the Sea. After the disciples fought the storm for hours on end, Jesus came to them by miraculously walking on water. Then Jesus miraculously calmed the sea. And then Jesus miraculously transported the disciples' boat to its destination on the shore near Capernaum.

So, the "next day" is the day following the feeding of the multitude and the calming of the storm. The scene returns to the northeastern shore of the Sea of Galilee, where some of the crowd still remains—the crowd that had been miraculously fed by Jesus.

John 6:22 continues: "the crowd that remained on the other side of the sea saw that there had been only one boat there, and that Jesus had not entered the boat with his disciples, but that his disciples had gone away alone" (ESV).

We don't know how many people remain on the northeast side of the Sea. It's possible most of the crowd had dispersed after the disciples departed by boat and Jesus went up into the hills. But some remain, having spent the night where Jesus had fed them, perhaps waiting for Jesus to come down from the hills. Those that do remain know the disciples took the only boat available the previous day. And they know Jesus didn't leave with them.

But they don't know Jesus miraculously joined his disciples during the night. The next day, they assume Jesus is still in the nearby hills. They wait for him to come down. While they wait, some other boats arrive.

John 6:23 continues: "Other boats from Tiberias came near the place where they had eaten the bread after the Lord had given thanks" (ESV). Tiberias is a town on the west side of the Sea of Galilee, several miles to the south of Capernaum. Since it is the largest city on the western shore, it would not be unusual for the boats to be from Tiberias. As those who remain see the boats arriving and the day unfolding, they realize that Jesus is probably not going to show and they decide to go look for him. John 6:24 says: "So when the crowd saw that Jesus was not there, nor his disciples, they themselves got into the boats and went to Capernaum, seeking Jesus" (ESV). This is a clue that the remaining crowd is probably not nearly as big as it once was because they are able to use the boats which had arrived from Tiberias to take them to Capernaum, about six or seven miles away.

John 6:25 continues: "When they found him on the other side of the sea, they said to him, 'Rabbi, when did you come here?'" (ESV). John 6:59 indicates the crowd found Jesus in the Jewish synagogue in Capernaum. Their question is an understandable one: "when did you come here?" They can't figure it out.

But Jesus does not seem eager to take this opportunity to flaunt his miraculous power. He could have explained the miracles of walking on water and stilling the sea and transporting the boat, and the disciples would certainly have corroborated the story. Instead, Jesus dodges the question entirely, and takes the conversation in a surprising direction.

Now consider, these people have gone to considerable lengths to seek Jesus. They have waited overnight for Jesus to come down from the hills on the northeastern shore of the Sea of Galilee. They have traveled by boat across the Sea in search of Jesus at Capernaum. And now they have come to the synagogue with questions. One would think that Jesus would be impressed with their seeking. But he's not. In fact, Jesus criticizes their motivations. John 6:26 says: "Jesus answered them, 'Truly, truly, I say to you, you are seeking me, not because you saw signs, but because you ate your fill of the loaves'" (ESV). This is an indictment. It's Jesus's way of saying: "You are seeking me because you're thinking with your belly." These seekers are not really interested in the deeper spiritual significance of the signs Jesus performed; they're more interested in satisfying their own physical appetites. They want to ride the Jesus gravy train, but the gravy they seek has little to do with spiritual things.

Jesus issues a corrective command in John 6:27: "Do not work for the food that perishes, but for the food that endures to eternal life" (ESV). Jesus is contrasting two types of food: "food that perishes" versus "food that endures to eternal life." It's physical nourishment versus spiritual nourishment. Without the one, you die physically; without the other, you die spiritually. Food that perishes symbolizes the things that satisfy physical appetites—things like groceries, clothing, shelter, sensual pleasure, exercise, and rest. These food items are good, but they don't endure forever. The benefits are temporary. In contrast, food that endures to eternal life symbolizes spiritual food given by God to satisfy the starvation of our souls. The phrase, "endures to eternal life" inextricably ties the spiritual food to eternal life so that they are essentially equated. The food that endures is eternal life. And this food lasts forever; the benefits are everlasting.

Jesus is challenging the crowd to stop working only for the food that perishes; spiritual food needs to be the priority. Jesus identifies himself as the source. In John 6:27, Jesus describes the "food that endures to eternal life" as that "which the Son of Man will give to you." It is Jesus the Son of Man who gives eternal life. Jesus is the sole provider of spiritual food. "The Son of Man" is a common self-designation of Jesus linked to the expected Messiah suggested in Daniel 7:13-14.[293] Jesus is identifying himself as the Son of Man and the ultimate source of spiritual food. To authenticate his claim as the source of eternal life, Jesus says in the last part of John 6:27, "For on him God the Father has set his seal" (ESV). The idea is that God the Father has authorized Jesus the Son to be his sole agent for providing this eternal spiritual food. (Do you sense the drawing?)

This prompts a good question in John 6:28: "Then they said to him,

---

[293] Borchert, *John 1-11*, 262n89; Walter A. Elwell and Barry J. Beitzel, *Baker Encyclopedia of the Bible* (Grand Rapids, MI: Baker Book House, 1998), 1983.

'What must we do, to be doing the works of God?'" (ESV). Jesus has just rebuked the crowd for seeking him only to satisfy their own physical appetites. He has just commanded them not to merely seek physical food, but to seek the spiritual food of eternal life that only he can give. Now the people are asking him how they can get this eternal life.

The people who are asking this question are Jews; they are in a synagogue. And they seem to be stuck on Jesus's use of the term "work" in association with the giving of eternal life. They assume there are works of God which must be done to earn eternal life. That they use the plural term "works" is understandable. After all, the Old Testament law given through Moses contains hundreds of commands to be obeyed.

Jesus clears up the confusion in John 6:29: "Jesus answered them, 'This is the work of God, that you believe in him whom he has sent'" (ESV). Jesus says, "this is the work." "Work" is singular. There aren't many works to be done in order to receive eternal life; there's just one work, and it's not a matter of human effort or intelligence or goodness: just believe in him. Believe in Jesus. Believe in the one whom God has sent. Notice Jesus casts human faith as a response to a divine initiative: the Father "sent" Jesus. Now, it's your move: believe. The incarnation is a part of the Father's work of drawing.

But the crowd resists the spiritual food Jesus is offering. They doubt that what he is saying is true and good. They quickly look for an excuse to reject it. John 6:30 continues: "So they said to him, 'Then what sign do you do, that we may see and believe you? What work do you perform?'" (ESV). The question, "What work do you perform?" is a common Old Testament expression of unbelief.[294] The implied but unspoken answer is, "you can't do such a work." This is a remarkable statement in light of the fact that, just the day before, these people had been miraculously fed by Jesus, and they were amazed. John 20:30-31 tells us that the signs included in this gospel are expressly intended to draw people to believe. But the crowd is resistant, demonstrating our human capacity to rationalize and avoid what we don't want to do. If

---

[294] Köstenberger, *John*, 208.

one is unwilling to believe in Jesus, then any excuse for not believing will do.

The crowd expands on their excuse in John 6:31: "Our fathers ate the manna in the wilderness; as it is written, 'He gave them bread from heaven to eat'" (ESV). This is an allusion to the Old Testament account of the people of Israel wandering in the wilderness under the leadership of Moses. In that account, bread called manna was miraculously provided each day from heaven. Apparently, this is how the crowd is rationalizing their unbelief. They're suggesting that Jesus's miracle the day before was insufficient to justify belief in him as the provider of eternal life. They reason Jesus fed a multitude for only one day, but Moses fed the entire nation of Israel for forty years. Therefore, Moses is the greater prophet. If Jesus wants to be believed as the source of eternal life, he better come up with a more convincing sign. That seems to be the rationalization of the crowd for their unbelief.

John 6:32 contains Jesus's reply: "Jesus then said to them, 'Truly, truly, I say to you, it was not Moses who gave you the bread from heaven, but my Father gives you the true bread from heaven" (ESV). Jesus corrects their idea three ways.

First, Jesus says it was God the Father who gave the manna in the wilderness, not Moses. The suggestion is that the crowd is overlooking the work of God in their midst. It could be argued that the work of God the crowd is overlooking is the work of the Father in drawing them through the signs and words of Jesus. Notice that Jesus uses the plural pronoun "you" in both of the parallel clauses: [1] "it was not Moses who gave *you* the bread from heaven, but [2] my Father gives *you* the true bread." One might have expected Jesus to use the pronoun "them" in the first clause to refer to forefathers, particularly since that is the pronoun the crowd uses in the immediately preceding verse. Jesus is apparently linking the identity of the unbelieving crowd with their wilderness ancestors who received the miracle of manna and also refused to trust God in spite of the miracle.[295]

---

[295] Charles R. Swindoll, *Insights on John*, Swindoll's New Testament Insights

Second, Jesus says that the Father didn't just give the physical manna in the past, he's also giving—present tense—*giving* the "true bread from heaven" right now. The "true bread" of which he speaks is spiritual, not physical.

The third correction comes in John 6:33, where Jesus identifies himself as the true bread from heaven, saying: "For the bread of God is he who comes down from heaven and gives life to the world" (ESV). Jesus is the one "who comes down from heaven." Jesus is the one who "gives life"—eternal life—"to the world." Verse 33 is the gospel in a nutshell. Jesus came to offer eternal life. Based on the atonement that would soon be accomplished on the cross, Jesus offers "life to the world." We receive it by simply believing him for it.

It is hard to escape the idea that the Father is working through the Son in this very moment in time to draw the hearers in the synagogue. Based on the word study for "draw" in John 6:44, it describes God drawing all people, not just the elect, in a non-physical, attractional, non-coercive, didactic way based on his great love, and that this divine overture can be received or rejected. Isn't that precisely what's happening in this story?

The crowd responds to Jesus in a way that makes it difficult to gauge their level of understanding and sincerity. "They said to him, 'Sir, give us this bread always'" (John 6:34, ESV). On the positive side, they address Jesus here in a new way. The Greek word translated, "sir" is κύριος. Usually it's translated, "Lord." At the very least, it is a word that shows respect, and sometimes it is a designation for God. That the translators of the *English Standard Version* render it "sir" suggests that they interpret it to be no more than respectful. Indeed, what Jesus says a little later in John 6:36 indicates that the crowd does yet not believe in him. Nevertheless, their respectful request, "Sir, give us this bread always," suggests at least some receptivity to the drawing that has occurred so far. Thus, Jesus reveals more, beginning in John 6:35. This reflects a pattern of divine drawing

---

(Grand Rapids, MI: Zondervan, 2010), 144

noted by Bing who says, "A receptive attitude towards God's Word is always rewarded with more truth (Mark 4:24-25)."[296] Similarly, in commenting on Matthew 13:10-17 as it relates to the issue of drawing, Anderson says, "light received brings more light; light rejected brings the night."[297]

Beginning in John 6:35, Jesus brings more light. Through careful repetition and imagery, Jesus provides a beautiful explanation of eternal salvation, presenting three parties who play important roles: God the Father, Jesus himself, and humankind.

The Role of the Father

I find at least four aspects to the Father's part in our salvation. First, the Father sent Jesus from heaven to earth to do his will. It was the Father's plan all along to have his son, Jesus, come to earth as a man. Jesus confirms this in John 6:38: "For I have come down from heaven, not to do my own will but the will of him who sent me" (ESV). Similarly, In John 6:57, Jesus says, "the living Father sent me, and I live because of the Father" (ESV). This is Jesus's way of saying that the Father sent him to do his will.

This leads to the second aspect of the Father's role in salvation: it is the Father's desire for us to have eternal life through Jesus. The Father wants us to have eternal life, and he sent his son, Jesus to provide it. Jesus affirms this in John 6:40: "For this is the will of my Father, that everyone who looks on the Son and believes in him should have eternal life" (ESV).

That leads us to the third aspect of the Father's role in our salvation: the Father draws us to Jesus according to his will. The Father attracts us, influences us, persuades us, compels us, enlightens us to come to Jesus for salvation, according to John 6:44: "No one can come to me unless the Father who sent me draws him" (ESV). The Father plays

---

[296] Bing, "How God Draws People to Salvation."

[297] David Anderson, "Regeneration and the *Ordo Salutis*."

an indispensable role in bringing us to Jesus. We don't come because we're smart enough or good enough or because we take the initiative; we come because the Father graciously enables us to come. The Father draws.

As has already been discussed, one of the ways the Father draws us is by teaching us. We hear and learn things that draw us. Jesus explains this in John 6:45: "It is written in the Prophets, 'And they will all be taught by God.' Everyone who has heard and learned from the Father comes to me" (ESV). The idea is that God the Father teaches or enlightens us in a way that draws us to Jesus.

There is a fourth aspect of the Father's role that is easy to miss or to confuse with other things. The Father gives believers to Jesus. "All that the Father *gives* me will come to me" (John 6:37, ESV, emphasis added). The Father giving persons to Jesus is reflected elsewhere this gospel (John 6:39; 10:29; 17:1-2, 6, 9, 24). This raises the question: whom does the Father give and when does he give them?

Storms argues that the elect of all time are in view and that the giving of the elect is a prerequisite for belief:

> On several occasions in John's Gospel divine election is described in terms of God the Father giving certain persons to God the Son (6:37, 39, 10:29; 17:1-2, 6, 9, 24). In each of these cases the giving of men to Christ precedes and is the cause of their receiving eternal life. Those who are given to the Son include not only the present company of disciples who believe in Jesus but also the elect of future ages who will come to faith through the gospel. Jesus looks upon them as already his ... even though they have not yet believed in his name. They are his because they were given to him by the Father in eternity past.[298]

In commenting on this same text, James White takes the same Reformed view: "But prior to man's action of believing comes the

---

[298] Storms, *Chosen for Life*, 91-92.

Father's action of giving those men who will believe to the Son. Christ's authority extends over *all flesh*, but the gift of eternal life is given only to those who the Father *has given* to the Son."[299]

Nevertheless, the idea that the giving in John 6 is about divine election is an assumption foreign to the text. In fact, evidence in the text itself argues for a simpler explanation without reading in something that is not there. Jesus gives back-to-back parallel statements in John 6:39-40, as shown in Table 9.

Table 9. Parallel Statements in John 6:39-40

	John 6:39	John 6:40
A	"And this is the will of him who sent me,"	"For this is the will of my Father,"
B	"that I should lose nothing of all that he has given me,"	"that everyone who looks on the Son and believes in him should have eternal life"
C	"but raise it up on the last day."	"and I will raise him up on the last day."

The unmistakable parallelism of parts "A" and "C" reveal that Jesus is restating the same idea. The "B" part of the parallelism strongly suggests that "all that he has given me" are the very same people as "everyone who looks on the Son and believes in him." Moreover, the parallelism suggests that the giving of believers to Jesus and the giving of eternal life to believers are concurrent, concomitant transactions triggered by faith. This contextual interpretation fits better than the Reformed importation of election.

---

[299] James R. White, *Drawn by the Father* (New York: Rotolo Media/Great Christian Books, 2000), 35.

Moreover, in John 6:37 the verb "gives" is in the present tense, which generally indicates ongoing, contemporary action, not something that happened in eternity past. So, in the midst of Jesus's discourse, the Father may be in the process of giving to the Son those who will believe in him.

The Role of Jesus

Jesus's part is in response to the Father's will: Jesus came to offer himself as the bread of life. Jesus offers himself as the source of eternal life—the life the Father wants us to have. In John 6:35, Jesus explains it this way: "I am the bread of life" (ESV). He says it again in Verse 48: "I am the bread of life."

Then Jesus explains the Bread of Life metaphor, making it clear that he's talking about spiritual bread and spiritual life. "Your fathers ate the manna in the wilderness, and they died" (John 6:49, ESV). This is a reference to the Jewish ancestors for whom God had miraculously provided physical bread called manna. But eventually they died, and the manna they ate is not the kind of bread that Jesus is talking about.

In contrast, the bread Jesus is talking about is spiritual bread that imparts spiritual life. Those who eat this bread will not die spiritually, but have eternal life. Jesus explains this in John 6:50-51: "This is the bread that comes down from heaven, so that one may eat of it and not die. I am the living bread that came down from heaven. If anyone eats of this bread, he will live forever" (ESV).

In the last part of John 6:51, Jesus reveals more information about the nature of this bread: "And the bread that I will give for the life of the world is my flesh" (ESV). This may sound cannibalistic, but it's simply Jesus's way of saying that he was soon going to give up his body—his flesh—to be crucified in payment for our sins. And so, Jesus's part in our eternal salvation is to offer the world eternal life on the basis of his death. While the original hearers likely did not understand this, we see in retrospect an allusion to Christ drawing all people when lifted up on the cross as the ultimate expression of love undeserved (John 12:32). Fischer explains the power of the cross to draw:

> The nucleus of everything that Christian theology says about God is to be found in the crucified Jesus. And in the crucified Jesus we learn that the God who pours out wrath is the God whose hands are nailed to the cross. The God who punishes sin is the God who takes the punishment. The God who judges is the God who looks upon those crucifying him and says, "Forgive them."[300]

Jesus came to offer himself as the bread of life sacrificed on our behalf. How do we receive this bread? How do we get this eternal life that Jesus offers? That brings us to our part in the way of eternal salvation.

The Role of Humanity

Jesus explains how we respond to his offer in three ways. But they are not three different things to do; they are just three different ways of explaining one important idea.

First, he says that our response is to simply believe in him. He says this several times for emphasis. "Whoever *believes* in me shall never thirst." (John 6:35, ESV, emphasis added). "For this is the will of my Father, that everyone who looks on the Son and *believes* in him should have eternal life" (John 6:40, ESV, emphasis added). "Truly, truly, I say to you, whoever *believes* has eternal life" (John 6:47, ESV, emphasis added).

Now, this seems quite clear. But it's apparently so important to Jesus that we know this that he states this truth a second way. In addition to the word "believe," Jesus uses the word, "come" to describe our part, as in "come to Jesus." For example, in John 6:35, Jesus says, "whoever *comes* to me shall not hunger" (ESV, emphasis added). Again, in John

---

[300] Austin Fischer, *Young, Restless, No Longer Reformed: Black Holes, Love, and a Journey In and Out of Calvinism* (Eugene, OR: Cascade Books, 2014), 46.

6:45: "Everyone who has heard and learned from the Father *comes* to me" (ESV, emphasis added). The Greek word used here for "come" is ἔρχομαι. In this context, it is the functional equivalent of coming to believe in Jesus, as discussed at the outset of this chapter. It's coming to accept by faith the bread of life Jesus offers. Our part in eternal salvation is to simply come to Jesus in faith, believing in him for eternal life.

To help us understand this idea, Jesus explains it a third way using a word picture to convey the idea of believing and coming. The word picture is something everyone can relate to: eating and drinking. For example, in John 6:51, Jesus says: "If anyone *eats* of this bread, he will live forever" (ESV, emphasis added). Again, in John 6:54: "Whoever *feeds* on my flesh and *drinks* my blood has eternal life" (ESV, emphasis added). Again, in John 6:57-58: "whoever *feeds* on me, he also will live because of me.... This is the bread that came down from heaven ... Whoever *feeds* on this bread will live forever" (ESV, emphasis added).

And just in case some may be wondering if eating and drinking really mean the same thing as believing and coming, Jesus removes all doubt in John 6:35: "I am the bread of life; whoever comes to me shall not hunger, and whoever believes in me shall never thirst" (ESV). This should be an encouragement to all who mix metaphors. In deliberately mixing his metaphors, Jesus is making the point that coming is the same thing as eating, and believing is the same thing as drinking.

Jesus is taking great pains to show how simple our part is. Just believe him. Just come to faith in him. He's offering himself as the bread of life. Just eat it. And live.

Moreover, Jesus says there aren't many ways to eternal salvation; there's only one way. In John 6:53, Jesus says, "Truly, truly, I say to you, unless you eat the flesh of the Son of Man and drink his blood, you have no life in you" (ESV). No belief, no life. Believe and live. It's that simple. To fortify the exclusiveness of Jesus's claims, throughout the discourse he repeatedly uses terms like "whoever" and "all" and "nothing" and "everyone" and "no one" and "anyone." It's a point of emphasis. According to Jesus, there is only one way. But that one way is wide open to all. In order to receive eternal life, we simply believe in Jesus for it. Is this not the Father drawing unbelievers through the Son preaching the good news?

The Role of Jesus Continued

The good news gets better. There's another part Jesus plays in response to our believing. Jesus ensures that once we have received eternal life through faith we will never lose it. In John 6:37, Jesus says, "whoever comes to me I will never cast out" (ESV). Similarly, in John 6:39, Jesus says: "And this is the will of him who sent me, that I should lose nothing of all that he has given me" (ESV). Once the Father has given us to Jesus through faith, we can never be lost again. Not ever.[301] This, of course, is problematic for many Arminians who hold that salvation can be lost.[302]

Also, in response to our faith, Jesus does something else. It's another point of emphasis because he says it four times in John 6:39, 40, 44, and 54. In every instance, Jesus is talking about what he will do for the believer. He says: "I will raise him up on the last day." The culmination

---

[301] It is beyond the scope of this study to fully defend the doctrine of eternity security. See Norman L. Geisler, "A Moderate Calvinist View," in *Four Views on Eternal Security*, ed. J. Matthew Pinson, Counterpoints Series, ed. Stanley N. Gundry (Grand Rapids, MI: Zondervan, 2002), 61-112; Steve Horn, "Article 9: The Security of the Believer," in *Anyone Can Be Saved*, 133-141.

[302] For example, F. Leroy Forlines, *Classical Arminianism: A Theology of Salvation* (Nashville, TN: Randall House, 2011), 303-335; I. Howard Marshall, *Kept by the Power of God: A Study of Perseverance and Falling Away* (Eugene, OR: Wipf and Stock, 2008); Thomas C. Oden, *The Transforming Power of Grace* (Nashville, TN: Abingdon Press, 1993), 157-158; Grant R. Osborne, "A Classical Arminian View," in *Four Views on the Warning Passages in Hebrews*, ed. Herbert W. Bateman IV (Grand Rapids, MI: Kregel, 2007), 86-128; Ben Witherington, "'Behavior Doesn't Interrupt Your Relationship with Christ': A Recipe for Disaster," *Christianity Today*, July 12, 2012, accessed November 3, 2017, http://www.christianitytoday.com/ct/2012/julyweb-only/behavior-relationship-with-christ.html.

of eternal life is the final resurrection of every believer. Receiving eternal life in the here and now is certainly a great crossing-over from condemnation to acceptance, from alienation to reconciliation, from enmity to harmony with God. But this is just a taste of eternal life. The fullness of the banquet begins on the last day, when Jesus will raise us up to be with him.

The Meaning of John 6:44 in Context

I contend that the entire Bread of Life discourse demonstrates how the Father draws. In the text, the Father draws through his Word, both inscripturated and incarnate, via the convicting ministry of the Holy Spirit. The Father draws through authenticating signs. The Father draws through progressive illumination. The Father draws through a clear and compelling presentation of the gospel from one person to another. The Father draws through a prophetic glimpse of his Son lifted up on the cross, defining the extent of his sacrificial love. This is not exhaustive but representative of the ways the Father draws.

So, when Jesus says, "No one can come to me unless the Father who sent me draws him" (John 6:44, ESV), he's not referring to a mysterious doctrine of election that would likely elude his original hearers. Instead, he's simply saying something like, "You won't believe unless the Father draws you, and the Father is lovingly drawing you right now, so I encourage you to believe while you have this opportunity." In commenting on John 6:44, Lennox seems to agree: "the initiative was God's; his was the drawing voice, and theirs was the responsibility to listen to him."[303] This interpretation dovetails nicely with the results of the word study for ἕλκω where its meaning in John 6:44 describes God drawing all people, not just the elect, in a non-physical, attractional, non-coercive, didactic way that can be received or rejected. This interpretation also comports well with the original question of the unbelieving crowd in the synagogue, "What must we

---

[303] Lennox, *Determined to Believe?*, 184.

do?" (John 6:28, ESV). It is decidedly more natural and logical and helpful in context than saying anything like, "In eternity past the Father has already determined who will come to Jesus, and you can't do a thing about it."[304] And it fits God's heart for the lost. Michael J. Anthony explains, "to see the heart of God, one need only look at the works of Jesus on the earth in the Gospel records. Here we see the heart of a heavenly Father who seeks the lost . . ."[305]

Objection Answered

From the same Bread of Life discourse, Storms disagrees, arguing from a traditionally Reformed point of view:

> It is *impossible* for someone whom the Father 'draws' *not* to come to him. . . . it is impossible that an elect person, a 'given-by-the-Father-to-the-Son person, should fail to come to faith in Christ. Or to put it positively, all the elect will come to faith in Christ. God's drawing of them is efficacious. The Father will never fail in drawing to salvation those whom he has given to the Son.[306]

Storms bases his argument on Jesus's statement in John 6:37, "All that the Father gives me will come to me" (ESV). Sproul argues from the same verse:

> Jesus is emphatic in His assertion that all whom the Father gives to Him will in fact come to Him. The order here is crucial. Jesus does not say that all who come to Him will then be given to Him

---

[304] This is essentially what Calvinist James White argues: "In response to the crowd's disbelief, Jesus also gives forth a clear explanation of their inability to understand, and their inability to come to Him as the one and only source of spiritual life." White, *Drawn by the Father*, 11.

[305] Michael J. Anthony, "Toward a Biblical Theology of the Heart of God," *Bibliotheca Sacra* 176 (January-March 2019): 13.

[306] Storms, *Chosen for Life*, 92-93.

by the Father. We do not determine by our response who will be the Father's gift to the Son. Rather our response is determined by the prior election of God for us to come to the Son as gifts to Him.[307]

James White joins the interpretive refrain from John 6:37:

What is also clearly presented is the simple fact that if God the Father gives a man to the Son, that man *will come to Christ in faith*. There is no contingency here, no possibility of this not coming to pass. The Father gives men to the Son for the express purpose of their salvation, and, because they are so given by the Father, they *will* be saved. . . . Nothing is said in Scripture about the Father's giving of people as being based upon anything in or of people themselves.[308]

More recently, Matthew Harmon gives a similar interpretation of John 6:37: "it is the Father's election of a specific group of people that defines who comes to the Son."[309]

At first blush, the arguments of Storms, Sproul, White, and Harmon seem compelling and airtight. But the arguments are based on a misunderstanding of what "will come to me" means in John 6:37. It is assumed that it means "will believe in me." It's an understandable assumption. At the outset of this chapter, I made the case that in John 6:44 and in the immediate context, Jesus uses the expressions, "come to me" and "believe in me" interchangeably. It is true but must be

---

[307] R. C. Sproul, "The Father's Gift to the Son," Ligonier Ministries, May 13, 2011, accessed July 12, 2017, http://www.ligonier.org/blog/fathers-gift-son/.

[308] White, *Drawn by the Father*, 31-32.

[309] Matthew Harmon, "For the Glory of the Father and the Salvation of His People: Definite Atonement in the Synoptics and Johannine Literature," in *From Heaven He Came and Sought Her: Definite Atonement in Historical, Biblical, Theological, and Practical Perspective*, ed. D. Gibson and J. Gibson (Wheaton, IL: Crossway, 2013), 270.

qualified. There is one exception that is not apparent in English, but conspicuous in Greek, as shown in Table 10.

Table 10. All Instances in John 6 Where Jesus Says, "Come to Me"

Verse	Translation (ESV)	Greek Verb Lemma & Tense	Meaning
John 6:35	"whoever *comes to me* shall not hunger"	ἔρχομαι (present)	Believe
John 6:37a	"All that the Father gives me will *come to me*"	ἥκω (future)	Ascend (cf. John 6:39, 40, 44, 54)
John 6:37b	"whoever *comes to me* I will never cast out"	ἔρχομαι (present)	Believe
John 6:44	"No one can *come to me* unless the Father who sent me draws him"	ἔρχομαι (aorist)	Believe
John 6:45	"Everyone who has heard and learned from the Father *comes to me*"	ἔρχομαι (present)	Believe
John 6:65	"no one can *come to me* unless it is granted him by the Father"	ἔρχομαι (aorist)	Believe

In five of six cases, the Greek word behind the English translation, "come(s)" is ἔρχομαι. Of these five cases, three are in the present tense (verses 35, 37b, 45), two are in the aorist tense (verses 44, 65). The two in the aorist tense are complementary infinitives[310] tied to the "helper" verb, "can" (δύναμαι),[311] which is also in the present tense in both cases. The point is: it's a homogenous group. In five of six cases, the verb is ἔρχομαι, and it reflects the present tense, either by direct conjugation or indirect association with a present-tense helper verb. And in every one of these five cases, it is the functional equivalent of "believe."

But in one case, John 6:37a, an entirely different verb is used (ἥκω) in an entirely different tense (future). It's a precursor of the Sesame Street game, "which one is not like the other ones?" The exception is intended to stand out and be identified as different. While ἥκω is generally synonymous with ἔρχομαι—it also means to come—it is reasonable to suspect that this one conspicuous change in word and tense signals that Jesus has in mind a different kind of coming. In this exception, I would argue that Jesus has in view not people coming to him in faith, but believers coming to him in the future last day when he will raise them up consistent with John 6:39, 40, 44, and 54. Therefore, in John 6:37, Jesus is saying in effect, "all that the Father gives me will ascend to me on the last day," or "all who believe in me I will raise up on the last day." If this is correct, then the arguments of Storms, Sproul, White, and Harmon that once seemed so airtight are utterly deflated. Election is nowhere in view. I am not alone nor the first to take this interpretation; Allen presents this view in his recent work.[312]

---

[310] Lukaszewski and Dubis, *The Lexham Syntactic Greek New Testament: Expansions and Annotations*, s.v. John 6:44, 65.

[311] Wallace describes them as "helper" verbs. Wallace, *Greek Grammar Beyond the Basics*, 598.

[312] Allen, *The Extent of the Atonement*, 697-698.

Some Other Ways God Draws

In the Bread of Life discourse God draws in multiple ways: through his Word, both incarnate and inscripturated; through authenticating signs; through progressive illumination—more truth given in response to receptivity; through the clear proclamation of the gospel, one person to others; and through a prophetic allusion to Christ's loving sacrifice on the cross. There are other means of divine drawing to be briefly noted, some of which were likely in play but not expressed during the Bread of Life discourse. And this list may not be exhaustive.

The Holy Spirit

Jesus explains the role of the Holy Spirit in drawing people to him in John 16:8-11: "And when he comes, he will convict the world concerning sin and righteousness and judgment: concerning sin, because they do not believe in me; concerning righteousness, because I go to the Father, and you will see me no longer; concerning judgment, because the ruler of this world is judged" (ESV).

Robert Pyne describes this as, "one aspect of the Spirit's evangelistic work."[313] He goes on to explain that this work extends to all people; it is not limited to the elect. "John's use of the word κόσμος [world] reinforces the idea that the Spirit's ministry of reproof is an expression of common grace.... The Spirit's ministry of reproof comes to every individual; all are charged with sin.... The passage does not distinguish between the elect and the nonelect in this aspect of the Spirit's ministry, which is directed toward the entire world."[314]

The nature of the Spirit's ministry of reproof is preparatory, according to Pyne. "In John 16:8 the Holy Spirit is involved in pointing out sin in order to bring about repentance.... the Holy Spirit shows

---

[313] Pyne, "The Role of the Holy Spirit in Conversion," 206.
[314] Ibid., 208-209, 211.

unbelievers their need for the gospel."³¹⁵ Specifically, "The Holy Spirit brings correction (ἐλέγχω) to the world, and does so by revealing sin, directing the way to righteousness, and warning of impending judgment. It is as if He says, 'You should not sin, but should pursue righteousness in the face of judgment.' All three are aspects of His ministry of correction and reproof."³¹⁶

Pyne also contends that the Spirit's ministry of reproof is resistible. "Such reproof is not irresistible; it is welcomed by the wise man but resisted by the fool.... The individual being reproved is usually present, and has freedom to accept or reject the reproof."³¹⁷

Creation

God also draws people through what he has created. God clearly reveals himself in creation to all and invites a Godward response. Of course, creation is an incomplete communicator; the gospel is not explained. But the existence of a Creator is clear, and it is intended to draw people, priming the progressive illumination process which can lead to eternal salvation.

Isaiah 40:26 directs our attention to the stars and asks a question that invites a response: "Lift up your eyes on high and see: who created these?" (ESV). Psalm 19:1-4 sings a winsome song: "The heavens declare the glory of God, and the sky above proclaims his handiwork. Day to day pours out speech, and night to night reveals knowledge. There is no speech, nor are there words, whose voice is not heard. Their voice goes out through all the earth, and their words to the end of the world" (ESV).

The theme of God's love as an attractional force is also reflected in creation. The splendor of the created order invites wonder: how could a majestic Creator like this love us? We are drawn by it. In Psalm 8:3-4,

---

[315] Ibid., 208, 211.
[316] Ibid., 211.
[317] Ibid., 208.

David muses: "When I look at your heavens, the work of your fingers, the moon and the stars, which you have set in place, what is man that you are mindful of him, and the son of man that you care for him?" (ESV).

Zedekia Marwa Kisare is a modern example of how God can use creation to draw people to himself. Kisare was a member of the Luo tribe of Tanzania, Africa. He was not raised in a Christian home. He didn't know who Christ was or what he had done. This is his story in his own words:

> I am five or six years old. It is early morning. I am sitting outside Mother's house, perched on the logs that support her granary. The morning is clear, cool; my black skin is soaking in the sun's early warmth. I fall into reverie. "Here I am sitting by Mother's granary," I muse. "How has this come about? How did I, Marwa, come to be a human being? How is it that I sit here feeling the warmth of the morning sun?"
>
> That morning, as I sat by Mother's granary, it came to me that God, in fact, was my reason for being, that beyond the village activity and relationships, there was one power in whom all things and all events had their beginning and purpose.
>
> Several years later two Christian evangelists, both Luo men, passed through. I was herding goats with several small boys on the savanna. The men, walking along the footpath, called us to come to the shade of a tree. These were the first Christians I had ever seen. I didn't think of them as men of God. These two men sang the most beautiful song for us. The tune was strange and ethereal, a melody drawing us out of the dusty savanna, lifting us beyond our circle of knowledge and experience. The words were in Luo, speaking of God; the music was like the wind whispering in the trees.
>
> Next they read from a book that said that God loves people and that he sent his Son to the world so that any person could have eternal life. Anyone who welcomed God's Son into the circle of his life would be accepted by God; those who made themselves

enemies of God's Son would be destroyed in everlasting fire. This was a new kind of life and death they were talking about—a reality beyond the circle of the village.[318]

Kisare received Christ as his Savior and became the longtime bishop of Tanzania Mennonite Church. He died in 1999 at the age of 90.

God reveals himself in creation to draw people. But not all are receptive; some suppress the truth revealed. Romans 1:18-21 explains,

> For the wrath of God is revealed from heaven against all ungodliness and unrighteousness of men, who by their unrighteousness suppress the truth. For what can be known about God is plain to them, because God has shown it to them. For his invisible attributes, namely, his eternal power and divine nature, have been clearly perceived, ever since the creation of the world, in the things that have been made. So they are without excuse. For although they knew God, they did not honor him as God or give thanks to him, but they became futile in their thinking, and their foolish hearts were darkened (ESV).

Pyne confirms, "according to Romans 1:18-21, unbelievers are capable of comprehending the truth of God's existence."[319] So they are without excuse in suppressing the evidence.

Neither the happy example of young Kisare nor the sad example of Romans 1 portrays the unregenerate as spiritual corpses unable to respond to God's initiative in drawing people to himself.

The Behavior of Believers

There is considerable scriptural evidence to suggest that God also uses the godly behavior of believers to draw unbelievers to himself. In The

---

[318] Zedekia Marwa Kisare in *More Reflections On The Meaning of Life*, ed. David Friend (New York: Little Brown & Co, 1992), 20.

[319] Pyne, "The Role of the Holy Spirit in Conversion," 203.

High Priestly Prayer, for example, Jesus prays for unity among all believers: "I do not ask for these only, but also for those who will believe in me through their word, that they may all be one, just as you, Father, are in me, and I in you, that they also may be in us" (John 17:20-21, ESV). And notice in particular the purpose of the unity for which Jesus prays: "so that the world may believe that you have sent me" (John 17:21, ESV). God intends to draw people to faith through the unity of believers.

Jesus follows this with a parallel prayer that effectively repeats the request for unity and then expands on the purpose: "The glory that you have given me I have given to them, that they may be one even as we are one, I in them and you in me, that they may become perfectly one, *so that the world may know that you sent me and loved them even as you loved me*" (John 17:21-22, ESV, emphasis added). God intends the unity of believers, which requires love for one another, to convey his love for all as a means of drawing people to faith.

The attractional force of love is also in view when Jesus gives his disciples a new commandment: "A new commandment I give to you, that you love one another: just as I have loved you, you also are to love one another. By this all people will know that you are my disciples, if you have love for one another" (John 13:34, ESV). The unspoken but unmistakable endgame is that the love of believers for one another will draw others to Christ.

In Titus 2:9-10, the apostle Paul also exhorts believers to behave in a godly way: "Bondservants are to be submissive to their own masters in everything; they are to be well-pleasing, not argumentative, not pilfering, but showing all good faith" (ESV). And here's the express purpose for such godly behavior: "so that in everything they may adorn the doctrine of God our Savior" (Titus 2:10, ESV). The Greek word translated "adorn" is κοσμέω. In its figurative use, it means to make something beautiful and attractive.[320] The godly behavior of believers

---

[320] BDAG, s.v. "κοσμέω."

makes the teaching about our Savior attractive. That is a way that God draws people to himself.

More Affirmations

To this point, a number of ways have been identified by which God the Father draws people to believe in Jesus: 1) the person of Jesus himself offered as the bread of life, 2) the Word of God from which we hear and learn, 3) authenticating signs, 4) progressive illumination, where human receptivity brings more divine truth, 5) interpersonal proclamation of the gospel, 6) Christ's loving sacrifice on the cross, 7) the Holy Spirit's ministry of reproof, 8) creation which testifies to God's existence, and 9) the godly behavior of believers.

Collectively, these drawing factors (and perhaps others not listed) are often called the general call to salvation because they apply to all people. It seems clear that God takes the initiative in our eternal salvation through these things. Without these divine initiatives, no one would believe. They are necessary. Each factor may not be necessary for every person, but the list is representative of God's essential work in calling people to salvation. Moreover, some factors seem more important than others; for example, the Word of God is indispensable, while the godly behavior of believers seems less so.

Of course, at the heart of all this is an offer of justification salvation, the good news that new life is available through faith in Christ. The apostle Paul makes the point with a rhetorical question: "and how are they to believe in him of whom they have never heard?" (Romans 10:14, ESV). The offer of the free gift of salvation today looks back on the death and resurrection of Christ that makes it possible (1 Corinthians 15:1-5). The gospel message is this: by his death and resurrection for our sins, Christ alone offers the free gift of eternal life to all who will simply believe him for it.

The nondeterministic modified view holds that, in its totality, the general call from God which includes the gospel message is enough help for any person to believe. When an unbeliever responds to light from God, more light is given by God. This view sees faith as coming from a person's genuine God-given freedom to accept or reject God's drawing and offer of salvation. Adherents say the general call including the gospel is sufficient and becomes effectual when a person believes; there is no intrinsically different and irresistible "effectual call" from God that goes out only to the elect. This nondeterministic modified view seems to be reflected in "A Statement of the Traditional Southern Baptist Understanding of God's Plan of Salvation" released in 2012. Article 8 says,

> We affirm that God, as an expression of his sovereignty, endows each person with actual free will (the ability to choose between two options), which must be exercised in accepting or rejecting God's gracious call to salvation by the Holy Spirit through the gospel.
>
> We deny that the decision of faith is an act of God rather than a response of the person. We deny that there is an "effectual call" for certain people that is different from a "general call" to any person who hears and understands the gospel.[321]

One of the things that makes the "Traditional Southern Baptist" view a modified position as opposed to an Arminian one is Article 9, which affirms the eternal security of the believer; once eternal salvation is received it cannot be lost.[322] The idea here is that God's general call which includes the gospel is sufficient for belief; it becomes effectual when one chooses to believe. The general call loaded with the gospel *is* the divine enablement needed; all a person needs to do is believe in Jesus to make it effective.

Radmacher explains, "In Philippi, Paul, Silas, Timothy and Luke preached the Word to women, including Lydia. That was the invitation,

---

[321] Eric Hankins, "A Statement of the Traditional Southern Baptist Understanding of God's Plan of Salvation," in *Anyone Can Be Saved: A Defense of "Traditional" Southern Baptist Soteriology*, ed. David L. Allen, Eric Hankins, and Adam Harwood (Eugene, OR: Wipf & Stock, 2016), 22.

[322] Ibid.

the general call. When Lydia responded, she was saved. That was what theologians call 'the effectual call.' The general call presents the message that 'Christ died for our sins.' But the hearer needs to believe."[323]

Roy Aldrich seems to hold a nondeterministic modified view as well, as he debates the view of Calvinist William Shedd that the lost should read the Bible, apply it, and pray for God to regenerate them as their only hope because, as spiritual corpses, they can't believe on their own:

> An unscriptural doctrine of total depravity leads to an unscriptural and inconsistent plan of salvation. Doubtless the sinner is "dead in trespasses and sins" (Eph. 2:1b). If this means that regeneration must precede faith, then it must also mean that regeneration must precede all three of the pious duties Shedd outlines for the lost. A doctrine of total depravity that excludes the possibility of faith must also exclude the possibilities of "hearing the word," "giving serious application to divine truth," and "praying for the Holy Spirit for conviction and regeneration." The extreme Calvinist deals with a rather lively spiritual corpse after all. If the corpse has enough vitality to read the Word, and heed the message, and pray for conviction, *perhaps it can also believe*" (emphasis added).[324]

Bing adds his nondeterministic take:

> God uses man's ability to respond. This does not diminish God's sovereignty, but recognizes that He has sovereignly designed man to have free will which allows him to respond to God. Since the Bible teaches that man does not seek God on his own (Rom. 3:11), God must take the initiative. He reveals Himself in creation, and though man knows this, he still refuses to honor

---

[323] Radmacher, *Salvation*, 106.

[324] Aldrich, "The Gift of God," 248.

God (Rom. 1:19-21). So God, in His love, seeks us out (Luke 19:10; John 3:16; 1 John 4:9-10). . . . God's will does not preclude man's will and freedom to respond, but includes it. . . . God does not force salvation on anyone.[325]

Jeremy Edmondson explains that a nondeterministic modified view is characteristic of Free Grace theology: "Free Grace affirms that mankind is totally depraved, unable to do anything to save himself, but we do not hold that mankind is unable to believe when presented the gospel. The Word of God is the agency by which faith is generated. Faith in Christ is man's response to the gospel presentation."[326]

Hodges gives an extended explanation that fits well within the nondeterministic modified view:

> Of course, we are not saying that men can come to God without any divine assistance at all. . . . God has a revelatory role in conversion (2 Cor 4:6). No conversion occurs until God breaks through the blindness induced by Satan and enlightens the heart with His truth. But where this enlightenment has occurred, it may be said to the believer that "flesh and blood has not revealed this to you, but My Father who is in heaven" (Matt 16:17).
>
> Thus the Bible does not say that man is constitutionally incapable of faith, only that faith cannot occur without divine illumination. In every realm of life, man cannot believe in what he regards as untrue. Only when he realizes the truth of any matter, only then does he believe it. The ability to believe things, we should say, is a capacity that man possesses, just like he possesses the ability to think or to speak. Only "ignorance of the truth" or "deception about the truth" stand in the way of man believing the Gospel. (. . . Satan knows this and acts accordingly: 2 Cor 4:4.)

---

[325] Bing, "How God Draws People to Salvation."

[326] Jeremy Edmondson, "Returning to Scripture as Our Sole Authority," *Free Grace Theology: 5 Ways It Magnifies the Gospel*, ed. Grant Hawley (Allen, TX: Bold Grace Ministries, 2016), 19.

But once a man realizes the truth of any matter, at the moment of realization he has believed it.

Consequently, saving faith occurs when it dawns on our hearts that Jesus Christ saves us forever the moment we believe that He does. (See John 11:25-27; John 20:30-31; 1 John 5:1.)

What then is the bottom line? Two things. (1) Man has the capacity to believe and is held responsible if he does not do so. (2) Man's faith can only occur in response to divine illumination.

Therefore, what should unsaved men be doing? They should be seeking the God who is revealed in creation (Rom 1:20-21). Since God rewards those who diligently seek Him (Heb 11:6), the search for God will lead to an examination of the claims of Christ. This, in turn, will lead to salvation truth since Jesus affirmed, "If anyone wills to do His will, he shall know concerning the doctrine, whether it is from God or whether I speak on My own authority" (John 7:17).

Paul's statement that "there is none who seeks after God" (Rom 3:11) may seem to contradict this, but it doesn't. This famous text does not say that man *cannot* seek God! He can and should seek God (Acts 17:26-27)! But he *doesn't* (unprompted by the Spirit) and, therefore, is responsible for not doing so.

Man's failure to believe, therefore, is something for which he can be held accountable by his Judge. If he had sought the truth, he would have found the truth!

But those who do find the truth are drawn to it, and thus taught, by God. The Savior declared: "No one can come to Me unless the Father who sent Me draws him; and I will raise him up at the last day. It is written in the prophets, 'And they shall all be taught by God.' Therefore everyone who has heard and learned from the Father comes to Me" (John 6:44-46; italics added).

As we evangelize men, we can become part of this drawing/teaching process until God illuminates the unsaved heart so that a response of faith results. But let us remember, even though God uses us in this process, it is still God—not us—who commands the light to shine into man's darkness (2 Cor 4:6). It is God who saves the lost![327]

The Deterministic Modified View Explained and Rebutted

Explanation of the Deterministic Modified View

The deterministic modified view sees faith as the unconditional gift of God given only to the elect such that they will surely believe and could not possibly do otherwise. In this view, there is no genuine human freedom which permits a person to choose freely between two options—to accept or reject, to believe or disbelieve—because God determines. Adherents say the general call which includes the gospel is not enough. An effectual call is needed that is intrinsically different and beyond the general call. The general call is insufficient and ineffectual because, in his still-depraved state, man remains unable to believe, even if he responds to the general call to some degree. Those who hold this view generally have Reformed leanings but are persuaded to break ranks with most Calvinists by believing that faith comes *before* regeneration, not after.

The deterministic modified view posits that God's enablement to believe comes through a special, selective, effectual call, not regeneration. Demarest explains that the divine initiative, "inheres in the Spirit's effectual call rather than in the new birth itself."[328] Also, "logically speaking, the called according to God's purposes convert, and so are regenerated. Not only is this position biblical, but we avoid the difficulty of positing, logically at least, that regeneration precedes personal belief in the Gospel, repentance from sin, and wholehearted trust in Christ."[329]

---

[327] Hodges, "God's Role in Conversion."

[328] Demarest, *The Cross and Salvation*, 227.

[329] Ibid.

Millard Erickson provides a good summary of the deterministic modified view and how it conceptualizes the relationship between effectual calling, faith (or conversion), and regeneration:

> Special or effectual calling, then, involves an extraordinary presentation of the message of salvation, sufficiently powerful to counteract the effects of sin and enable the person to believe. It is also so appealing that the person will believe. Special calling is in many ways similar to the prevenient grace of which Arminians speak. It differs from that concept, however, in two respects. It is bestowed only upon the elect, not upon all humans, and it leads infallibly or efficaciously to a positive response by the recipient.[330]
>
> If we sinful humans are unable to believe and respond to God's gospel without some special working of his within us, how can anyone, even the elect, believe unless first rendered capable of belief through regeneration? To say that conversion is prior to regeneration would seem to be a denial of total depravity. Nonetheless, the biblical evidence favors the position that conversion is logically prior to regeneration. Various appeals to respond to the gospel imply that conversion results in regeneration. Among them is Paul's reply to the Philippian jailor (we are here assuming that regeneration is part of the process of being saved): "Believe in the Lord Jesus, and you will be saved—you and your household" (Acts 16:31). Peter makes a similar statement in his Pentecost sermon: "Repent and be baptized, every one of you, in the name of Jesus Christ for the forgiveness of your sins. And you will receive the gift of the Holy Spirit" (Acts 2:38). This appears to be the pattern throughout the New Testament.[331]

The conclusion here, then, is that God regenerates those who repent and believe. But this conclusion seems inconsistent with

---

[330] Erickson, *Christian Theology*, 863.

[331] Ibid., 863-864.

the doctrine of total inability. Are we torn between Scripture and logic on this point? There is a way out. That is to distinguish between God's special and effectual calling on the one hand, and regeneration on the other. Although no one is capable of responding to the general call of the gospel, in the case of the elect God works intensively through a special calling so that they do respond in repentance and faith. As a result of this conversion, God regenerates them. The special calling is simply an intensive and effectual working by the Holy Spirit. It is not the complete transformation that constitutes regeneration, but it does render the conversion of the individual both possible and certain. Thus the logical order of the initial aspects of salvation is special calling—conversion—regeneration.[332]

Lewis and Demarest concur with Erickson and expand the case for a modified view, describing it as "moderately Reformed":

> On the related issue of the logical order of the divine and human factors three major options need consideration: (1) Some find the Scriptures to teach that God's calling of all in prevenient grace and their response in conversion precedes regeneration (Arminians). (2) Others find the Scriptures to teach that the special call and regeneration precede conversion (traditional Calvinists). (3) A third view finds that the special call precedes conversion and conversion precedes regeneration (Millard Erickson and ourselves).[333]
>
> This modified Calvinistic hypothesis . . . best coheres with the Bible's teachings of (1) the unwillingness and inability of sinners to receive the Good News and (2) the need to receive the Good News to be born again. . . . The teaching that regeneration must precede faith seems to contradict the teaching that we must

---

[332] Ibid., 864.

[333] Lewis and Demarest, *Integrative Theology*, 3:56.

believe in Christ to receive eternal life, justification, and adoption as children of God.[334]

This moderately Reformed scheme agrees with Arminianism in holding that human conversion precedes divine regeneration (Miley, Wiley) and disagrees with high Calvinism in its claim that the Spirit's regeneration takes logical precedence over conscious, human conversion (Strong, Berkhof, Murray). In contrast to Arminianism, however, the only sinners who convert to Christ are effectually called by the Spirit. Whereas theologians such as L. Berkhof seem to equate special calling and regeneration, we distinguish the one from the other; they are as distinct as conception and birth. It is one thing to conceive the truth of the Gospel by the Spirit and another to be born of the Spirit, although the one leads to the other.[335]

Are we regenerated in order that we may convert? Or do we convert in order to be regenerated? The usual Calvinist view maintains that a conversion that does not logically follow regeneration is not a true conversion. In place of regeneration in that statement we would insert the Spirit's effectual calling. This better fits the biblical passages indicating that sinners convert in order to become children of God (John 1:12-13) and receive eternal life (John 3:16, 18, 36; 5:24). As John later explained: "By believing you may have life in his name" (20:31). So in our moderately Reformed *ordo salutis*, sinners who convert are regenerated. Spiritual conception (calling and conversion) precedes the spiritual birth of a child of God (1 Cor. 3:6).[336]

It seems that Chafer also holds a deterministic modified view, but in some of his writing it is not as obvious, partly because he doesn't use the term "effectual call" quite as much as one might expect, and partly

---

[334] Ibid., 3:57.

[335] Ibid.

[336] Ibid., 3:104.

because he sometimes uses terms characteristic of the nondeterministic view, such as "divine influence" and "enlightens." His determinism is evident, however, in statements which limit the enabling work of the Spirit to the elect as over against "the Arminian notion of a general bestowment of grace whereby all men are able to respond to the gospel appeal."

> ... man cannot of himself turn to God ... he must be enabled to do so. ... It is as definitely contended that, apart from this divine influence, no unregenerate person will ever turn to God. ... It is in connection with this specific enabling work of the Spirit that the sovereign election of God is manifested. Only those are included whom God *calls*, *draws*, and *enlightens*. ... No ground is found in the Bible for the Arminian notion of a general bestowment of grace whereby all men are able to respond to the gospel appeal ...
>
> To a degree which allows of no exception, the Scriptures assert the supernatural inability of fallen men to turn to God in saving faith, apart from the supernatural unveiling of the mind which Satan has darkened.[337]

In commenting on John 16:7-11, Chafer describes the effectual call this way:

> The Holy Spirit undertakes a work in the hearts of unregenerate men which is quite evidently not their regeneration, but may be defined as a preparation of the mind to the end that an intelligent choice of Christ as Savior may be made. ... there would be no hope of the salvation of any individual in this age apart from this particular ministry of the Spirit.[338]

---

[337] Chafer, *Systematic Theology*, 3:210-211, 223.

[338] Ibid., 3:217.

According to Chafer, it is through the Spirit's effectual call that one comes to believe in Jesus, and in turn, "regeneration is conditioned simply on faith (John 1:12-13; Gal. 3:26)."[339] In his interpretation of John 6:44, Chafer removes all doubt about whether he is in the deterministic camp:

> No Scripture is more absolute about *divine determination* than verse 44 [John 6:44] . . . It is here in the sphere of an *effectual call* that the *divine election* is realized. . . . The Arminian practice of intruding into this passage the human element by such phrases as, 'if they will to hear the call" . . . deserves the rebuke which belongs to those who distort the Word of God by adding thereto (emphasis added).[340]

The deterministic modified view is commonly based on a deterministic understanding of Romans 8:29-30: "For those whom he foreknew he also predestined to be conformed to the image of his Son, in order that he might be the firstborn among many brothers. And those whom he predestined he also called, and those whom he called he also justified, and those whom he justified he also glorified" (ESV). Traditionally, Roman 8:29-30 is seen as revealing what has been called "the golden chain of salvation," depicting God's sequential work leading to salvation as shown in Figure 5:

Figure 5: The Golden Chain of Salvation from Romans 8:29-30

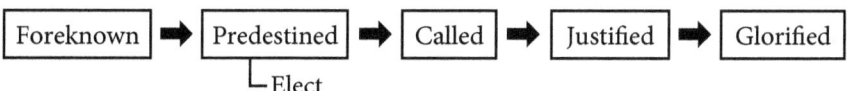

The elect are not mentioned specifically in Romans 8:29-30, but in this context, they are commonly considered to be the same as the

---

[339] Ibid., 7:265.

[340] Ibid., 3:223.

"predestined," as shown in Figure 5. Regarding election, Erickson (who holds a deterministic modified view) explains, "Scripture speaks of election in several different senses. Election sometimes refers to God's choice of Israel as his specially favored people. It occasionally points to the selection of individuals to special positions of privilege and service, and, of course, to selection to salvation."[341] It is the latter aspect of election that is commonly linked to the "golden chain." Specifically, election is a specific aspect of predestination. Erickson explains, "'Predestination' refers to God's choice of individuals for eternal life or eternal death. 'Election' is the selection of some for eternal life, the positive side of predestination."[342] The golden chain of Romans 8:29-30 has the positive side in view. The elect are those who have been predestined or chosen by God to be eternally saved.

In a Calvinistic paradigm, the predestination or election or choosing by God is deterministic and unconditional. Erickson explains, "in our Calvinistic scheme there is no basis for God's choice of some to eternal life other than his own sovereign will. There is nothing in the individual that persuades God to grant salvation to him or her."[343] In commenting on Romans 8:30, Erickson explains, "Here the classes of those predestined, called, justified, and glorified seem coextensive. If that is the case, the calling must be efficacious—those who are called are actually saved."[344] Pyne (who also holds a deterministic modified view) agrees: "Since only those who are predestined for salvation are called, and all those who are called are justified and ultimately glorified, it seems obvious that the apostle refers only to the elect."[345]

The logic of the deterministic modified view may be represented by a pair of syllogisms shown in Table 11.

---

[341] Erickson, *Christian Theology*, 856.

[342] Ibid., 842.

[343] Ibid., 859.

[344] Ibid., 862.

[345] Pyne, "The Role of the Holy Spirit in Conversion," 212.

Table 11. Logic of the Deterministic Modified View

Syllogism A:

Premise 1:	According to Romans 8:30, all those "called" by God are saved.
Premise 2:	Those drawn by the general call from God are not all saved.
Conclusion:	The "calling" of Romans 8:30 must describe an effectual call from God that goes beyond the general call to cause the elect to believe.

Syllogism B:

Premise 1:	Contrary to the prevailing Calvinist view, regeneration comes after faith, not before.
Premise 2:	The effectual call logically comes before faith, not after.
Conclusion:	Therefore, the effectual call cannot be the same as or a part of regeneration.

Premise 1 of syllogism B makes this view modified, and it forces Calvinists who agree with it to find another way for God to make people believe, consistent with their deterministic view of election. This leaves them having to explain how God produces belief in a person who is otherwise unable to believe. Regeneration is off the table, so a special effectual call limited to the elect and leading inexorably to faith is inferred. This makes this view deterministic. Within this camp, the effectual call is also referred to as "efficacious grace" or a "special calling" or an "internal call," or "special grace."

In defending this view, Walvoord explains,

> The Scriptures bear faithful testimony to the fact that efficacious grace is an act of God. Every reference to divine calling presumes

or states that it is an act of God. . . . Never in the Scriptures is divine calling attributed to human choice. . . . efficacious grace is an immediate act of God which by its nature cannot be resisted. . . . Efficacious grace is irresistible not in the sense that it is resisted and all such resistance is overcome, but it is irresistible in the sense that it is never resisted. Its nature forbids it. It is irresistible in that it is certainly effectual.[346]

Erickson affirms, "Special calling means that God works in particularly effective way with the elect, enabling them to respond in repentance and faith, and rendering it certain that they will."[347]

Pyne adds,

Romans 8, however, is describing a narrower form of divine invitation [relative to the general call]. As already noted, this invitation is extended only to the elect, to those who have already been predestined to salvation in Christ. If this call is limited to the elect it cannot be rejected. . . . This work of God can be referred to as "irresistible grace" in that it is never refused, or "efficacious grace" in that it is always successful in accomplishing its purpose.[348]

It is interesting that some who hold the deterministic modified view seem to want to dodge the determinism of it. For example, Walvoord says, "Even the work of efficacious grace, though simultaneous with regeneration, and indispensable to it, does not in itself effect regeneration. Efficacious grace only makes regeneration possible and certain. . . ."[349] If this is an attempt to distance efficacious grace from determinism, it doesn't work. How can there be an efficacious

---

[346] Walvoord, *The Holy Spirit*, 121, 123.

[347] Erickson, *Christian Theology*, 862.

[348] Pyne, "The Role of the Holy Spirit in Conversion," 213.

[349] Walvoord, *The Holy Spirit*, 133.

grace that doesn't effect regeneration but makes it certain? How can an efficacious grace be efficacious and not efficacious at the same time?

Lewis and Demarest also hold the deterministic modified view, and also seem to want to soften the determinism by denying the irresistibility of the effectual call:

> The Spirit's internal call is *effectual*, but not irresistible. Prior to the Spirit's calling, slaves to sin not only *can* resist special grace but invariably *do* so. The point of effectual grace is that the Holy Spirit lovingly overcomes insolence in the elect and delivers them from bondage to sinful unbelief. The spiritually dead, like Lazarus, cannot come forth from their tombs, but the Holy Spirit grants the beginnings of new life. Although efficacious for salvation and service, the Spirit's modes of operation are not irresistible in an impersonal, automatic way. Since the word, 'irresistible' often connotes a mechanical coercion, it is inapplicable to personal relationships.[350]

Saying the "internal call is effectual, but not irresistible" does not save it from being deterministic. It just sounds nicer. The fact remains; in this view, God unconditionally imposes an effectual call on the elect that causes them to believe whether they resist or not. There is no real human choice in the matter.

Rebuttal of the Deterministic Modified View

The deterministic modified view seems flawed in a number of ways. The following flaws are not unique to the deterministic modified view, but are generally reflected in Reformed theology as well.

---

[350] Lewis and Demarest, *Integrative Theology*, 3:55-56.

Election and Romans 8:29-30 Need Not Be Interpreted Deterministically

An Alternative Interpretation

The calling of Romans 8:29-30 may not be unconditional after all; God's calling may be conditioned on his foreknowledge of those who will believe. Dillow argues this point from Romans 8:29-30:

> These five terms link, as in a chain, the history of the same group of people from foreknowledge to glorification. The same group that was foreknown will also ultimately be glorified. . . . The word "foreknowledge" could mean, as our Experimentalist [Calvinist] friends maintain, "prior choice." However, there is no obvious reason for rejecting the more common meaning—simple prior knowledge of future events. God knows who will believe and, based on this prior knowledge, He predestines them to salvation. To predestine is simply to plan in advance.
>
> The call referred to here is the efficacious call to come to Him. . . . All those whom God foreknew would believe are predestined. Because God foreknew they would believe, He calls them efficaciously. All those who are predestined are called, and all those who are called are justified. The calling is an effectual calling.[351]

Lemke agrees and expands the argument:

> Applied to salvation, Traditionalists[352] believe that God elects and predestines those whom he foreknows will respond to the proclamation of the gospel through the conviction of the Holy

---

[351] Dillow, *Final Destiny*, 742.

[352] The Traditionalist view is summed up by Eric Hankins: "anyone can be saved and, once saved, is secure forever," Hankins, "Savability: Southern Baptists' Core Soteriological Conviction and Contribution," *Anyone Can Be Saved*, 10.

Spirit with repentance and faith in Christ as Savior and Lord. This pattern is stated nowhere more clearly than in Rom. 8:29-30... Note that predestination, calling, and justification are conditional upon God's foreknowledge of those who would be led by the Holy Spirit to respond to the gospel with repentance and faith. God does not first decree or predestine those who are elect and then foreknow those who would be saved based on his decree. Rather, God's foreknowledge of human responses comes first, with God's election, calling, and justification flowing from his foreknowledge.... God desires the salvation of not just a chosen few, but of anyone and everyone in the world who responds to him in faith. He sovereignly and graciously elects and predestines all those who believe.[353]

Other Interpretations

The above arguments of Dillow and Lemke fit within a view Bing calls "pre-temporal, conditional election."[354] This is just one of seven common views on election summarized by Bing, another being "monergistic, unconditional, pre-temporal election," which generally describes the deterministic modified view.[355] The remaining five views

---

[353] Steven W. Lemke, "Commentary on Article 7: The Sovereignty of God," *Anyone Can Be Saved*, 106-107, 116.

[354] Charles C. Bing, "Free Grace and Views of Election," *GraceNotes*, no. 72, n.d., accessed May 5, 2017, http://gracelife.org/resources/gracenotes/?id=72.

[355] Ibid. Here are the seven views: 1) monergistic, unconditional, pre-temporal election (Reformed, deterministic); 2) synergistic, pre-temporal election (see Norman L. Geisler, *Chosen But Free*, 15-21, 130-159); 3) pre-temporal, conditional election (Dillow and Lemke cited above); 4) pre-temporal, corporate election (see Brian J. Abasciano, "Corporate Election in Romans 9: A Reply to Thomas Schreiner," *Journal of the Evangelical Theological Society* 49, no. 2 (June 2006): 351-371); 5) pre-temporal, middle-knowledge election (see Kenneth Keathley, *Salvation and Sovereignty: A Molinist Approach* (Nashville: B&H Publishing Group, 2010), 138-163); (6) atemporal, qualitative election (see Robert N. Wilkin, "The Doctrine of

are not deterministic. It is beyond the scope of this work (and the current capacity of this author) to explain all these views of election. They are mentioned here only to show that there are numerous alternatives to a deterministic interpretation.

In addition to these seven views, Flowers offers yet another angle on the golden chain of Romans 8. He points out that all the verbs in Romans 8:30 are in the aorist tense, suggesting that Paul may have in view believers who had already died.[356] Flowers explains,

> Notice the apostle's use of the past tense in this verse. If Paul intended to speak about the future salvation of every elect individual then why would he use the past tense verbs? When writing these words, Paul and his readers had not yet been glorified, so there is no explicit reason to use the past tense. Thus, there is no reason to assume Paul has in mind the future glorification of all believers.
>
> The past tense suggests that Paul is referring to former generations of those who have loved God and were called to fulfill His redemptive purpose....
>
> Calvinists must interpret Paul's use of the past tense (aorist indicative) as meaning 'it is as good as done' because it was predestined. But this is a very rare usage in the original language

---

Divine Election Reconsidered: Election to Service, Not to Everlasting Life." *Journal of the Grace Evangelical Society* 25, no. 49 (Autumn 2012): 3-22); and 7) trans-temporal, congruent election (see Richard Land, "Congruent Election: Understanding Salvation from an 'Eternal Now' Perspective," in *Whosoever Will: A Biblical-Theological Critique of Five-Point Calvinism*, ed. David L. Allen and Steve W. Lemke (Nashville, TN: B&H Publishing Group, 2010), 45-59).

[356] Of course, the use of the aorist tense in Romans 8:30 does not prove that all the action described happened in the past. The use of the proleptic or futuristic aorist is possible here, though it is rare. Wallace cites Romans 8:30 as a possible example of the proleptic aorist (Wallace, *Greek Grammar Beyond the Basics*, 563-564).

and the immediate context does not clearly support a Calvinistic rendering. . . .

Instead of introducing a complex concept of divine prescience, unconditional election, and effectual salvation never once clearly expounded upon in the Scriptures, could it be that Paul may intend simply to communicate that those who were previously loved and known by God were also predestined to be conformed to the image of the One to come? Paul seems to be giving a brief history lesson of what God had done in former generations as a reference for God's trustworthiness for all who come to Him in faith.[357]

The point is: election need not be interpreted deterministically; there are good, biblical options that are non-deterministic.

The Deterministic Modified View Renders the General Call Meaningless

The deterministic modified view calls into question the meaningfulness of the general call. What purpose does the general call serve if an intrinsically different effectual call from God is needed? In the deterministic modified view, the general call seems pointless. Braxton Hunter explains the problem:

> The problems of compatibilism[358] are further compounded by the questionable separation of the 'general' and 'effectual' calls of

---

[357] Leighton Flowers, *The Potter's Promise: A Biblical Defense of Traditional Soteriology*, (San Bernardino, CA: Trinity Academic Press, 2017), 92-95. Flowers' interpretation of Romans 8:30 sets up his non-Calvinistic interpretation of Romans 9 (pp. 97-148).

[358] Compatibilism is the view that "God's sovereignty determines whatsoever will come to pass . . . including the sinful acts of his creatures." In contrast, libertarianism is the view that "God's sovereignty is limited by and consistent with the libertarian choices of his creatures," such that "the

God. . . . If the effectual call goes out only to the elect, and only the elect can respond to it, then what of the general call? Two possible reasons for the general call come into view. It could be that the general call is merely the byproduct of the preaching of the word for the elect. In attempting to spread the gospel so that the elect might respond the message spills over to the non-elect. They hear, but cannot respond to the message. After all, Calvinists agree that they should evangelize every person because of their ignorance of who is and is not elect. Still, on this view the general call does not even actually go out to every man. It goes out to the elect and is heard by others. Perhaps the general call exists so that the guilt of those who do not respond to it is made even more apparent. However, if this is the case, we must loop back to the problem previously mentioned. They are still being punished for choosing A rather than C, when C was not available to them. Either way, what is the purpose of the general call? It seems a strange byproduct for a compatibilistic view of biblical freedom. Such a division between a general and effectual call is not necessary for those who see biblical freedom as libertarian . . . Common proof texts related to the division of the effectual and general calls such as Rom 8:29-30 do not require readers to fall into a framework which is fraught with the philosophical problems mentioned. Is the Calvinistic explanation of such texts the only possible understanding? Does it represent a position that can be demonstrated with overwhelming certainty? No.[359]

---

efficient cause of evil is not God but free creaturely choices." J.P. Moreland and William Lane Craig, *Philosophical Foundations for a Christian Worldview* (Downers Grove, IL: InterVarsity Press, 2003), 281-282.

[359] Braxton Hunter, "Commentary on Article 8: The Free Will of Man," *Anyone Can Be Saved*, 125-126.

The Deterministic Modified View Calls into Question the Goodness of God

God's Love

The deterministic modified view suggests that God does not love all people, at least not in the same way. Allen explains:

> All Calvinists, because of their doctrine of unconditional election, must talk about God's love in ways that distinguish between different kinds of God's love for the elect and non-elect. Some prefer to say that God has a "special" or "saving" love for the elect that he does not have for the non-elect. . . .
>
> All non-Calvinists find this notion of God's "saving love" or "special love" as defined by Calvinists to be problematic. God's love is expressed in actual relationship with all believers in a way that is not the case with unbelievers. But it is a different matter to suggest, as all Calvinists do, that God places a saving love on some individuals and not on others. From a non-Calvinist perspective, Scripture does not make such a distinction.[360]

Jerry Walls (an Arminian) is more forceful: "Calvinism simply cannot make coherent sense of God's love for all persons and it would be better to forthrightly admit that, than to maintain a posture of love for all that is utterly hollow when carefully examined."[361] A. W. Pink (a Calvinist) just comes right out and admits it: "God loves whom He chooses. He does not love everybody."[362] Of course, it would be unfair to paint all Calvinists Pink. In John 3:16, Carson does not take, "For God so loved the world" (ESV) to mean God loves the elect

---

[360] Allen, *The Extent of the Atonement*, 779-780.

[361] Jerry L. Walls, *Does God Love Everyone? The Heart of What is Wrong with Calvinism*, (Eugene, OR: Cascade Books, 2016), 83.

[362] Arthur W. Pink, *The Sovereignty of God* (Grand Rapids, MI: Baker, 1930), 29-30.

only.[363] But he does admit that God loves the elect differently. "The elect may be the entire nation of Israel or the church as a body or individuals. In each case, God sets his affection on his chosen ones in a way in which he does not set his affection on others.... God's love... is peculiarly directed toward the elect."[364] This idea of God loving the elect "peculiarly," sounds like just a nice way of saying "better." Wright (a Calvinist) says, as if to reassure, "We also need to remember that our God loves different objects with different sorts of love."[365] The implication is that one "sort" of love determines some "objects," before they were ever created, will go to hell without ever having a chance to be saved because Jesus never loved them with the same "sort" of love that drove him to the cross in payment for sin; he only did that for some other people for whom he had a different "sort" of love.[366] This unsettling idea chased me back to one of the most formative books of my early Christian life, J. I. Packer's *Knowing God*, to reread the section on the love of God.[367] It was just as eloquent as I remembered, but I detect no definitive stance on whether God loves the non-elect.

---

[363] D. A. Carson, *The Difficult Doctrine of the Love of God* (Wheaton, IL: Crossway Books, 2000), 17.

[364] Ibid., 18-19.

[365] Wright, *40 Questions about Calvinism*, 52.

[366] I recognize that there are indeed different aspects of God's love. Allen says, "There is both a conditionality and unconditionality to God's love, corresponding to objective and subjective aspect of His love.... In the subjective sense, God's love is described in Scripture as eternal, unconditionally constant, and grounded in His eternal character of love. The objective aspects of God's love are relational and predicated on human response to God's prevenient, unmerited love." See Allen, *The Atonement*, 190. But this is not the distinction Calvinists such as Carson and Wright have in mind.

[367] J. I. Packer, *Knowing God* (Downers Grove, IL: InterVarsity Press, 1973), 106-115.

God's Integrity

In the deterministic paradigm, the non-elect have no chance whatsoever of believing and being saved. How then could Jesus legitimately offer himself as the Bread of Life to the unbelieving crowd in the synagogue in John 6—a crowd that surely included some who were non-elect? To the non-elect, the offer of eternal life is not good news; it's a false hope. It's disingenuous. Bing avers, "God's invitation to be saved through the gospel is a sincere and legitimate offer only if any and every person can believe it."[368] Hankins adds: "If some are chosen without respect to their response of faith, then no hope of salvation ever existed for others."[369] Allen says, "the logic here is simple. If there is no atonement for some people, then those people are not savable. . . . Only universal atonement guarantees the genuineness of the offer of salvation made to all people through the preaching of the gospel."[370]

God's Fairness & Association with Sin

The deterministic modified view also raises questions about God's fairness and his connection with sin. How can humans be held responsible for something that is impossible for them to do?[371] Dillow

---

[368] Bing, "Can an Unregenerate Person Believe the Gospel?"

[369] Hankins, "Savability: Southern Baptists' Core Soteriological Conviction and Contribution," *Anyone Can Be Saved*, 11.

[370] Allen, *The Atonement*, 181.

[371] A common Reformed argument traced to Jonathan Edwards is that the unregenerate have no *moral ability* to believe in Jesus. They will not believe because, in their unregenerate state, they do not *want* to believe, and it cannot be otherwise. Nevertheless, it is argued that the unregenerate do have a *natural ability* to believe in the sense that there are no physical constraints preventing belief; if they *wanted* to believe, theoretically they could. It's just that their moral inability prevents them from ever *wanting* to believe. Therefore, it is argued, human responsibility for unbelief rests on the *natural ability* to do otherwise. Daniel Whedon argues persuasively that the Edwardsian distinction between moral ability and natural ability

says, "The Experimentalist view [a deterministic view] is a blasphemous conception of God which says that in eternity past He predestined the vast majority of the human race to eternal torment before they were even born and had a chance to accept or reject Him."[372]

Austin Fischer (a former Calvinist) is pointed:

> The reprobate. This is the technical term used to describe those humans who, according to Calvinism, have been unconditionally predestined to hell. To say it another way, the reprobate are those humans who, before they existed, were chosen by God to spend eternity in hell for sins God ordained they would commit. In summary, then, the reprobate are all those humans who will experience a fate dreadful beyond comprehension (hell) as they are eternally punished by God for sins he ordained they would commit before they existed—*they were created so they could be damned*. If you don't cringe a little, you don't have a pulse....
>
> How can humans be held responsible for their sins when God is the ultimate cause of their sins? *Can you come up with a single analogy or illustration that makes the slightest sense of this?* ...
>
> Calvinism attempts to stress sin and magnify grace by emphasizing our depravity: we are so depraved that God has to do every single bit of our salvation. God even determines our acceptance of the gift of salvation because we could not otherwise do so.
>
> But ... for me this undermined both sin and grace because God is the ultimate cause of our sinfulness and depravity and as

---

is fallacious and fails to be a valid ground for human responsibility in a deterministic paradigm. In sum, "if there is no moral ability, there is no physical ability." See Daniel D. Whedon, *Freedom of the Will: A Wesleyan Response to Jonathan Edwards,* ed. John D. Wagner (Eugene, OR: Wipf & Stock, 2009), 202-212.

[372] Dillow, *Final Destiny,* 741n2374.

such his saving us is not an act of grace—God is merely fixing the problem he caused.[373]

Modern historian and philosopher Will Durant recounts the perspective of Erasmus, an influential scholar during the Renaissance who helped prepare the way for the Reformation and then came to oppose the extreme deterministic theology of some of the Reformers:

> To Erasmus it seemed obvious that a God who punished sins that His creatures as made by Him could not help committing, was an immoral monster unworthy of worship or praise; and to ascribe such conduct to Christ's "Father in heaven" would be the direst blasphemy.... Erasmus confessed that a man's moral choice is fettered by a thousand circumstances over which he has had no control; yet man's consciousness persists in affirming some measure of freedom, without which he would be a meaningless automaton. In any case, Erasmus concluded, let us admit our ignorance, our incapacity to reconcile moral freedom with divine prescience or omnipresent causality; let us postpone the solution to the Last Judgment; but meanwhile let us shun any hypothesis that makes man a puppet, and God a tyrant crueler than any in history.[374]

For these reasons, the goodness of God does not support the deterministic modified view.

The Deterministic Modified View Is Unclear about What the Effectual Call Involves

Walvoord says, "the doctrine of efficacious grace must remain essentially inscrutable to human minds."[375] There's truth to this, especially as it

---

[373] Fischer, *Young, Restless, No Longer Reformed*, 22, 24, 78.

[374] Will Durant, *The Reformation*, The Story of Civilization, vol. 6 (New York: Simon & Schuster, 2011), 9677-9684, Kindle.

[375] Walvoord, *The Holy Spirit*, 127.

relates to the deterministic modified view. As shown in the earlier study of John 6, there is ample biblical information describing what the general call involves. Nevertheless, I am unaware of any references that describe specifically what a special, intrinsically different effectual call involves. It is commonly characterized as a mystical inner work of the Holy Spirit that enables faith in a way that the general call doesn't. But this seems to be based on a logical inference of a deterministic system, not biblical data.

When proponents of the deterministic modified view try to explain what their effectual call involves, there is a tendency to reach for biblical ideas that actually relate to the general call to all people, which is understandable because there is little else available. For example, Lewis and Demarest explain the effectual or internal call this way:

> In summary, the Spirit's mission in internal calling involves (1) convicting a worldly person of sin, righteousness, and judgment; (2) illuminating the mind to understand the observed facts and revealed meanings of the Gospel message; (3) persuading of the Gospel's objective validity for all; and (4) witnessing to the Gospel's applicability for one's repentant self.[376]

This sounds an awful lot like the general call. Isn't the first factor tied to the Holy Spirit's ministry of reproof in John 16:8-11—the reproof that goes out to "the world"? Isn't the second factor the progressive illumination seen in John 6, where the receptivity of unbelievers prompted more light from Jesus, which may have converted some but not all? Isn't the third factor also reflected in John 6, where the entire Bread of Life discourse represents Jesus's attempt to persuade the unbelieving crowd, at least some of whom were not persuaded? (It's hard to comment on the fourth factor because it is not at all clear what "one's repentant self" is.)

---

[376] Lewis and Demarest, *Integrative Theology*, 3:56.

Chafer also takes a crack at explaining the effectual call:

> No Scripture is more absolute about divine determination than verse 44 [John 6:44]. . . . It is here in the sphere of an effectual call that the divine election is realized. . . . The Arminian practice of intruding into this passage the human element by such phrases as, 'if they will to hear the call" . . . deserves the rebuke which belongs to those who distort the Word of God by adding thereto.[377]

These are strong words from a venerable theologian. But I contend that John 6:44 is better understood to be describing the general call to salvation. If this is correct, Chafer's own comment, "[n]o Scripture is more absolute about divine determination than verse 44," ironically points up the weakness of his own view.

Compton takes a slightly different approach to an effectual call. He takes the idea of illumination and divides it into two types: a non-efficacious illumination that is part of the general call, and an efficacious illumination that is part of the effectual call. He explains the distinction:

> It must be granted that there is a general illuminating work of the Spirit accomplished in connection with the proclamation of the gospel that is non-efficacious, that is, it does not result in conversion/salvation. This illuminating activity of the Spirit is an expression of common grace and is part of the general call of the gospel (e.g., John 16:8-11). It is to be distinguished from the more specific work of illumination that the Spirit accomplishes in connection with the conversion of the elect as part of God's special grace exercised in the effectual call.[378]

Compton appeals to Acts 16:14 (where God opens Lydia's heart) and 1 Corinthians 2:12-14 (where the Spirit gives believers understanding

---

[377] Chafer, *Systematic Theology*, 3:223.

[378] Compton, "The *Ordo Salutis* and Monergism: The Case for Faith Preceding Regeneration, Part 3," 295-296.

that unbelievers do not have) in arguing for an illumination that is effectual.[379] Nevertheless, neither reference provides any basis for distinguishing an effectual type of illumination (see chapter 1 for a discussion of both Acts 16:13-15 and 1 Corinthians 2:14). It seems that these references are simply the best proof texts he can find to try to support the idea of something effectual preceding and causing faith—a special illumination or a call—that is required by his prior commitment to the doctrine of total inability, a doctrine already shown to be unsupported. In his own words: "The need for a work of God logically preceding repentance and faith or conversion is based on passages that describe the unconverted as incapable of responding savingly to the gospel."[380]

Beyond the four reasons articulated above (one, election and Romans 8:29-30 need not be interpreted deterministically; two, the deterministic modified view renders the general call meaningless; three, it calls into question the goodness of God; and four, it is unclear about what the effectual call involves), it is interesting to note that the deterministic modified view is generally rejected by traditional Reformed theologians. Inasmuch as these Reformed theologians have already been shown to hold a scripturally weak conception of how God draws people to believe, their rejection of the deterministic modified view is not exactly persuasive. Nevertheless, it is informative to see why the deterministic modified view is considered out-of-step with traditional Reformed theology.

Barrett argues against the deterministic modified view for at least two reasons. First, he argues that the partial nature of the effectual call in the deterministic modified view is unscriptural:

> The Bible teaches that the sinner is called into fellowship with Christ (1 Cor. 1:9; John 6:44), called out of darkness into Christ's marvelous light (1 Peter 2:9), and called into Christ's kingdom

---

[379] Ibid., 294.

[380] Ibid., 295.

and glory (1 Thess. 2:12; 2 Thess. 2:14; 1 Peter 5:10). One does not get the impression from passages like these that calling is merely initial and partial, only to be completed by a regeneration that comes subsequent to man's will in conversion. Rather ... the effectual call both consists of and is followed by the regeneration of the sinner. Only then can the sinner respond with faith and repentance.[381]

Moreover, Barrett argues that a partial effectual call diminishes the proper biblical view of regeneration:

What then remains to be accomplished in regeneration? Has not the sinner already been renewed and restored in all areas (mind, will, desires)? ... Consequently, Lewis and Demarest have minimized and depleted regeneration of its full power to awaken the sinner. As a result, regeneration no longer is the first and primary event that brings new life into the dead sinner as Scripture affirms (Ezek. 36-37; John 3:5-8; Eph. 2:5; Titus 2:3-7; 1 Peter 1:23).[382]

Second, Barrett argues that the modified view is inherently synergistic and, therefore, stands well outside the Reformed tradition.[383]

It is crucial to recognize that placing conversion before regeneration is synergistic because in this arrangement God's act of regeneration is logically and causally dependent upon and conditioned upon man's act of belief and repentance.[384]

---

[381] Barrett, *Salvation by Grace*, 295-296.

[382] Ibid., 296-297.

[383] Ibid., 308-313.

[384] Ibid., 308.

> ... the consensus among Calvinists, both past and present, is that *regeneration precedes faith* in the *ordo salutis* and this is essential to monergism.[385]

In rejecting the deterministic modified view for being outside the Reformed tradition, I believe Barrett arrives at the right conclusion for the wrong reason.

For the above reasons, the deterministic modified view is flawed.

The Arminian View Explained and Rebutted

At this point it would be fair to ask: is the general call of the nondeterministic modified view essentially the same thing as the prevenient grace of the Arminian view? I confess to not knowing a lot about prevenient grace previously, and I'm not an expert now. My background and training are moderately Calvinistic and so I hadn't read much on the subject of prevenient grace. In my research, I discovered that not much has been written about it. Brian Shelton (an Arminian) reveals, "there remains no seminal works on prevenient grace in the two-hundred-year legacy of John Wesley."[386]

Shelton defines prevenient grace this way: "The doctrine of prevenient grace is the belief that God enables all people to exercise saving faith in Christ by mitigating the effects of sinful depravity."[387] He explains that original sin prevents us from believing in Christ on our own, and so prevenient grace represents God's enabling initiative without which no one would believe.[388] He carefully distinguishes the divine enablement of prevenient grace from two alternatives: 1) the deterministic enablement of the Reformed tradition, and 2) the semi-

---

[385] Ibid., 312.

[386] W. Brian Shelton, *Prevenient Grace: God's Provision for Fallen Humanity* (Anderson, IN: Francis Asbury Press, 2014), i.

[387] Ibid., 259.

[388] Ibid.

Pelagian view of the Orthodox (Catholic) tradition that asserts that people can come to faith on their own, at least initially, apart from God's initiative and enablement.[389] This seems to harmonize with the nondeterministic modified view.

F. Leroy Forlines also summarizes how God draws people to believe from an Arminian viewpoint.

> If we say that, without the work of the Holy Spirit (Jn. 6:44), no one will ever believe in Christ, I would agree. However, such a statement, as I understand it, still leaves room for the individual's response of belief or unbelief. . . .
>
> For a person to be *caused* to believe violates what it means to be a person. Faith is a personal experience. *It is a choice.* Divine *assistance* and *influence*, yes. Divine *cause*, no.
>
> I have given considerable attention to the fact that the words *cause* and *effect* are not appropriate in describing personal relationships. *Influence* and *response* are the words to use in describing interpersonal relationships. There is no such thing as a person doing something without having a genuine involvement in the action.[390]

The explanation from Forlines certainly does contradict the deterministic modified view, but his words could well be those of pretty much anyone in the nondeterministic camp.

Olson explains that the Arminian view, "reserves all the power, ability and efficacy in salvation to grace, but allows humans the God-granted ability to resist or not resist it. The only 'contribution' humans make is non-resistance to grace. This is the same thing as accepting a gift. Arminius could not fathom why a gift that must be freely received

---

[389] Ibid.

[390] Forlines, *Classical Arminianism: A Theology of Salvation*, 132.

is no longer a gift, as Calvinists contend."391 Again, this sounds fairly consistent with the nondeterministic modified view.

Based on the descriptions of Shelton, Forlines, and Olson, there does indeed seem to be considerable overlap between what I have described as the general call in the nondeterministic modified view and the Arminian doctrine of prevenient grace.

Nevertheless, some aspects of the Arminian view and prevenient grace give me pause. For example, Olson says,

> For Arminius, however, there is an intermediate stage between being unregenerate and regenerate. The intermediate stage is when the human being is not so much free to respond to the gospel (as the semi-Pelagians claimed) but is freed to respond to the good news of redemption in Christ. Arminius thus believes not so much in free will but in a freed will, one which, though initially bound by sin, has been brought by the prevenient grace of the Spirit of Christ to a point where it can respond freely to the divine call. The intermediate stage is neither unregenerate nor regenerate, but perhaps post-unregenerate and pre-regenerate. The soul of the sinner is being regenerated but the sinner is able to resist and spurn the prevenient grace of God by denying the gospel.392

I'm not sure how one can be unregenerate and regenerate at the same time, and I'm unaware of any scriptural evidence to support this claim. Similarly, I don't know where to find support for the notion that a sinner could be in the very process of being regenerated by God and then stop the regenerative process by denying the gospel. Conversely, in the case of one who accepts the gospel, this seems to suggest that regeneration somehow starts before faith and then is completed after faith. If so, the Arminian view would be considered a faith-

---

[391] Olson, *Arminian Theology: Myths and Realities*, 165.

[392] Ibid., 164-165.

before-regeneration view only if regeneration is taken to mean "fully regenerated." What's more, this suggests that everyone is in the process of being regenerated. If I'm understanding all this correctly, this is a point where the nondeterministic modified view parts company with the Arminian view. In the introduction, regeneration was defined as an instantaneous act of new birth, not a process—a point which Anderson has argued persuasively.[393]

And there are other concerns. Thomas Oden describes the Arminian connection between prevenient grace and baptism: "Sacramentally viewed, prevenient grace is that grace that leads to baptism and the solemn voluntary reaffirmation of baptism. Baptism bestows saving grace upon those who have been readied to respond to it in faith, either by one's own faith or the anticipatory faith of the worshiping and parenting community."[394] I don't understand and cannot affirm as biblical this aspect of prevenient grace, and it makes me suspect there may be other aspects I'm not aware of and could not support. Therefore, while there seems to be considerable overlap between the conception of the general call I'm advocating and the Arminian conception of prevenient grace, they do not appear to be the same thing.

Moreover, Forlines summarizes yet another common Arminian view that distinguishes it from all the other views considered: "it is possible for a person who has been saved to commit apostasy and become once again lost and under the wrath of God."[395] I believe this flies in the face of what Jesus says in John 6:37, "whoever comes to me I will never cast out" (ESV). Similarly, in John 6:39, Jesus says: "And this is the will of him who sent me, that I should lose nothing of all that he has given me" (ESV). Once a person believes in Jesus and has been given by the Father to Jesus, that person will never be lost again. Not ever.

---

[393] Anderson, *Free Grace Soteriology*, 245-246.

[394] Oden, *The Transforming Power of Grace*, 50.

[395] Forlines, *Classical Arminianism: A Theology of Salvation*, 303.

Concluding Evaluation of the Nondeterministic Modified View

Compared to other faith-before-regeneration views, the nondeterministic modified view of how God draws people to believe harmonizes the most biblical data and makes the fewest assumptions.

The word "draws" (ἕλκω) as it is used in John 6:44 describes God drawing all people, not just the elect, in a non-physical, attractional, non-coercive, didactic way that can be received or rejected. And this is modeled clearly and beautifully in the Bread of Life discourse, where the Father draws through his Word, both inscripturated and incarnate; the Father draws through authenticating signs; the Father draws through progressive illumination; the Father draws through a clear and compelling presentation of the gospel from one person to another; and the Father draws through a prophetic glimpse of his Son lifted up on the cross. With the added influences of the Holy Spirit's ministry of reproof, the creation which testifies to God's existence, and the godly behavior of believers, we see a powerful constellation of light God uses to penetrate the darkness and draw people to believe in Jesus.

This divine illumination is at the heart of the nondeterministic modified view. As presented in this research, it outshines the problems posed by the determinism of the alternative modified view which renders the general call to salvation meaningless and the goodness of God questionable. And it outshines the Arminian view which undermines Jesus's ability to keep those the Father has given him and posits a strangely continuous view of regeneration connected to a prevenient grace freighted with unscriptural baggage.

CHAPTER 4

PASTORAL IMPLICATIONS OF THE NONDETERMINISTIC MODIFIED VIEW

Implications for What God Is Like

I AGREE WITH A. W. Tozer on this: "The gravest question before the Church is always God Himself, and the most portentous fact about any man is not what he at a given time may say or do, but what he in his deep heart conceives God to be like. We tend by a secret law of the soul to move toward our mental image of God."[396]

I believe pastors have a responsibility to work hard to present to their congregations an accurate, biblical, accessible picture of what God is like. An undershepherd needs to represent the Chief Shepherd well. And I can think of no issue more telling than how God draws people to himself. Hebrews 1:3 tells us that, "He [the Son] is the radiance of the glory of God and the exact imprint of his nature" (ESV). So, what better place to begin than to consider how Jesus draws people to himself?

For me, one of the most delightful discoveries of this study is the

---

[396] Aiden Wilson Tozer, *The Knowledge of the Holy, The Attributes of God: Their Meaning in the Christian Life*, gift ed. (New York: HarperCollins, 1992), 1-2.

model of Jesus drawing people to believe in him provided in John 6. The study of what Jesus says in John 6:44, "No one can come to me unless the Father who sent me draws him" (ESV), is well documented. The study of what Jesus does in the immediate context as a model of drawing is not as well attested, and it's not something I had fully considered before.[397]

The question of how God draws can easily be taken to a level that makes my head spin. How refreshing and helpful for me as a pastor to be able to begin the discussion by saying, "Let's look at how Jesus draws people in John 6," and to allow the text to show what God is like because Jesus is the "exact imprint." Isn't it just like Jesus to make a complicated issue more accessible? Perhaps a sharper focus on Jesus as our model for drawing can help us avoid pushing doctrine in a direction or to an extent that calls into question God's character.

Implications for the Primacy of Scripture

Things change. And, according to Pulitzer-prize-winning author Thomas Friedman, the rate of change in the world is accelerating: "the rate of technological change is now accelerating so fast that it has risen above the average rate at which most people can absorb all these changes."[398] Such technological change is directly tied to the electronic dissemination of information and ideas. And that includes theology.

The potential for sweeping changes in the popularity of certain theological ideas has never been greater, and this can be good or bad. As I mentioned at the outset of this work, Calvinism seems to be on the rise, at least in America. Carson's endorsement of a recent compendium of

---

[397] C. Gordon Olson briefly alludes to the context but does not fully unpack it in C. Gordon Olson, *Beyond Calvinism and Arminianism: An Inductive Mediate Theology of Salvation*, 3rd ed. (Lynchburg, VA: Global Gospel Ministries, 2012), 275.

[398] Thomas L. Friedman, *Thank You For Being Late: An Optimist's Guide to Thriving in the Age of Accelerations*, (New York: Farrar, Straus, and Giroux, 2016), 480, Kindle.

Reformed essays is telling: "I cannot imagine that this book could have been published twenty-five years ago: there were not at that time enough well-informed theologians working in the Reformed heritage."[399] I have experienced the rise of Calvinism first-hand. Phoenix Seminary has become decidedly more Reformed since I began attending in the early 90s. My point is not to decry the direction of the shift, but to marvel at the swiftness and magnitude of it, and to acknowledge it as one of the reasons for doing this research. I wanted to go back to Scripture and re-evaluate my own thinking, and of course, I wanted to be in a better position to interpret for my congregants the Calvinistic shift in the theological landscape. By the way, I remain grateful for Phoenix Seminary and remain friends with faculty and staff members, some of whom I presume embrace the theological shift as good progress.

I have emerged with a fresh appreciation for the primacy of Scripture in a world where change is fast but not always good. In this research, as I returned again and again to Scripture, I found some of my own preconceptions challenged. I never thought I would find myself disagreeing with some of my heroes. How could I disagree, for example, with Dallas Theological Seminary patriarchs, Chafer and Walvoord? I was surprised also at the weakness of the faith-after-regeneration view. Frankly, I expected the biblical arguments for it to be more persuasive.

Of course, I might be surprised because I am wrong. I don't pretend to be in the same league as many of the theologians I've cited in terms of knowledge or intelligence. But the most important thing is not what any theologian says, or what any theological system dictates, or what any theological trend popularizes. The most important thing is what the Bible says. This study has brought me back to that. And that is where I will encourage my congregants to return.

I do see the need to respectfully consider the historical faith of our fathers, and I acknowledge this is not a strength of mine nor is it a point of emphasis in this work. I am nonetheless intrigued by the recent work of Patristics scholar Ken Wilson relating to Augustine. Wilson confirms

---

[399] Carson, endorsement in *From Heaven He Came and Sought Her*, 1.

Augustine is a patriarch of Calvinism: "Augustine's five points of total inability, unconditional election, limited atonement, irresistible grace, and perseverance are now recognized as the TULIP of Calvinism. Thus Augustine was the inventor of the five points of Calvinism."[400] Wilson argues that Augustine's deterministic thinking, which came to him later in life and which now finds expression in modern Calvinism, was informed to a large extent by the pagan heterodox philosophies of Manichaeism (Gnosticism), Stoicism, and Neoplatonism.[401] Wilson concludes, "Current Calvinist interpretations of 'deterministic' scripture passages are pagan interpretations brought into Christianity through Augustine."[402] This is a bombshell for those who trace their theological heritage to Augustine. But at the end of the day, Augustine is not our authority. Scripture is.

Implications for Giving an Answer

I have friends and colleagues who are Calvinists. I've hired a Calvinist to our pastoral staff. We've had a Calvinist on our elder board. They are brothers and sisters in Christ, not enemies. I consider our disagreements to be intramural and friendly.

In the course of conversation, there is one question I've been asked repeatedly. Flowers describes it as the Calvinist's most popular question, and he should know; he was one.[403] The question goes something like this: "Why did you believe the gospel, but your friend

---

[400] Ken Wilson, "A Theological and Historical Investigation," in *A Defense of Free Grace Theology: With Respect to Saving Faith, Perseverance, and Assurance*, 47. The aforementioned chapter is a summary of Wilson's doctoral thesis at the University of Oxford, 2012. For a complete record of his research see Kenneth Wilson, *Augustine's Conversion from Traditional Free Choice to "Non-free" Free Will: A Comprehensive Methodology* (Tubingen: Mohr Siebeck, 2018).

[401] Ibid., 61.

[402] Ibid., 65.

[403] Flowers, *The Potter's Promise*, 155.

did not? Are you wiser or smarter or more spiritual or better trained or more humble?"[404] White (a Calvinist) is typical when he asks, "Why do some see and yet not believe? Why do others see and believe? Are those who believe 'better' than those who do not?"[405] In my experience, this usually comes across as a "gotcha" question. Behind that question I imagine there are other implied questions: "So, you think you're better than other people? You think you're somebody special? You think you can take some credit for your own salvation?"

Of course, I don't think any of these things, but I suspect my friends are trying to get me to see what they perceive to be an inherent pridefulness in my non-Calvinist thinking, as if I'm trying to grab some glory that belongs to God. But in my non-Calvinist thinking, I fail to see how anybody can take credit for simply receiving a gift by faith. Faith is not a meritorious work. Can Scripture be any clearer in distinguishing faith from works? I can't take credit for anything.

Well, I never really felt satisfied with my answers to the "gotcha" question of my Calvinist friends. But over the course of my study, I have learned the tables may be turned. Flowers explains,

> God created both individuals with genuine responsibility (ability-to-respond), whereas the consistent Calvinist must admit that one individual was made "better" than the other by means outside of either individual's control (i.e. irresistible grace or effectual regeneration).
>
> Therefore, it is the Calvinist who ultimately has to admit to all the unbelievers of the world, "We chose to believe in Christ because God made us morally better people than the rest of you." Whereas the Traditionalist would say, "No, everyone has the same God given moral capacity to believe in Christ, no one is made morally 'better' by God. If you refuse to believe there is no

---

[404] Ibid.

[405] White, *Drawn by the Father*, 28.

one to blame but yourself, because God gave you everything you needed."[406]

Thank you, Leighton Flowers, for giving me a better answer. I'm also grateful to Flowers for providing an answer for my grandchildren in the form of a story. These days an important litmus test for my own theological understanding is: can I explain this to my grandchildren? Here's the story:

> Back when my kids were younger we did a family activity that our church had suggested. I stood at the top of the stairs with my three children at the bottom.
> I said to them, "Here are the rules. You must get from the bottom of the stairs to the top of the stairs without touching any of the railing, the wall or even the stairs. Ready, go!"
> My kids looked at me and then each other and then back at their mother. With bewilderment in their eyes, they immediately began to whine and complain saying, "Dad, that is impossible!"
> I told them to stop whining and figure it out.
> The youngest stood at the bottom and started trying to jump, slamming himself into the steps over and over. The more creative one of the bunch began looking for tools to help build some kind of contraption. Another sat down on the floor while loudly declaring, "This is just stupid, no one can do that!"
> Finally, in exasperation one of the kids yelled out, "Dad, why don't you just help us?" I raised my eyebrows as if to give them a clue that they may be on the right track. The eldest caught on quickly.
> "Can you help us dad?" he shouted.
> I replied quietly, "No one even asked me."
> "Can you carry us up the stairs?" he asked.
> "I will if you ask me," I said.

---

[406] Flowers, *The Potter's Promise*, 159-160.

And one by one, I carried each child to the top after they simply asked. Then, we sat down and talked about salvation. We talked about how it is impossible for us to get to heaven by our own efforts, but if we ask Christ for help then He will carry us. It was a great visual lesson of God's grace in contrast with man's works.

But suppose that my children's inability to get to the top of the stairs also meant they were incapable of asking me for help. Imagine how this story would have played out if it was impossible for my children not only to get to the top of the stairs but equally impossible for them to recognize that inability and request help when it was offered. . . .

The whole purpose of presenting my kids with that dilemma was to help them to discover their need for help. To suggest that they cannot realize their need and ask for help on the basis that they cannot get to the top of stairs completely undermines the very purpose of the giving them that dilemma.

The purpose of the father in both instances is to get others to trust him. The law was not sent for the purpose of getting mankind to heaven. Just as the purpose of the activity was not to get the kids to the top of the staircase. The purpose was to help them to see that they have a need and that they cannot make it on their own.

Calvinists have wrongly concluded that because mankind is unable to attain righteousness by works through the law, they must also be equally unable to attain righteousness by grace through faith. In other words, they have concluded that because mankind is incapable of "making it to the top of the stairs," then they are equally incapable of "recognizing their inability and asking for help." It does not follow and it is not biblical.[407]

---

[407] Ibid., 171-173.

Now, that's a story I can adapt for my grandchildren. (But, I'll need to buy or borrow a place with stairs.)

Implications for Humility

Eating Humble Pie and Crow

For me, this study was a big slice of humble pie. There are many intelligent, erudite, godly people on every side. I feel as though I didn't finish but merely abandoned the work for lack of time; I have a church to pastor and a wife who feels widowed. I have walked through some personal doors of learning only to discover bigger rooms with more doors yet to be opened—doors that could change my thinking significantly. This is humbling and exciting.

In my early seminary days, I considered myself to be a moderate Calvinist. At one time, I was up to four points on the TULIP test.[408] I could never quite embrace limited atonement. (And I know in some circles a four-point Calvinist is an Arminian.) I say this to confess my own former prejudice against Arminians. Yes, they were in the family of God, I thought, but they weren't my closer Calvinist brothers; they were my distant, weird cousins—the unscholarly ones who were too light on God's sovereignty and human depravity, too heavy on human achievement, and out to lunch on eternal security. My theological debates were almost always with my brothers, not my cousins.

I was wrong. I still don't agree with all tenets of Arminianism, but I was wrong. In researching for this work, I likely read more Arminian works than I had read in all my years before. I discovered that Arminianism is not unscholarly. And Arminianism holds a strong view of human depravity; it just posits prevenient grace instead of the regeneration

---

[408] TULIP stands for 1) total depravity, 2) unconditional election, 3) limited atonement, 4) irresistible grace, and 5) perseverance of the saints. The five points minus the third point of limited atonement is sometimes referred to as Amyraldianism.

of Calvinism as God's gracious way of drawing the unregenerate who would otherwise have no hope. After doing my research and building a case for how God draws from John 6 and elsewhere, it was then that I began to ask myself: is what I'm finding all that different from prevenient grace? From what I can tell, there is considerable overlap.

I still don't believe, as most Arminians do, that a regenerate person can lose his eternal salvation. I don't see regeneration as a process. I don't see how prevenient grace leads to a baptism that bestows saving grace.[409] And I'm still wondering whether election based on foreseen faith is the best option. But I've come away humbled, with a deeper respect for my Arminian brothers and sisters.

Middle Ground

Theological categories aren't tidy. While the terminology of Calvinism and Arminianism is in some ways unavoidable and needs to be addressed, in my opinion, it need not and should not frame all our theological thinking and conversation. There is a tendency shared by both Calvinists and Arminians to dismiss the possibility of a middle ground. For example, Michael Horton (a Calvinist) says, "There is no such thing as Calminianism."[410] On the other side, Roger Olson (an Arminian) tries to dispel the "myth" that "a hybrid of Calvinism and Arminianism is possible."[411] I get it. Some important differences seem irreconcilable.

But isn't it possible to build a biblical soteriology from the ground up with neither Calvinistic nor Arminian templates and end up with a system that in some ways resembles each? Allen contends, "in light of the historical evidence, extreme claims of some high Calvinists and Arminians that no middle ground exists between Calvinism and

---

[409] Oden, *The Transforming Power of Grace*, 50.

[410] Michael Horton, foreword to *Against Calvinism* by Roger Olson (Grand Rapids, MI: Zondervan, 2011), 10

[411] Olson, *Arminian Theology: Myths and Realities*, 61-77.

Arminianism are unfounded."[412] In fact, the simple statement of Eric Hankins representing the "traditional" Southern Baptist soteriology, "anyone can be saved and, once saved, is secure forever" is a middle or modified view that resonates with me.[413]

Food for Thought from a Calvinist and a Liberal

There are two sides to the deterministic coin. On the one side, there is the humble acknowledgement that the elect are completely unworthy of being chosen and had absolutely no part in it. On the other side, however, is the unavoidable idea that God seems to love the elect in a different way than the non-elect, even though it's unmerited. It is this other side that has the potential to engender pridefulness.

This is not my idea. I got it from a Calvinist. And a big one. G. C. Berkouwer describes "the great misunderstanding" regarding the doctrine of election:

> We wish to point to that great misunderstanding which so directly concerns the nature of divine election that for many generations it has fallen like a shadow over the doctrine of election.... We are thinking of that misunderstanding of election whereby man takes his election for granted so that it becomes an occasion for subtle self-justification. Election is accepted as a matter of course and it is no longer seen as truly free, sovereign, and gracious....
>
> The humility which in Scripture is the correlate of election, and which is incorporated in the warning which is part of the message of God's electing act, changes into self-awareness, self-justification, and self-distinction. God's gracious and free election is obscured by man's pretentiousness.[414]

---

[412] Allen, *The Extent of the Atonement*, 769.

[413] Hankins, "Savability: Southern Baptists' Core Soteriological Conviction and Contribution," *Anyone Can Be Saved*, 10.

[414] G. C. Berkouwer, *Divine Election*, Hugo Bekker trans., Studies in

Of course, Berkouwer contends that the potential "pretentiousness" is born of a "misunderstanding." He may be right. But I wonder if it is rather an unwanted side effect of Reformed theology that's just more palatably described as a "misunderstanding." I want to be careful here. I'm not saying that all Calvinists are pretentious. Nor am I saying I'm better; I struggle mightily with pridefulness and I can be a sinful jerk. I'm just wondering if the "pretentiousness" Berkouwer mentions is actually a *systemic* vulnerability of Calvinism.

I had almost decided to leave this touchy subject alone when I ran across an article by Christian Piatt that tipped the scales the other way. I had never heard of Piatt before. As far as I can tell, he is not a conservative evangelical, and has no horse in the Calvinism-versus-Arminianism race. But he, too, sees the propensity of Calvinism to engender pridefulness. So, I'll just quote him and leave it at that.

> If you believe humanity ultimately is depraved, and that only a preordained few are to receive God's sovereign grace, this is fertile ground for seeing much of the world as "less than." And what's more, Calvinists can divest themselves of the culpability for such supremacist thinking, because, after all, it's God's will! This isn't how we want it, they say, but it just is how it is.... It seems more of a "Daddy loves me best" argument.[415]

Implications for Evangelism

The charge that Calvinism discourages evangelism is an old saw. That Calvinists affirm the need for evangelism is well attested.[416]

Dogmatics, (Grand Rapids, MI: Wm B. Eerdmans, 1960), 307-308.

[415] Christian Piatt, "Driscoll, Piper, Calvin and God's Gift of ... Racism?", Huffington Post, January 10, 2013, accessed July 19, 2017, http://www.huffingtonpost.com/christian-piatt/driscoll-piper-calvin-and-gods-gift-of-racism_b_2050070.html.

[416] See for example, J. I. Packer, *Evangelism and the Sovereignty of God* (Downers Grove, IL: IVP Academic, 1991).

Nevertheless, I can say that studying and arriving at a nondeterministic modified view of God drawing people to salvation has refreshed my own fervor for evangelism. In particular, as I considered how God uses the unity, love, and godliness of believers to draw people to himself, I felt a renewed desire to be the kind of person and to shepherd the kind of church that God can use to draw unbelievers. It also occurs to me that this is supportive of the church striving to be attractional within the bounds of biblical orthodoxy.

I can also say that it has refreshed my concern for the logical extent of certain Calvinistic views. For example, if I believe in limited atonement, what do I say when the unbeliever to whom I am witnessing asks, "Did Christ die for me?" Or, "Am I savable? Do I say, "maybe"? And if I hold a deterministic view of election, what do I say to the unbeliever who asks, "Does God love me as much as he loves you?" Do I say, "potentially"? And if I hold a deterministic view of salvation, what do I say to the unbeliever who asks, "If, according to God's sovereignty, I was born with a sinful condition that makes it impossible for me to believe in Jesus, then how can God condemn me to hell for not believing?" I have no answer.

In my opinion, the nondeterministic modified view supported in this work is the biblical alternative that poses the fewest problems. I have a hard-enough time motivating myself and my congregation to evangelize without having to deal with Calvinistic wrenches in the evangelistic machine.

Implications for Assurance

In the study of the Bread of Life discourse as a model for drawing, it was shown that the one who comes to Jesus in faith will never be cast out (John 6:37b). That's strong, clear assurance. The terms are plain and simple. There's a promise: "I will never cast you out." And there's a proviso: "if you come to me in faith."

Wayne Grudem (a Calvinist) criticizes Free Grace theology for giving false assurance: "Free Grace theology gives false assurance of eternal life to many people who profess faith in Christ but then show no evidence in their pattern of life."[417] The idea seems to be that the Free Grace gospel peddles an easy believism that produces and coddles a bunch of professing-but-counterfeit believers whose behavior is not good enough to prove that they are truly saved. Grudem says, "they are lost" and should be challenged to have genuine faith that produces works.[418] Packer, in his enthusiastic endorsement of Grudem's book just cited, characterizes Free Grace theology as "unbiblical," "anti-evangelical," and "sub-Christian."[419]

My purpose here is not to defend Free Grace theology. Instead, I want to reveal the irony and inconsistency of this accusation of false assurance coming from any Calvinist brother such as Grudem or Packer who believes in limited atonement.[420] As I understand it, in their system, there are basically two possibilities for the professing believer who bears little or no apparent fruit: he is either elect or non-elect. If he's non-elect, the challenge to have genuine faith unto salvation is a *false hope* because there's no possibility that he could ever be saved; there's no atoning provision for it. On the other hand, if he's elect, there are two possibilities for him: he is either regenerate or unregenerate. If he is regenerate, then insinuating that he's lost is a *false accusation* and a misdiagnosis of the problem that may engender legalism. And if he is unregenerate, then he is still a spiritual corpse and cannot possibly respond in any positive way to any spiritual challenge unless and until God regenerates him, apart from which any challenge to have genuine faith will be a *false start* that goes nowhere. And besides all this, why

---

[417] Grudem, *"Free Grace" Theology: 5 Ways It Diminishes the Gospel* (Wheaton, IL: Crossway, 2016), 77. For a thorough and convincing rebuttal of all Grudem's criticisms of Free Grace Theology see *A Defense of Free Grace Theology: With Respect to Saving Faith, Perseverance, and Assurance*, ed. Fred Chay.

[418] Ibid., 78-79.

[419] J. I. Packer, endorsement in *"Free Grace" Theology: 5 Ways It Diminishes the Gospel*, by Wayne Grudem, 2.

[420] Grudem, *Systematic Theology*, 594-603; Packer, *Concise Theology*, 137-139.

get so worked up about *false assurance* because, in Reformed thinking, nobody's salvation is truly jeopardized by it anyway? It's a *false alarm*. This seems a rather rickety catapult from which to launch stones at the appearance of falsity.

In commenting on the assurance of John 6:37 that all who come to Jesus in faith will never be cast out, White (a Calvinist) is careful to qualify this assurance as if to dissuade people from linking it to simple, ordinary faith in Jesus for eternal life. Like Grudem, White is concerned about false professions:

> But lest we overlook, in our proper zeal for the truth of the eternal nature and security of salvation, the danger of false profession, let us remark again that the tremendous promise that is here given, and which will be further amplified in the following verses, is not for those who do not truly trust, truly believe, and truly *follow* Jesus Christ. There is no foundation in this passage (or any in God's Word) for one who does not truly love Christ, does not truly desire to follow Him, to be with Him, to honor Him and to glorify Him, to claim "eternal security."[421]

What White seems to be claiming is that when Jesus says, "whoever comes to me," what he *really* means is "whoever truly trusts me, and truly believes in me, and truly follows me, and truly loves me, and truly desires to follow me, and be with me, and honor me, and glorify me." To be sure, following and loving and desiring and honoring and glorifying Jesus are wonderful things every believer should do. But the crucial question is this: are these presented by Jesus in John 6 as conditions for receiving eternal life and for having the assurance of never being cast out?

In John 6, Jesus presents one and only one condition for receiving the eternal life that he offers: faith in Jesus. In the text, this faith is variously expressed as believe, come, eat, and drink. All these convey the very

---

[421] White, *Drawn by the Father*, 47-48.

Pastoral Implications 221

same idea summed up by Jesus in John 6:47, who issues a "truly" of his own: "Truly, truly, I say to you, whoever believes has eternal life" (ESV).

It's hard to see how, by any lexical or exegetical wizardry, the concepts of following, loving, desiring, honoring, and glorifying Jesus could possibly be shoehorned into Jesus's simple statement: "whoever believes."[422] I agree that merely professing something does not necessarily make it so; therefore, I do not deny the presence of "false professors" in the church. But I fear that in trying to fix the problem of *false professions*, White and others like him have created the much bigger problem of *false additions*. It is no longer faith alone in Christ alone; it's faith plus something else.

And caught up in the error of false additions is the unfortunate side effect of *false jeopardy*. What truly self-aware believer can honestly be assured by the supposedly salvific requirements of continually following, loving, desiring, honoring, and glorifying the Lord? By these criteria, I'm toast. One might argue that such false jeopardy might not be such a bad thing if it motivates godly behavior. But by that same logic I should probably threaten to disown my adoptive child or warn her that her misbehavior may prove that my adoption of her never really happened. False jeopardy is unhealthy and unbiblical.[423]

Wright insists that full assurance of eternal salvation is available to

---

[422] I say this knowing full well that I am not just arguing against White, but also others (e.g. Bates, Fuller, Greear, Shepherd, Snoeberger, and Theilman) who import these kinds of things into the concept of faith as explained in the introduction under "faith."

[423] I am aware of the argument from 2 Corinthians 13:5-6 that professing believers ought to examine themselves and their lifestyles to find out whether they are truly regenerated, as argued by Grudem for example (Grudem, *Free Grace Theology*, 130-132). I am persuaded that there are better interpretations of this passage as explained by Fred Chay, "Examine Yourself to See If You Are in the Faith," *A Defense of Free Grace Theology*, 535-547.

Calvinists as they look to the "tricycle" of their salvation (an illustration he first heard from fellow Calvinist, Thomas Schreiner).

> We can think of these three means of salvation as the wheels on a big wheel tricycle. The tricycle needs all three wheels (evidence of sanctification, testimony of the Spirit, saving work of Christ) to function well. But the big wheel, the one that pulls the other two along, is the most significant one. The tricycle can limp along without one or both of the small wheels in the back, but it won't work at all without the large wheel. In the same way, our experience of assurance of salvation will be weak and limpid if we're only looking at the small wheels. But when we look to the finished work of Christ on the cross for us, along with the assurance of the saving character of God that accompanies it, we have real assurance of salvation.[424]

Besides the dubious mechanics of the tricycle illustration (can you really limp along with two back wheels missing?), how do I interpret back wheels that behave as though they are missing for me, a believer? Does the "evidence of sanctification" wheel seem not to be working because I am in a difficult season, or because I am backsliding, or because I am too introspective and hard on myself, or because I am not among the elect and therefore a hopeless counterfeit? And what if I die with one or both of the rear wheels malfunctioning? Have I failed to persevere to the end, thus failing the Calvinistic test of true salvation? And even if both my back wheels are working just fine right now, what assurance do I have that they will function to the end? What if they malfunction? The cute-but-confusing tricycle illustration is unconvincing.

Our assurance is based on the person and promise of Christ, not our performance.[425]

---

[424] Wright, *40 Questions about Calvinism*, 289.
[425] For a solid Free Grace view of assurance, see Joseph Dillow, "Finding

Implications for Further Study

Where to begin? As I've said, I have so much to learn. I suppose the area that stands out to me as needing more work and clarification, at least in my own mind, is the doctrine of election. As an example, I've very briefly touched on eight different viewpoints in this work in connection with Romans 8:29-30. So far, all I have been able to do with some confidence is rule out one of them.

Also, it seems to me that there's work to be done in articulating Arminian tenets through the exegesis of specific biblical texts. Perhaps this is an idea borne of my own ignorance; my knowledge of the Arminian view is comparatively thin, and it's reflected in this work. But it does seem that Calvinists are piling up more dead trees (writing more and bigger books), and by comparison, Arminians look environmentally friendly. And in some of the Arminian works I consulted, I was at times frustrated by the lack of a Scripture index.

Concluding Comment on Implications

I hope I have conveyed in this section what I believe to be true: this matters. Our convictions concerning how God draws people to believe have sweeping implications. These convictions shape our view of some of the most important things in life: the nature of God, the interpretation of Scripture, the way of salvation, the rationale for evangelism, the basis of assurance, and the nature of humankind in relationship to our Creator.

The challenge before us is to make sure our convictions are informed by Scripture and not merely by some popular theological system touted by those who seem smart and sincere.

Assurance," in *A Defense of Free Grace Theology*, 193-238.

CONCLUSION

Jesus says, "No one can come to me unless the Father who sent me draws him" (John 6:44, ESV). But exactly how does the Father draw people such that they come to believe in Jesus for eternal life? Traditional answers have been varied, contradictory, and confusing.

Reformed theology is becoming increasingly popular, at least in America, and its adherents have traditionally held that God draws people to faith by regenerating the ones he chooses. This regeneration is defined as the moment one moves from spiritual death to new spiritual life in Christ; it's being born again. According to this view, God unconditionally and unilaterally chooses a subset of humanity who will believe, and then he makes them believe by giving them new life. Faith in Jesus inevitably and instantly springs from within the chosen when God regenerates them. As such, they believe *after* they have been born again, not before. It is argued that belief in Jesus can happen no other way because, in their fallen, unregenerate state, humans are spiritual corpses unable to respond to God in any good way, much less believe. God must make them new. So he regenerates the ones he chooses, according to his grace, and he leaves the rest hopelessly unregenerate, according to his sovereignty. This is the faith-after-regeneration view of how God draws people to believe in Jesus, and it has been described as perhaps "the very hinge of the Calvinist position."[426]

In this work, biblical arguments given in support of the faith-after-regeneration view have been found wanting. It seems the "very hinge"

---

[426] Barrett, *Salvation by Grace*, xxi.

of Calvinism is unhinged. After examining all the Scriptures given as proof texts for faith coming *after* regeneration, not one of them truly supports this idea. In fact, a significant number of the given proof texts boomerang in favor of a faith-before-regeneration view. While most evangelical scholars would agree with human depravity such that the unregenerate cannot believe without God's help, it simply does not follow that his help must be regeneration; other options are possible. Moreover, the notion that the unregenerate cannot respond to God in any good way has been refuted by numerous biblical texts that show that the unregenerate can and do respond to God's initiatives. This makes sense; otherwise, how could God condemn a person for failing to respond, if it was never possible for that person to respond?

The faith-*before*-regeneration view is the most biblically defensible. Numerous Scriptures point to faith in Jesus as the sole prerequisite for receiving new life in Christ and the many spiritual blessings that come with it. Nevertheless, within the general faith-before-regeneration view, there are three alternative views concerning how God draws people to believe, two modified and one Arminian. These are as shown in Table 12 below—a table used throughout this work to help keep the views straight.

Table 12. Concluding Summary of Views on How God Draws People to Believe

Faith-After-Regeneration View: (Calvinism/ Reformed Theology)	Faith-Before-Regeneration View:		
	Modified View:		Arminian View:
	Deterministic:	Nondeterministic:	
Regeneration (irresistible)	*Effectual Call (irresistible)*	*Divine Illumination (resistible)*	*Prevenient Grace (resistible)*

First, there is a deterministic modified view which is so much like the traditional Reformed view that some of its adherents still consider themselves to be Reformed. In this view, proponents are persuaded by biblical evidence that faith does indeed precede regeneration. In an effort to reconcile the traditional Reformed view with the idea that faith comes *before* regeneration, proponents of the deterministic modified view introduce an effectual call from God as the way he draws people to believe. It is much the same Reformed argument, except regeneration is replaced by an effectual call as the cause of faith. God unconditionally and unilaterally determines a subset of humanity who will believe, and then he makes them believe by effectually calling them. This calling is effectual in the sense that it inevitably and irresistibly produces faith; there is no genuine human choice to believe or not believe. That is why this is called a deterministic view.

The determinism of this modified view is largely its undoing. All the problems inherent in the determinism of Reformed theology are carried by this deterministic modified view as well. The goodness of God is in question. If, according to God's sovereignty, I was born with a sinful condition that makes it impossible for me to believe in Jesus, then how can God condemn me to hell for not believing? Such determinism renders meaningless the general call for all people to be saved. Moreover, proponents of the deterministic modified view have failed to come up with any clear biblical data that explains exactly what their effectual call entails. It seems to be an assumption required to make their Reformed theological system work rather than an idea grounded in hard biblical evidence.

A second faith-before-regeneration view is the Arminian view. The Arminian answer to how God draws people to believe is prevenient grace. Through prevenient grace, God overcomes the effects of the Fall, enabling all people to choose belief or unbelief.

While avoiding the problems of determinism, the Arminian view has some problems of its own. First and perhaps foremost is the belief that because we can opt into eternal salvation we can also opt out. Once received, eternal life can be lost, suggesting the unbiblical idea that this new life may not be so "eternal" after all. Moreover, against the weight of biblical evidence and evangelical scholarship, the Arminian view of regeneration seems to be more of a process than a one-time spiritual birth. Indeed, prevenient grace seems to be viewed by some as a regenerative *process* such that all people are being regenerated but can bail out on the process before it is completed. This is hard to square with biblical data which present spiritual life and death as discrete positions.

The final view, the nondeterministic modified view harmonizes the most biblical data and makes the fewest assumptions. The study of what Jesus says in John 6:44, "No one can come to me unless the Father who sent me draws him" (ESV), is well documented. But the study of what Jesus does in the immediate context as a model of drawing is not as well attested. This study shows that the word "draws" (ἕλκω) as used in John 6:44 describes God drawing all people, not just the elect, in a non-physical, attractional, non-coercive, didactic way based on his great love, and this divine overture can be received or rejected. This is modeled clearly and beautifully in the Bread of Life discourse in John 6, where the Father draws through his Word, both inscripturated and incarnate; the Father draws through authenticating signs; the Father draws through progressive illumination; the Father draws through a clear and compelling presentation of the gospel from one person to another; and the Father draws through a prophetic glimpse of his Son lifted up on the cross. With the added influences of the Holy Spirit's ministry of reproof, the creation which testifies to God's existence, and the godly behavior of believers, we see a powerful and essential constellation of light God composes to penetrate spiritual darkness and draw people to believe in Jesus. Such divine illumination is at the heart of the nondeterministic modified view.

Therefore, when Jesus says, "No one can come to me unless the Father who sent me draws him" (John 6:44, ESV), he's not referring to a mysterious doctrine of election that would likely elude his original hearers. Instead, he's simply saying something like, "You won't believe unless the Father draws you, and the Father is lovingly drawing you right now, so I encourage you to believe while you have this opportunity."

In sum, God does not manufacture faith, he lovingly invites it through an essential constellation of lights he composes to draw us to believe in Jesus, and he embraces our faith with the giving of eternal life that can never be lost. "God is light, and in him there is no darkness at all" (1 John 1:5, ESV).

APPENDIX
UNDERSTANDING JOHN 2:23-25

Now when he was in Jerusalem at the Passover Feast, many believed in his name when they saw the signs that he was doing. But Jesus on his part did not entrust himself to them, because he knew all people and needed no one to bear witness about man, for he himself knew what was in man (John 2:23-25, ESV).

Barrett does not present John 2:23-25 as a text that explicitly teaches that faith follows regeneration; nevertheless, he does contend that it is necessary to understand this passage as a context for properly interpreting John 3:3-8, a text he does offer in support of the faith-after-regeneration view. According to Barrett, John 2:23-25 establishes a context in which Jesus is "troubled" by a lack of regeneration among some who believed in his name but were counterfeits. Barrett says:

> In order to understand John 3 we must begin with the context of the passage [in John 2]. . . . John states that "many believed in his name when they saw the signs that he was doing" (John 2:23). However, what appeared to be belief was mere superficiality. They "believed" because they saw the miracles, but John reveals that Jesus knew what was within them, namely, unbelief and wickedness. Jesus refused to entrust himself to the people

because "he knew all people and needed no one to bear witness about man, for he himself knew what was in man" (John 2:25). As John 3 will show, it was not only what was in man (unbelief and wickedness) that troubled Jesus but also what was not within man, namely, a new spirit. In John 3 Jesus will get right to the point with Nicodemus: there is a lack of regeneration by the Spirit."[427]

While understanding the context is certainly important to proper interpretation, I believe Barrett misunderstands the context in John 2:23-25. A better interpretation of John 2:23-25 is that it describes people who have been genuinely regenerated. And so, the contextual focus is not on the need for regeneration among professing-but-counterfeit believers.

There are two primary parts to this passage. The first part is in John 2:23, and the main assertion of this first part is that, "many believed in his name." This, of course, is referring to Jesus as the object of faith. Many believed in Jesus. There is little or no debate on this point, at least on the surface.

Also, the many who believed in Jesus, did so because "they saw the signs he was doing." The signs include the miraculous things Jesus did, including turning water into wine at the wedding of Cana, recorded earlier in John 2. There is little or no debate on this point.

The second part of the passage comes in John 2:24-25. The main assertion of this second part is that "Jesus . . . did not entrust himself to them." That is to say, Jesus did not entrust himself to the many who believed in him. There is little or no debate on this point, at least on the surface.

And the reason that Jesus didn't entrust himself to these believers is that he had supernatural insight into all people. Jesus understands people as only God can. That's what John means when he says, "he knew all people and needed no one to bear witness about man, for he

---

[427] Barrett, *Salvation by Grace*, 145.

himself knew what was in man." There is little or no debate on this point.

The controversy has to do with the spiritual status of the many who believed in Jesus back in John 2:23. Barrett's view and the view of many other commentators is that the many who believed are not eternally saved. They are not genuinely converted. They have not received new, eternal life in Christ. They are counterfeit Christians.

The reason given is that, while these people may have believed in Jesus, their faith is not good enough. Their faith is inadequate. It's superficial. It's not genuine, saving faith. Two lines of evidence are commonly given for the inadequacy of their faith.

First, it is claimed that, if their faith were genuine saving faith, then Jesus would have surely entrusted himself to them. Since he did not, it must be because Jesus knew that their faith was inadequate for eternal salvation.

Second, it is claimed that faith in Jesus that comes from seeing miraculous signs performed is not a good enough faith. Such faith is superficial and fails to rise to the level of faith required to receive eternal life.

Carson touches on these points succinctly in his commentary on these verses. He says, "To exercise faith on the grounds of having witnessed miraculous signs is precarious. . . . Sadly, their faith was spurious, and Jesus knew it. . . . He therefore did not entrust himself to these spurious converts."[428]

Remember, there are two basic parts to the text. There's the first part that asserts that "many believed in his name." Then, there's the second part that says that, "Jesus did not entrust himself to them." Let's consider the meaning of each part, starting with John 2:23 that says, "many believed in his name."

The word, "believed" is a translation of the Greek verb, πιστεύω. It means pretty much the same thing as the English word, "believed." There's nothing mysterious or hard to understand about it. To believe

---

[428] Carson, *The Gospel According to John*, 184.

means to be convinced that something is true. When the object of belief is a person, it conveys belief or trust in who the person is and what the person says.[429]

The phrase, "in his name," makes Jesus the personal object of belief. The name of Jesus is his reputation. It's who he is reputed to be and what he is reputed to have done. Who Jesus is reputed to be is made clear by the preceding context. He is the long-awaited Messiah, the Savior of the world. In John 1:29, John the Baptist says of Jesus, "Behold, the Lamb of God, who takes away the sin of the world!" (ESV). In John 1:41, Andrew says of Jesus, "We have found the Messiah" (ESV). In John 1:45, Philip says of Jesus, "We have found him of whom Moses in the Law and also the prophets wrote, Jesus of Nazareth, the son of Joseph" (ESV). In John 1:49, Nathanael says to Jesus, "you are the Son of God! You are the King of Israel!" (ESV).

So, back in John 2:23, it seems quite clear the "many" believed in Jesus as the Messiah, the Savior of the world.

It also seems clear that whenever John speaks of believing in the name of Jesus, he's talking about a faith that saves. This is true in every instance. Every time John speaks of those who have believed in Jesus's name, he's referring to those who have been born of God, those who have become children of God, those who are eternally saved and going to heaven. For example, in John 1:12-13, it says, "But to all who did receive him, who believed in his name, he gave the right to become children of God, who were born, not of blood nor of the will of the flesh nor of the will of man, but of God" (ESV). It is quite clear in this passage that those who have "believed in his name" have become "children of God." They are born again.

John 3:18 says, "Whoever believes in him is not condemned, but whoever does not believe is condemned already, because he has not believed in the name of the only Son of God" (ESV). Here, the distinction between those who are condemned to hell and those who

---

[429] I am essentially following Bing, Chay, and Correia in this definition contra others, as explained in the introduction under "faith."

are destined for heaven is crystal clear. The decisive factor is belief in the name of Jesus, the only Son of God.

Finally, John 20:30-31 says, "Now Jesus did many other signs in the presence of the disciples, which are not written in this book; but these are written so that you may believe that Jesus is the Christ, the Son of God, and that by believing you may have life in his name" (ESV). This passage makes it clear that eternal life comes to those who believe in Jesus's name. Moreover, a faith in Jesus based on signs he has performed is not viewed as insufficient or inadequate. On the contrary, John says here that he wrote about selected signs in this gospel for the express purpose of encouraging belief in Jesus—a belief that results in eternal life in his name.

Accordingly, back in John 2:23, when John says, "many believed in his name when they saw the signs that he was doing," this is clear and compelling evidence from John himself that he is describing believers who have been genuinely saved from the penalty of their sins through their authentic faith in Jesus.[430] The evidence is so strong that even Calvinist Wayne Grudem is persuaded by it: "It seems to me that there is room for disagreement over the meaning of 'many believed in his name' in John 2:23, but I would take it to refer to genuine trust in Christ, because believing 'in his name' is believing in him, in biblical usage."[431]

But what about second part of the text—the part in John 2:24 that says Jesus did not entrust himself to these believers? Barrett and others assume that Jesus did not entrust himself to these people because their faith was inadequate for eternal salvation. But this is merely an assumption. Does this assumption have any biblical support?

The Greek word translated "entrust" is πιστεύω, which happens to be the very same verb translated "believed" in the text. But the construction of the sentence calls for a different translation. A painfully

---

[430] For more thorough argument for the "many" being genuine believers see Zane C. Hodges, "Untrustworthy Believers—John 2:23-25: Part 2: Problem Passages in the Gospel of John," *Bibliotheca Sacra* 135 (1978): 138-152.

[431] Grudem, *"Free Grace" Theology: 5 Ways It Diminishes the Gospel*, 110n14.

literal translation of John 2:24 could be something like, "Jesus did not believe himself to them." But that's not very clear in English. So, translators pick up the personal element of trust in πιστεύω and render it "entrust," which is a perfectly good translation. But it's still not exactly clear why Jesus is not entrusting himself.

We can also look to the writings of John for all the instances where he uses the same word, πιστεύω, or something synonymous to describe Jesus entrusting or not entrusting himself to others. What do we find? Nothing. This text is the only instance where John speaks of Jesus entrusting or not entrusting himself to others.[432]

Accordingly, the second part of the text is more difficult to understand than the first, because we don't have other Scriptures by John that use the same language to help us figure it out. We can't be as confident about what it really means for Jesus to not entrust himself to people. There's room for debate.

The analogy of faith suggests that we should interpret that which unclear in light of that which is clear. So let's go in the direction of the analogy of faith, starting with the interpretation of the clear part. As previously shown, there is very clear evidence that the many who believed in his name in John 2:23 are indeed eternally saved. They are genuine believers, not counterfeits. In light of this clear first part, what are the possible explanations for Jesus not entrusting himself to these believers in the second part?

Hodges argues that Jesus did not "disclose" himself or "commit" himself to the many who genuinely believed in him because "the level of their knowledge of him remained rudimentary," and they were not yet ready to follow him because of "competing interests."[433] Similarly, Dillow and Wilkin argue that Jesus did not entrust himself to the many

---

[432] Wilkin argues that "manifest" (John 14:21) and "made known" (John 15:14-15) are synonymous with "entrust," and show that entrusting is conditioned on obedience. This is possible but seems unlikely. Wilkin, "The Gospel According to John," 373.

[433] Zane C. Hodges, *Faith in His Name: Listening to the Gospel of John* (Corinth, TX: Grace Evangelical Society, 2015), 50-51.

believers because they were not yet willing to obey.[434] Their explanation of John 2:24 is certainly plausible, and they may be right. I believe it is true that fellowship with Jesus is indeed compromised when believers are not willing to obey, but I'm not convinced that this is the point of John 2:24.

Perhaps a simpler, better explanation is that, while the many people in Jerusalem trusted in Jesus for their future, Jesus wasn't trusting in people for his. And rightly so. Jesus was entrusting his future to his faithful Father, not to unreliable people.

Perhaps that is why John uses the very same verb, πιστεύω, to describe both the believers and Jesus. It sets up a contrast: believers entrust themselves to Jesus, but Jesus doesn't entrust himself to them; instead, Jesus entrusts himself to the Father. Charles Swindoll explains it this way: "Jesus wasn't depending on a favorable response from anyone—the religious leaders or the masses—to complete his mission. He wasn't running for election; He didn't need popular support to claim the throne; He had no plans to train an army. He didn't entrust Himself, His mission, or His future to humanity; He trusted His Father"[435]

This view has scriptural support. For example, 1 Peter 2:23 says of Jesus that during times of suffering he entrusted himself to his Father, not to other people. It says, "When he was reviled, he did not revile in return; when he suffered, he did not threaten, but continued *entrusting himself to him who judges justly*" (ESV, emphasis added). And Luke 23:46 describes Jesus on the cross, crying out, not to other people, but to his Father: "Father, I *entrust* my spirit into your hands!" (NLT, emphasis added).

In summary, John 2:23-25 does not provide a context in which Jesus is troubled by a lack of regeneration among professing-but-counterfeit believers. Instead, it provides a context in which the direction of trust is Godward not manward.

Barrett's interpretation of this passage seems to be an example of

---

[434] Dillow, *Final Destiny*, 146; Wilkin, "The Gospel According to John," 373.
[435] Swindoll, *Insights on John*, 63.

how faith is often diminished and questioned by those who hold to the faith-after-regeneration view. This propensity makes sense. If one holds that through regeneration God unilaterally gives the capacity to believe and, indeed, faith itself is a gift from God, then it is reasonable to expect the belief to be fruitful, because God gives good gifts. And so, if there is some evidence that faith may be less fruitful than one might expect, then regeneration is questioned. The focus naturally shifts, then, to the need for regeneration and away from the need for faith.

In summary, John 2:23-25 does not show that Jesus is "troubled" by a lack of regeneration among some who believed in his name but were counterfeits. A better interpretation is that it describes people who had been genuinely regenerated, and while they were trusting Jesus for their future, Jesus was not trusting them for his.

SCRIPTURE INDEX

OLD TESTAMENT

Genesis
1:27 43
3:8-10 45
3:10 44
4:3 45
4:3-7 45
6:5 .... 27, 29
8:21 .... 27, 29
9:6 43
12:3 47
15:6 67
21:33 67
41:8 46

Exodus
3:14 108
12:37-38 47

Numbers
14:14 108
21 112
21:4-9 75
21:8-9 .... 67, 112
24:9 108

Deuteronomy
10:12 64
13:4 64
21:3 138
30:6 .... 59, 63, 64

Judges
5:14 138
20:2 138
20:15 138
20:17 138
20:25 138
20:35 138
20:46 138

1 Samuel
14:22 108

2 Samuel
7:12-16 74
22:5 141
22:7 141
22:17 .... 138, 141, 142

1 Kings
21:5 .... 46, 47

1 Chronicles
5:26 .... 46, 47

2 Chronicles
36:22 .... 46, 47

Nehemiah
9:30 138

Job
20:28 138
28:18 138
39:10 138

Psalms
8:3-4 169
10:9 .... 138, 142, 143, 144, 145
14:1-3 30
14:3 .... 27, 30
19:1-4 169
118:131 139

Proverbs
25:20 139
28:18 108

Ecclesiastes
1:5 139
2:3 139

Song of Solomon
1:4 .... 139, 142,143, 144, 145

Isaiah
10:15 139
14:14 108
22:3 108
40:26 169
53:14 148
54:6-8 148
54:13 148

Jeremiah
14:6 139
24:7 58
31:3 .... 139, 144, 145, 146, 147
31:31-34 64
31:33 .... 59, 60
32:39-40 .... 59, 60
38:13 .... 139, 142, 143

Ezekiel
7:4 108
11:19 .... 61, 64
11:19-21 60
18:30-32 128
18:31 64
36:22-29 64
36:26-27 .... 60, 61
36-37 201
37:1-14 .... 61, 62

Daniel
2:1 .... 46, 47
4:14 139
5 47
5:5-6 .... 46, 47
7:10 139
7:13-14 152

Hosea
11:1-4 148

Habakkuk
1:15 .... 139, 142, 144, 145

Zephaniah
3:9 ....58, 65, 66, 67

NEW TESTAMENT

Matthew
8:26 13
13 49
13:10-17 .... 48, 156
16:17 99

Mark
4:24-25 156
6:14 .... 107, 108
10:17 118
10:29-30 118
14:42 108
16:15-16 123

Luke
7:50 12
8:4-15 .... 49, 50
8:12 50
10:25-37 101
19:10 176
23:46 237

John
1:7 78
1:12 .... 70, 71, 123
1:12-13 ....68, 70, 71, 112, 181, 183, 234
1:13 .... 21, 68, 69, 70, 71
1:29 234
1:41 234
1:45 234
1:49 234
1-11 .... 69, 152
2 .... 231, 232
2:23 .... 231, 232, 233, 234, 235, 236
2:23-25 ....72, 231, 232, 235, 237, 238
2:24 .... 235, 236, 237

2:24-25	232
2:25	232
3	231, 232
3:2	74
3:3	71, 72, 73, 74
3:3-8	71, 72, 73, 75, 76, 112, 231
3:3-21	73
3:5-8	201
3:9	75
3:9-21	73
3:14-15	68, 75
3:14-16	116
3:15-16	111
3:16	73, 176, 181, 193
3:18	93, 107, 108, 181, 234
3:36	111, 116, 181
4:9-10	176
4:14	111
5:1	177
5:24	111, 117, 119, 181
5:34	79
5:35	79
5:36-47	79
5:39-40	117
5:40	111
6	21, 31, 157, 165, 195, 198, 206, 208, 220, 228
6:22	149, 150
6:22-59	149
6:23	151
6:24	151
6:25	151
6:26	151
6:27	152
6:28	152, 164
6:29	153
6:30	153
6:31	154
6:32	154
6:33	155
6:34	155
6:35	134, 155, 156, 159, 160, 161, 166
6:36	155
6:37	134, 157, 159, 162, 164, 165, 166, 167, 205, 218, 220
6:38	156
6:39	157, 158, 162, 166, 167, 205
6:39-40	21, 158
6:40	156, 158, 160, 162, 166, 167
6:44	i, ii, 1, 30, 31, 32, 134, 135, 136, 137, 139, 144, 145, 146, 147, 148, 149, 155, 156, 162, 163, 165, 166, 167, 183, 199, 200, 203, 206, 208, 225, 228
6:44-45	149
6:44-46	177
6:45	148, 157, 166
6:47	111, 160, 221
6:49	159
6:50-51	159
6:51	117, 159, 161
6:51-54	111
6:53	161
6:53-54	117
6:54	161, 162, 167
6:57	117, 156
6:57-58	161
6:59	151
6:65	30, 32, 166, 167
7	50
7:17	50, 51, 177
7:38-39	120, 122
8:12	89
8:36	32
10:29	157
11:25	117
11:25-27	177
12:32	135, 139, 144, 146, 147, 149, 160
12:36	129
13:34	172
14:21	236
15:5	33
15:13	146
15:14-15	236
16:7-11	182
16:8	168
16:8-11	168, 198, 199

17:1-2	157
17:3	92
17:6	157
17:9	157
17:20-21	172
17:21	172
17:21-22	172
17:24	157
18:10	135, 140
20:30-31	153, 177, 235
20:31	111, 117, 181
21:6	135, 140
21:11	135, 140

Acts

1:17	86
2:38	120, 122, 179
5:31	76, 77
9	80
9:1-4	33, 34
9:1-20	79, 80, 81
10:1-2	51, 52
10:34-48	51
10:43	51
11:14	52
11:17	51
11:18	76, 77, 113, 129
13:39	124
13:48	81, 82
15:9	129
16:13-15	86, 200
16:14	199
16:19	135, 140, 142
16:30-31	91
16:31	124, 179
17:26-27	99, 177
18:8	124
21:30	135, 140, 142
26:14	33

Romans

1	171
1:1	38
1:5	14
1:6	38
1:7	38
1:16	124
1:16-17	56
1:18	34
1:18-20	52, 53
1:18-21	171
1:19-21	176
1:20-21	177
2:6-7	118
2:23	118
3:10	27, 30
3:10-19	29, 30
3:11	175, 177
3:21-22	54
4:4-6	22
4:21	99
6	93
6:1-14	93
6:12-14	93
6:17	53, 54, 55
8	185, 190
8:6	27, 34
8:9	123
8:28	38
8:29-30	183, 184, 188, 192, 200, 223
8:30	38, 184, 185, 190, 191
9	189, 191
9:11	38
9:14-16	34
9:16	35
9:24	38
10:9-10	124
10:14	173
11:29	38
13:2	108
16:25	55
16:25-27	55
16:26	14

1 Corinthians

1:1	38
1:2	38
1:9	38, 200
1:21	125

1:24	38
1:26	38
2:12-14	199
2:14	35, 200
3:6	181
7:15	38
7:17	38
7:18	38
7:20	38
7:21	38
7:22	38
7:24	38
12:12-13	123
13:2	14
15:1-5	173

2 Corinthians
3:5	27, 35
3:14-16	130
4:3-6	56, 88, 113
4:4	176
4:6	89, 99, 176, 178
5:17	40, 89
6:7	100
13:5-6	221

Galatians
1:6	38
1:15	38
1:15-16	81
3:2	129, 130
3:5	129, 130
3:13	122
3:13-14	120
3:26	129, 183
4:6	121, 122
5:8	38
5:13	38
6:8	118
6:15	89

Ephesians
1:13	100, 122
1:13-14	121, 123
1:18	38

2	36, 91
2:1	90, 91, 92, 93, 94, 175
2:1-5	35, 36
2:1-7	89, 90
2:2	92
2:5	36, 84, 113, 201
2:8	12, 32, 83, 84, 113
2:8-9	81, 82, 83, 84
4:1	38
4:4	38
4:18	92

Philippians
1:6	36
1:29	85
1:29-30	81
2:13	37

Colossians
1:5	100
2:11-14	94, 95, 96
2:12	130
2:12-13	96
3:15	38
12:11-14	113

1 Thessalonians
2:12	38, 201
4:7	38
5:24	38

2 Thessalonians
2:14	38, 201

1 Timothy
1:16	130
2:4	78
4:3	78
6:12	38
6:19	118

2 Timothy
1:9	38
2:15	100
2:24	77
2:24-26	76, 77, 113
2:25	77

Titus
1:2 118
2:3-7 201
2:9-10 172
2:10 172
3:3-7 .... 96, 98
3:5 .... 72, 97, 119
3:5-7 119
3:7 118

Hebrews
1:3 207
3:1 38
4:16 97
7:6 108
9:15 38
11:6 .... 99, 125, 177

James
1:12 118
1:17 99
1:18 .... 98, 99, 100, 113, 131
2:6 .... 135, 140, 142
2:26 14
3:9 43

1 Peter
1:3-5 101
1:15 38
1:23 201
2:9 .... 38, 200
2:21 38
2:23 237
3:9 38
5:10 .... 38, 201

2 Peter
1:1 .... 81, 85
1:3 38
1:4 40
1:10 38

1 John
1:5 229
2:29 .... 70, 109
3:2 70
3:9 .... 70, 109
3:10 70
3:23 14
4:7 109
4:9-10 176
5:1 .... 58, 70, 102, 103, 104, 105,
107, 108, 109, 110, 111, 118, 177
5:1-2 70
5:4 109
5:10 108
5:18 109

Jude
1:3 12

Revelation
2:10 118
14:6-7 57

APOCRYPHA

1 Maccabees
10:82 .... 140, 142, 143

3 Maccabees
4:7 .... 140, 142
5:49 140

4 Maccabees
11:9 .... 140, 142
14:13 .... 140, 144, 147
15:11 .... 140, 144, 147

Wisdom
19:4 .... 140, 144

Sirach
28:19 140

Scripture Index is created by: GraceLife.org

Scripture Indexing tool is accessed at: http://www.gracelife.org/resources/bibletools/

AUTHOR INDEX

A

Abasciano, Brian 4, 70, 71, 105, 106, 107, 108, 110, 189, 261
Aldrich, Roy L. 6, 10, 83, 175, 261
Allen, David i, xiv, xvi, 6, 42, 84, 93, 94, 96, 100, 112, 116, 126, 128, 146, 147, 167, 174, 176, 190, 193, 194, 195, 215, 216, 249, 254, 255, 256, 261, 264
Anderson, David 6, 10, 11, 13, 16, 17, 21, 22, 23, 42, 47, 48, 49, 52, 53, 57, 78, 79, 91, 106, 107, 156, 202, 205, 249, 261, 264
Anthony, Michael J. 164, 261
Arminius, Jacobus 16, 17, 41, 203, 204, 249
Arndt, W. F. xxiii, 98, 136, 250

B

Badger, Anthony 44, 250, 262
Barrett, Matthew 3, 5, 10, 11, 18, 20, 35, 39, 58, 59, 60, 61, 62, 67, 72, 73, 74, 76, 77, 80, 82, 83, 86, 87, 88, 89, 94, 95, 97, 98, 99, 100, 101, 102, 105, 106, 107, 109, 113, 118, 119, 121, 122, 125, 126, 127, 128, 200, 201, 202, 225, 231, 232, 233, 235, 237, 250, 264
Bateman, Herbert W. IV 162, 258

Bates, Matthew 14, 15, 221, 250
Bauer, W. xxiii, 98, 136, 250
Beale, G. K. 104, 250
Beitzel, Barry J. 152, 252
Bekker, Hugo 216, 250
Berkhof, L. 13, 181, 250
Berkouwer, G.C. 216, 217, 250
Bing, Charles ii, xvi, 6, 15, 16, 44, 49, 156, 175, 176, 189, 195, 234, 264
Bolt, John 77, 250
Borchert, Gerald L. 69, 152, 251

C

Calvin, John 8, 16, 17, 27, 29, 30, 31, 32, 34, 35, 36, 37, 217, 251, 263, 266
Carson, D.A. 3, 65, 69, 71, 83, 146, 193, 194, 208, 209, 233, 251, 254, 257
Chafer, Lewis Sperry 6, 10, 17, 19, 21, 43, 83, 84, 181, 182, 183, 199, 209, 251
Chandler, Matt 9
Chay, Fred i, xvi, 6, 13, 15, 219, 221, 234, 249, 251, 252, 261
Christiano, Donna 102, 264
Compton, R. Bruce 6, 11, 64, 67, 71, 85, 96, 119, 120, 199, 262
Correia, John 15, 234, 252, 265
Craig, William Lane 192, 257

Crisp, Oliver 2, 252
Culver, Robert 105, 252

D

Danker, F. W. xxiii, 98, 136, 250
Davids, Peter H. 98, 100, 252
Delitzsch, Franz 47, 48, 255
Demarest, Bruce 2, 6, 10, 11, 17, 40, 41, 178, 180, 187, 198, 201, 252, 256
DeYoung, Kevin 9
Dillow, Joseph ii, xvi, 6, 63, 78, 124, 188, 189, 195, 196, 222, 236, 237, 252
Driscoll, Mark 8, 217, 265, 266
Dubis, Mark 84, 95, 167, 265
Durant, Will 197, 252

E

Edmondson, Jeremy 176, 252
Edwards, Jonathan 2, 195, 196, 260
Elwell, Walter A. 152, 252
Erickson, Millard 6, 10, 11, 17, 18, 179, 180, 184, 186, 253

F

Fee, Gordon D. 78, 253
Fischer, Austin 160, 196, 197, 253
Flowers, Leighton 6, 42, 43, 45, 46, 55, 56, 128, 190, 191, 210, 211, 212, 253, 265
Forlines, F. Leroy 4, 162, 203, 204, 205, 253
Friberg, Barbara 85, 86, 91, 253
Friberg, Timothy 85, 253
Friedman, Thomas 208, 253
Fuller, Daniel 14, 221, 253

G

Geisler, Norman 43, 83, 91, 162, 189, 253, 260, 265

Gerstner, John 40, 253
Gingrich, F. W. xxiii, 98, 136, 250
Glas, John 10
Greear, J. D. 13, 14, 221, 254, 265
Green, Bradley 64, 254
Grudem, Wayne 3, 17, 218, 219, 220, 221, 235, 254
Gundry, Stanley N. 162, 253

H

Hankins, Eric 6, 174, 188, 195, 216, 254, 255, 256
Hansen, Collin 9, 265
Harmon, Matthew 165, 167, 254
Harwood, Adam 174, 254, 255, 256
Hemphill, Ken 42, 254
Hodge, Charles 18, 80, 254
Hodges, Zane 6, 89, 91, 93, 99, 100, 101, 124, 176, 178, 235, 236, 254, 262, 265
Hoehner, Harold 83, 84, 90, 255
Hoekema, Anthony 105
Horn, Steve 162, 255
Horton, Michael 215, 255
Hunter, Braxton 191, 192, 255

J

Johnston, O.R. 21, 29, 33, 256, 258

K

Kaiser, Walter C. Jr 65, 255
Kärkkäinen, Veli-Matti 11, 255
Keathley, Kenneth 189, 255
Keil, Carl Friedrich 47, 48, 255
Keller, Tim 8, 9
Kisare, Zedekia Marwa 170, 171, 255
Köstenberger, Andreas J. 69, 148, 153, 256

L

Land, Richard 190, 256

Author Index

Lemke, Steve 6, 116, 118, 121, 122, 125, 128, 188, 189, 190, 249, 256
Lennox, John C. 21, 163, 256
Lewis, Gordon 6, 10, 11, 17, 180, 187, 198, 201, 256
Lincoln, Andrew T. 83, 256
Litfin, A. Duane 78, 256
López, Réne A. 85, 256, 262
Lukaszewski, Albert L. 84, 95, 167, 265
Luther, Martin 21, 33, 34, 68, 256, 258

M

MacArthur, John F. Jr. 3, 90, 82, 256
Marshall, I. Howard 162, 257
McLean, Archibald 10
McNeil, John T. 17, 251
Meisinger, George E. 6, 42, 50, 51, 52, 53, 54, 55, 56, 263
Merkle, Benjamin L. 112, 261
Metzger, Bruce M. 83, 256
Miller, Neva 85, 253
Mohler, Albert 9
Moo, Douglas J. 100, 257
Moreland, J.P. 192, 257
Muller, Richard A. 2, 3, 257
Murray, John 73, 181, 257

N

Newman, Barclay 134, 257
Nichols, James 263
Nichols, William 17, 249
Nida, Eugene 134, 257

O

O'Brien, Peter T. 83, 257
Oden, Thomas 4, 162, 205, 215, 257
Ogilvie, Lloyd J. 65, 255
Olson, Gordon C. 208, 257
Olson, Roger 4, 41, 77, 203, 204, 215, 255, 257, 266

Oppenheimer, Mark 8
Osborne, Grant R. 162, 258

P

Packer, J.I. 3, 21, 28, 29, 33, 194, 217, 219, 256, 258
Peterson, Robert 105
Piatt, Christian 217, 266
Pink, A.W. 193, 258
Pinson, Matthew 162, 253
Piper, John 3, 8, 9, 17, 31, 36, 103, 104, 106, 217, 258, 266
Pringle, William 32, 251
Pyne, Robert 6, 10, 11, 168, 169, 171, 184, 186, 263

R

Radmacher, Earl xvi, 6, 17, 174, 175, 258
Rahlfs, Alfred xxiii, 137
Robertson, A.T. 107, 258
Robertson, O. Palmer 66, 259

S

Sandeman, Robert 10, 263
Sapaugh, Gregory P. 83, 263
Schaeffer, Francis 9
Schreiner, Thomas R. 3, 54, 55, 102, 104, 110, 189, 222, 259, 261, 266
Shedd, William 175
Shelton, Brian W. 4, 202, 204, 259
Shepherd, Norman 13, 221, 266
Snoeberger, Mark 3, 10, 11, 13, 59, 66, 68, 69, 70, 221, 263
Sproul, R. C. 3, 9, 17, 19, 20, 21, 22, 23, 27, 28, 34, 36, 82, 123, 136, 164, 165, 167, 259, 266
Storms, Samuel C. 86, 157, 164, 165, 167, 259
Stott, John R. W. 90, 103, 104, 106, 259
Swindoll, Charles 154, 237, 258, 259

T

Thielman, Frank 14, 259
Townsend, Jim 83, 263
Tozer, A.W. 207, 260

V

Valdés, Alberto 87, 260
Vance, Laurence 94, 260

W

Wagner, John D. 196, 260
Wallace, Daniel B. 74, 83, 95, 106, 107, 167, 190, 260
Walls, Jerry 193, 260
Walvoord, John 6, 10, 17, 21, 38, 39, 63, 78, 185, 186, 197, 209, 256, 260, 263
Ware, Bruce 105
Whedon, Daniel 195, 196, 260
White, James R. 3, 90, 91, 105, 157, 158, 164, 165, 167, 211, 220, 221, 260
Wilkin, Robert 7, 69, 78, 87, 100, 124, 146, 189, 236, 237, 254, 255, 260, 263, 266
Williams, Michael 105
Williamson, Paul 147, 260
Wilson, Ken 26, 136, 143, 209, 210, 261, 266
Witherington, Ben 4, 162, 266
Wright, Shawn D. 112, 194, 221, 222, 261

Y

Yarbrough, Robert 105

BIBLIOGRAPHY

Books

Allen, David L. *The Atonement: A Biblical, Theological, and Historical Study of the Cross of Christ.* Nashville, TN: B&H Academic, 2019.

_____. *The Extent of the Atonement: A Historical and Critical Review.* Nashville, TN: B&H Academic, 2016.

Allen, David L. and Steve W. Lemke, eds. *Whosoever Will: A Biblical-Theological Critique of Five-Point Calvinism.* Nashville: B&H Publishing Group, 2010.

Anderson, David R. *Free Grace Soteriology.* 3rd ed. N.p.: Grace Theology Press, 2018. Kindle.

_____. "The Faith That Saves." In *A Defense of Free Grace Theology: With Respect to Saving Faith, Perseverance, and Assurance*, edited by Fred Chay, 67-87. N.p.: Grace Theology Press, 2017.

_____. "Fellowship with the Father." In *A Defense of Free Grace Theology: With Respect to Saving Faith, Perseverance, and Assurance*, edited by Fred Chay, 604-607. N.p.: Grace Theology Press, 2017.

Arminius, James. *The Public Disputations of James Arminius, D.D.* In James Arminius, *The Works of James Arminius: The London Edition.* 3 vols. Translated by James and William Nichols. 1825-75. Reprint, Grand Rapids, MI: Baker, 1986.

Augustine. *The Enchiridion: On Faith, Hope and Love*. Translated by J.F. Shaw. In Augustine, *Basic Writings of Saint Augustine*. Edited by Whitney J. Oates. 2 vols. 1948. Reprint, Grand Rapids: Baker, 1980.

_____. *On Grace and Free Will*. In Augustine, *Basic Writings of Saint Augustine*. Edited by Whitney J. Oates. 2 vols. 1948. Reprint, Grand Rapids: Baker, 1980.

Badger, Anthony B. *Confronting Calvinism: A Free Grace Refutation and Biblical Resolution of Radical Reformed Soteriology*. N.p.: Anthony B. Badger, 2013.

Barrett, Matthew. *Salvation by Grace: The Case for Effectual Calling and Regeneration*. Phillipsburg, NJ: P&R Publishing, 2013.

Bates, Matthew W. *Salvation by Allegiance Alone: Rethinking Faith, Works, and the Gospel of Jesus the King*. Grand Rapids, MI: Baker Academic, 2017.

Bauer, W., F. W. Danker, W. F. Arndt, and F. W. Gingrich. *A Greek-English Lexicon of the New Testament and Other Early Christian Literature*. 3rd ed. Chicago: University of Chicago Press, 2000.

Bauer, Walter, William F. Arndt, F. Wilbur Gingrich, and Frederick W. Danker. *A Greek-English Lexicon of the New Testament and Other Early Christian Literature*. 2nd ed. Chicago: University of Chicago Press, 1979.

Bavinck, Herman. *Reformed Dogmatics*. Vol. 4. Edited by John Bolt. Translated by John Vriend. Grand Rapids: Baker, 2008.

Beale, G. K. *A New Testament Biblical Theology: The Unfolding of the Old Testament in the New*. Grand Rapids, MI: Baker Academic, 2011.

Berkhof, Louis. *Systematic Theology*. Grand Rapids, MI. Wm. B. Eerdmans, 1939.

Berkouwer, G. C. *Divine Election*. Translated by Hugo Bekker. In *Studies in Dogmatics*. Grand Rapids: Eerdmans, 1960.

_____. *Faith and Justification*. Translated by Lewis B. Smedes. In *Studies in Dogmatics*. Grand Rapids: Eerdmans, 1954.

Borchert, Gerald L. *John 1-11*. Vol. 25a. The New American Commentary. Nashville: Broadman & Holman Publishers, 1996.

Calvin, John. *Commentary on the Gospel According to John*. Translated by William Pringle. 2 vols. 1857-48. Reprint, Grand Rapids: Baker, 1979.

_____. *Institutes of the Christian Religion*. 2 vols. Edited by John T. McNeil. Translated by Ford Lewis Battles. Library of Christian Classics, vols. 20-21. Philadelphia: Westminster John Knox, 1960.

_____. *Institutes of the Christian Religion*. 2 vols. Translated by Henry Beveridge. Grand Rapids, MI: Eerdmans, 1975.

_____. *Selected Works of John Calvin: Tracts and Letters*. 7 vols. Edited by Henry Beveridge and Jules Bonnet. 1858. Reprint, Grand Rapids: Baker, 1983.

Carson, D. A. *The Difficult Doctrine of the Love of God*. Wheaton, IL: Crossway Books, 2000.

_____. Endorsement in *From Heaven He Came and Sought Her: Definite Atonement in Historical, Biblical, Theological, and Practical Perspective*, edited by D. Gibson and J. Gibson, 1. Wheaton, IL: Crossway, 2013.

_____. *The Gospel According to John*. The Pillar New Testament Commentary. Leicester, England; Grand Rapids, MI: Inter-Varsity Press; W.B. Eerdmans, 1991.

Chafer, Lewis Sperry. *Systematic Theology*. Vols. 3 and 7. Grand Rapids: Kregel, 1993.

Chay, Fred, ed. *A Defense of Free Grace Theology: With Respect to Saving Faith, Perseverance, and Assurance*. N.p.: Grace Theology Press, 2017.

_____. "Examine Yourself to See If You Are in the Faith—2 Corinthians 13:5-6." In *A Defense of Free Grace Theology: With*

Respect to Saving Faith, Perseverance, and Assurance, edited by Fred Chay, 535-547. N.p.: Grace Theology Press, 2017.

Chay, Fred and John Correia. *The Faith That Saves: The Nature of Faith in the New Testament—An Exegetical and Theological Analysis on the Nature of New Testament Faith.* Eugene, OR: Wipf & Stock, 2012.

Crisp, Oliver D. *Saving Calvinism: Expanding the Reformed Tradition.* Downers Grove, IL: InterVarsity Press, 2016.

Crossway Bibles. *ESV: Study Bible: English Standard Version.* Wheaton, IL: Crossway Bibles, 2007.

Culver, Robert Duncan. *Systematic Theology: Biblical & Historical.* Geanies House, Fearn, Ross-shire, Great Britain: Mentor Imprint, 2005.

Davids, Peter H. *The Epistle of James: A Commentary on the Greek Text.* New International Greek Testament Commentary. Grand Rapids, MI: Eerdman's, 1982.

Demarest, Bruce. *The Cross and Salvation: The Doctrine of Salvation.* Foundations of Evangelical Theology, edited by John S. Feinberg, vol. 1. Wheaton, IL: Crossway, 1997.

Dillow, Joseph. *Final Destiny: The Future Reign of the Servant Kings.* 4th ed. N.p. Grace Theology Press, 2018.

_____. "Finding Assurance." In *A Defense of Free Grace Theology: With Respect to Saving Faith, Perseverance, and Assurance*, edited by Fred Chay, 193-238. N.p.: Grace Theology Press, 2017.

Durant, Will. *The Reformation.* The Story of Civilization. vol. 6. New York: Simon & Schuster, 2011. Kindle.

Edmondson, Jeremy. "Returning to Scripture as Our Sole Authority." In *Free Grace Theology: 5 Ways It Magnifies the Gospel*, edited by Grant Hawley, 1-29. Allen, TX: Bold Grace Ministries, 2016.

Elwell, Walter A. and Barry J. Beitzel. *Baker Encyclopedia of the Bible.* Grand Rapids, MI: Baker Book House, 1998.

Erickson, Millard. *Christian Theology*. 3rd ed. Grand Rapids: Baker Book House, 2013.

Fischer, Austin. *Young, Restless, No Longer Reformed: Black Holes, Love, and a Journey In and Out of Calvinism*. Eugene, OR: Cascade, 2014.

Fee, Gordon D. *1 and 2 Timothy, Titus*. New International Biblical Commentary. Peabody, MA: Hendrickson Publishers, 1988.

Flowers, Leighton. *God's Provision for All: A Defense of God's Goodness*. N.p.: Trinity Academic Press, 2019.

_____. *The Potter's Promise: A Biblical Defense of Traditional Soteriology*. San Bernardino, CA: Trinity Academic Press, 2017.

Forlines, F. Leroy. *Classical Arminianism: A Theology of Salvation*. Nashville, TN: Randall House, 2011.

Friberg, Timothy, Barbara Friberg and Neva Miller. *Analytical Lexicon of the Greek New Testament*. Grand Rapid, MI: Baker Academic, 2000.

Friedman, Thomas L. *Thank You For Being Late: An Optimist's Guide to Thriving in the Age of Accelerations*. New York: Farrar, Straus, and Giroux, 2016. Kindle.

Fuller, Daniel P. *The Unity of the Bible: Unfolding God's Plan for Humanity*. Grand Rapids, MI: Zondervan, 1992.

Geisler, Norman L. *Chosen But Free: A Balanced View of God's Sovereignty and Free Will*. 3rd ed. Bloomington, MN: Bethany House Publishers, 2010.

_____. "A Moderate Calvinist View." In *Four Views on Eternal Security*, edited by J. Matthew Pinson, 61-112. In the Counterpoints series, edited by Stanley N. Gundry. Grand Rapids, MI: Zondervan, 2002.

Gerstner, John H. *Wrongly Dividing the World of Truth: A Critique of Dispensationalism*. 3rd ed. Draper, VA: Apologetics Group Media, 2009.

Gonzalez, Justo L. *Essential Theological Terms.* Louisville: Westminster John Knox Press, 2005.

Greear, J. D. *Stop Asking Jesus Into Your Heart: How To Know For Sure You Are Saved.* Nashville: B&H, 2013.

Green, Bradley G. *Covenant and Commandment: Works, Obedience and Faithfulness in the Christian Life.* New Studies in Biblical Theology. Edited by D. A. Carson. Nottingham, England: Apollos, 2014. Downers Grove, IL: InterVarsity Press, 2014.

Grudem, Wayne A. *"Free Grace" Theology: 5 Ways It Diminishes the Gospel.* Wheaton, IL: Crossway, 2016.

_____. *Systematic Theology.* Grand Rapids: Zondervan, 1994.

Hankins, Eric. "A Statement of the Traditional Southern Baptist Understanding of God's Plan of Salvation," In *Anyone Can Be Saved: A Defense of "Traditional" Southern Baptist Soteriology,* edited by David L. Allen, Eric Hankins, and Adam Harwood, 16-24. Eugene, OR: Wipf & Stock, 2016.

_____. "Savability: Southern Baptists' Core Soteriological Conviction," In *Anyone Can Be Saved: A Defense of "Traditional" Southern Baptist Soteriology,* edited by David L. Allen, Eric Hankins, and Adam Harwood, 9-15. Eugene, OR: Wipf & Stock, 2016.

Harmon, Matthew, "For the Glory of the Father and the Salvation of His People: Definite Atonement in the Synoptics and Johannine Literature." In *From Heaven He Came and Sought Her: Definite Atonement in Historical, Biblical, Theological, and Practical Perspective,* edited by D. Gibson and J. Gibson, 267-288. Wheaton, IL: Crossway, 2013.

Hemphill, Ken. *Unlimited: God's Love, Atonement, and Mission.* Traveler's Rest, SC: Auxano Press, 2018.

Hodge, Charles. *Systematic Theology.* Vol. 3. New York: Scribner, 1877.

Hodges, Zane C. "The Epistle of James." In *The Grace New Testament Commentary.* Edited by Robert N. Wilkin, 1098-1142. Denton, TX: Grace Evangelical Society, 2010.

———. *Faith in His Name: Listening to the Gospel of John*. Corinth, TX: Grace Evangelical Society, 2015.

———. *Romans: Deliverance from Wrath*. Edited by Robert N. Wilkin. Corinth, TX. Grace Evangelical Society, 2013.

———. *Six Secrets of the Christian Life*. Corinth, TX: Grace Evangelical Society, 2016.

Hoehner, Harold. *Ephesians: An Exegetical Commentary*. Grand Rapids, MI: Baker Academic, 2002.

Horn, Steve "Article 9: The Security of the Believer." In *Anyone Can Be Saved: A Defense of "Traditional" Southern Baptist Soteriology*, edited by David L. Allen, Eric Hankins, and Adam Harwood, 133-141. Eugene, OR: Wipf & Stock, 2016.

Horton, Michael. *For Calvinism*. Grand Rapids, MI: Zondervan, 2011.

———. Foreword to *Against Calvinism* by Roger Olson, 9-11. Grand Rapids, MI: Zondervan, 2011.

Hunter, Braxton. "Commentary on Article 8: The Free Will of Man." In *Anyone Can Be Saved: A Defense of "Traditional" Southern Baptist Soteriology*, edited by David L. Allen, Eric Hankins, and Adam Harwood, 119-131. Eugene, OR: Wipf & Stock, 2016.

Kaiser, Walter C. and Lloyd J. Ogilvie. *Micah, Nahum, Habakkuk, Zephaniah, Haggai, Zechariah, Malachi*. Vol. 23. The Preacher's Commentary Series. Nashville, TN: Thomas Nelson, 1992.

Kärkkäninen, Veli-Matti. *Spirit and Salvation*. Vol. 4. A Constructive Christian Theology for the Pluralistic World. Grand Rapids, MI: Eerdmans, 2016.

Keathley, Kenneth. *Salvation and Sovereignty: A Molinist Approach*. Nashville: B&H Publishing Group, 2010.

Keil, Carl Friederich and Franz Delitzsch. *Commentary on the Old Testament*. Vol. 1. Peabody, MA: Hendrickson, 1996.

Kisare, Zedekia Marwa. In *More Reflections On The Meaning of Life*, edited by David Friend, 20. New York: Little Brown & Co, 1992.

Köstenberger, Andreas J. *John*. Baker Exegetical Commentary on the New Testament. Grand Rapids, MI: Baker Academic, 2004.

Land, Richard. "Congruent Election: Understanding Salvation from an 'Eternal Now' Perspective." In *Whosoever Will: A Biblical-Theological Critique of Five-Point Calvinism*, edited by David L. Allen and Steve W. Lemke, 45-59. Nashville, TN: B&H Publishing Group, 2010.

Lemke, Steve W. "A Biblical and Theological Critique of Irresistible Grace." In *Whosoever Will: A Biblical-Theological Critique of Five-Point Calvinism*, edited by David L. Allen and Steve W. Lemke, 109-162. Nashville: B&H, 2010.

———. "Commentary on Article 7: The Sovereignty of God." In *Anyone Can Be Saved: A Defense of "Traditional" Southern Baptist Soteriology*, edited by David L. Allen, Eric Hankins, and Adam Harwood, 103-117. Eugene, OR: Wipf & Stock, 2016.

Lennox, John C. *Determined to Believe? The Sovereignty of God, Freedom, Faith, & Human Responsibility*. Grand Rapids, MI: Zondervan, 2017.

Lewis, Gordon R. and Bruce A. Demarest. *Integrative Theology*. Vol. 3. Grand Rapids, MI: Zondervan, 1994.

Lincoln, Andrew T. *Ephesians*. Word Biblical Commentary. Vol. 42. Edited by Bruce M. Metzger. Dallas: Word Books, 1990.

Litfin, A Duane. "2 Timothy." In *The Bible Knowledge Commentary: An Exposition of the Scriptures*. Vol. 2. Edited by J.F. Walvoord and R.B. Zuck. Wheaton, IL: Victor Books, 1985.

López, Réne A. *Romans Unlocked: Power to Deliver*. Springfield, MO. 21st Century Press, 2005.

Luther, Martin. *The Bondage of the Will*. Translated by J. I. Packer and O. R. Johnston. New York: Revell, 1957.

MacArthur, John F. Jr. *Faith Works: The Gospel According to the Apostles*. Dallas, TX: Word Publishing, 1993.

_____. *The Gospel According to Paul*. Nashville: Nelson Books, 2017.

Marshall, I. Howard. *Kept by the Power of God: A Study of Perseverance and Falling Away*. Eugene, OR: Wipf and Stock, 2008.

Moo, Douglas J. *The Letter of James*. The Pillar New Testament Commentary. Edited by D. A. Carson. Grand Rapids, MI: Wm B. Eerdmans Publishing and Leicester, England: Apollos, 1999.

Moreland, J.P. and William Lane Craig. *Philosophical Foundations for a Christian Worldview*. Downers Grove, IL: InterVarsity Press, 2003.

Muller, Richard A. *Divine Will and Human Choice: Freedom, Contingency, and Necessity in Early Modern Reformed Thought*. Grand Rapids, MI: Baker Academic, 2017.

Murray, John. "Redemption Accomplished and Applied." *Collected Writings of John Murray*. Edinburgh: Banner of Truth, 1976.

Newman, Barclay Moon and Eugene Albert Nida. *A Handbook on the Gospel of John*. UBS Handbook Series. New York: United Bible Societies, 1993.

O'Brien, Peter T. *The Letter to the Ephesians*. The Pillar New Testament Commentary. Edited by D. A. Carson. Grand Rapids, MI: Wm B. Eerdmans Publishing and Leicester, England: Apollos, 1999.

Oden, Thomas C. *The Transforming Power of Grace*. Nashville, TN: Abingdon Press, 1993.

Olson, C. Gordon. *Beyond Calvinism & Arminianism: An Inductive, Mediate Theology of Salvation*. 3rd ed. Lynchburg, VA: Global Gospel Publishers, 2012.

Olson, Roger E. *Against Calvinism*. Grand Rapids, MI: Zondervan, 2011.

_____. *Arminian Theology: Myths and Realities*. Downers Grove, IL: InterVarsity Press, 2006.

_____. "Repentance." In *The Westminster Handbook to Evangelical Theology*, 250-251. Louisville: Westminster John Knox, 2004.

Osborne, Grant R. "A Classical Arminian View." In *Four Views on the Warning Passages in Hebrews*, edited by Herbert W. Bateman IV, 86-128. Grand Rapids, MI: Kregel, 2007.

Packer, J. I. *Concise Theology: A Guide to Historic Christian Beliefs*. Wheaton, IL: Tyndale House, 1993.

_____. Endorsement in *"Free Grace" Theology: 5 Ways It Diminishes the Gospel*, 2. Wheaton, IL: Crossway, 2016.

_____. *Evangelism and the Sovereignty of God*. Downers Grove, IL: IVP Academic, 1991.

_____. *Knowing God*. Downers Grove, IL: InterVarsity Press, 1973.

Packer, J. I. and O. R. Johnston. "Historical and Theological Introduction." Luther, Martin. *The Bondage of the Will*. Translated by J. I. Packer and O. R. Johnston. New York: Revell, 1957.

Pink, Arthur W. *The Sovereignty of God*. Grand Rapids, MI: Baker, 1930.

Piper, John. *Does God Desire All to Be Saved?* Wheaton, IL: Crossway, 2013.

_____. *Finally Alive*. Grand Rapids: Desiring God, 2009.

_____. *Future Grace: The Purifying Power of the Promises of God*. Rev. ed. New York: Multnomah, 2012.

Radmacher, Earl D. *Salvation*. Swindoll Leadership Library, edited by Charles R. Swindoll and Roy B. Zuck. Nashville: Word Publishing, 2000.

Robertson, A. T. *A Grammar of the Greek New Testament in the Light of Historical Research*. Nashville, TN: Broadman Press, 1934.

Robertson, O. Palmer. *The Books of Nahum, Habakkuk and Zephaniah.* The New International Commentary on the Old Testament. Grand Rapids, MI: Wm. B. Eerdmans, 1990.

Schreiner, Thomas R. *1, 2 Peter, Jude.* The New American Commentary. Nashville: Broadman & Holman Publishers, 2003.

_____. *New Testament Theology: Magnifying God in Christ.* Grand Rapids, MI: Baker Academic, 2008.

_____. *Romans.* Vol. 6. Baker Exegetical Commentary on the New Testament. Grand Rapids, MI: Baker Books, 1998.

Shaw, J.F. trans., *Saint Augustine of Hippo: The Enchiridion.* Edited by Paul A. Böer, Sr. N.p.: Veritatis Splendor Publications, 2012. Kindle.

Shelton, W. Brian. *Prevenient Grace: God's Provision for Fallen Humanity.* Anderson, IN: Francis Asbury Press, 2014.

Sproul, R. C. *Chosen by God.* Wheaton, IL: Tyndale, 1986.

_____. *What Does It Mean to Be Born Again?* Crucial Questions Series. Sanford, FL: Reformation Trust Publishing, 2010.

_____. *What Is Reformed Theology: Understanding the Basics.* Grand Rapids, MI: Baker, 1997

_____. *Willing to Believe: The Controversy Over Free Will.* Grand Rapids, MI: Baker Books, 1997.

Storms, C. Samuel. *Chosen for Life: The Case for Divine Election.* Wheaton, IL: Crossway, 2007.

Stott, John R. W. *The Letters of John.* Grand Rapids, MI: Eerdmans, 1988

_____. *Message of Ephesians: God's New Society.* Edited by John R. W. Stott. Downers Grove, IL: InterVarsity Press, 1979),72.

Swindoll, Charles R. *Insight on John.* Swindoll's New Testament Insights. Grand Rapids, MI: Zondervan, 2010.

Thielman, Frank. *Theology of the New Testament: A Canonical and Synthetic Approach.* Grand Rapids, MI: Zondervan, 2005.

Tozer, Aiden Wilson. *The Knowledge of the Holy, The Attributes of God: Their Meaning in the Christian Life.* Gift ed. New York: HarperCollins, 1992.

Valdés, Alberto S. "The Acts of the Apostles." In *The Grace New Testament Commentary*, edited by Robert N. Wilkin, 481-620. Denton, TX: Grace Evangelical Society, 2010.

Vance, Laurence M. *The Other Side of Calvinism.* Rev. ed. Orlando, FL: Vance Publications, 2014.

Wallace, Daniel B. *Greek Grammar Beyond the Basics.* Grand Rapids, MI: Zondervan, 1996.

Walls, Jerry L. *Does God Love Everyone? The Heart of What Is Wrong with Calvinism.* Eugene, OR: Cascade Books, 2016.

Walvoord, John. *The Holy Spirit.* Wheaton, IL: Van Kampen Press, 1954.

Whedon, Daniel D. *Freedom of the Will: A Wesleyan Response to Jonathan Edwards.* Edited by John D. Wagner. Eugene, OR: Wipf & Stock, 2009.

White, James R. *Drawn by the Father.* New York: Rotolo Media/Great Christian Books, 2000.

_____. *The Potter's Freedom: A Defense of the Reformation and a Rebuttal of Norman Geisler's Chosen But Free.* Merrick, NY: Calvary Press Publishing, 2000.

Wilkin, Robert N. "The Gospel According to John." In *The Grace New Testament Commentary*, edited by Robert N. Wilkin, 357-479. Denton, TX: Grace Evangelical Society, 2010.

_____. "The Second Epistle of Paul the Apostle to Timothy." In *The Grace New Testament Commentary*, edited by Robert N. Wilkin, 993-1012. Denton, TX: Grace Evangelical Society, 2010.

Williamson, Paul R. "Because He Loved Your Forefathers: Election, Atonement, and Intercession in the Pentateuch." In *From Heaven He Came and Sought Her: Definite Atonement in Historical, Biblical,*

Theological, and Practical Perspective, edited by D. Gibson and J. Gibson, 227-245. Wheaton, IL: Crossway, 2013.

Wilson, Kenneth. *Augustine's Conversion from Traditional Free Choice to "Non-free" Free Will: A Comprehensive Methodology.* Tubingen: Mohr Siebeck, 2018.

_____. "A Theological and Historical Investigation." In *A Defense of Free Grace Theology: With Respect to Saving Faith, Perseverance, and Assurance,* edited by Fred Chay, 33-65. N.p.: Grace Theology Press, 2017.

Wright, Shawn D. *40 Questions about Calvinism,* edited by Benjamin L. Merkle. Grand Rapids, MI: Kregel Academic, 2019.

Zaspel, F.G. "Effectual Calling," In *Lexham Survey of Theology,* edited by M. Ward, J. Parks, B. Ellis, & T. Hains. Bellingham, WA: Lexham Press, 2018.

Journal Articles

Abasciano, Brian J. "Corporate Election in Romans 9: A Reply to Thomas Schreiner." Journal of the Evangelical Theological Society, 49, no. 2 (June 2006): 351-371.

_____. "Does Regeneration Precede Faith? The Use of 1 John 5:1 As a Proof Text." Evangelical Quarterly, 84, no. 4 (2012): 307-322.

Aldrich, Roy L. "The Gift of God." Bibliotheca Sacra 122, no. 487 (July 1965): 248-253.

Allen, David L. "Does Regeneration Precede Faith?" Journal for Baptist Theology and Ministry. 11. no. 2 (Fall 2014): 34-52.

Anderson, David R. "Regeneration: A Crux Interpretum." Journal of the Grace Evangelical Society 13, no. 2 (Autumn 2000): 43-65.

Anthony, Michael J. "Toward a Biblical Theology of the Heart of God." Bibliotheca Sacra 176 (January-March 2019): 3-17.

Badger, Anthony B. "TULIP: A Free Grace Perspective Part 1: Total Depravity." Journal of the Grace Evangelical Society 16, no. 1 (Spring 2003): 35-61.

_____. "TULIP: A Free Grace Perspective Part 4: Irresistible Grace." Journal of the Grace Evangelical Society 17, no. 33 (Autumn 2004): 19-40.

Combs, William W. "Does the Bible Teach Prevenient Grace?" Detroit Baptist Seminary Journal 10 (2005): 3-18.

Compton, R. Bruce. "The Ordo Salutis and Monergism: The Case for Faith Preceding Regeneration, Part 1." Bibliotheca Sacra 175 (January-March 2018): 34-39.

_____. "The Ordo Salutis and Monergism: The Case for Faith Preceding Regeneration, Part 2." Bibliotheca Sacra 175 (April-June 2018): 159-173.

_____. "The Ordo Salutis and Monergism: The Case for Faith Preceding Regeneration, Part 3." Bibliotheca Sacra 175 (July-September 2018): 284-303.

Countess, Robert H. "Thank God for the Genitive!" Journal of the Evangelical Theological Society 2 (1969): 115-123.

Dodds, Adam. "Regeneration and Resistible Grace: A Synergistic Proposal." Evangelical Quarterly 83, no. 1 (2011): 29-48.

Hart, John F. "Is Faith a Gift from God According to Ephesians 2:8?" Chafer Theological Seminary Journal 12, no. 2 (Fall 2006): 44-57.

Hodges, Zane C. "Untrustworthy Believers—John 2:23-25: Part 2: Problem Passages in the Gospel of John." Bibliotheca Sacra 135 (1978): 138-152.

Lewis, Steve. "What is the Nature of Saving Faith? Conservative Theological Journal 9, no. 27 (August 2005): 170-191.

López, Réne A. "Is Faith A Gift From God Or A Human Exercise? Bibliotheca Sacra 164, no. 655 (July-September 2007): 256-276.

Makidon, Michael D. "From Perth to Pennsylvania: The Legacy of Robert Sandeman. Journal of the Grace Evangelical Society 15, no. 28 (2002): 75-92.

Marko, Jonathan S. "'Free Choice' in Calvin's Concepts of Regeneration and Moral Agency: How Free Are We?" Ashland Theological Journal 42 (2010): 41-60.

Meisinger, George E. "The Issue of One's Ability to Believe: Total Depravity/Inability." Chafer Theological Seminary Journal 11, no. 1 (Spring 2005): 66-96.

Nichols, Timothy R. "A Free Grace Critique of Irresistible Grace." Chafer Theological Seminary Journal 11, no. 2 (Fall 2005): 52-63.

Putra, Yuhard R. D. "The Relation of Faith and Regeneration." Stulos Theological Journal 9, no. 1 (2001): 43-55.

Pyne, Robert A. "The Role of the Holy Spirit in Conversion." Bibliotheca Sacra 150, no. 598 (April 1993): 203-218.

Sapaugh, Gregory P. "Is Faith a Gift? A Study of Ephesians 2:8. Journal of the Grace Evangelical Society 7, no. 7 (1994). 31-43.

Snoeberger, Mark A. "The Logical Priority of Regeneration to Saving Faith in a Theological Ordo Salutis." Detroit Baptist Seminary Journal 7 (Fall 2002): 49-93.

Townsend, Jim. "Saved by Grace Alone—This is All My Plea." Emmaus Journal 7 (1998): 229-240.

Walvoord, John F. "The Prophetic Context of the Millennium." Bibliotheca Sacra 114 (1957): 97-101.

Warren, Scott C. "Ability and Desire: Reframing Debates Surrounding Freedom and Responsibility." Journal of the Evangelical Theological Society 52, no. 3 (2009): 551-567.

Wilkin, Robert N. "The Doctrine of Divine Election Reconsidered: Election to Service, Not to Everlasting Life." Journal of the Grace Evangelical Society 25, no. 49 (Autumn 2012): 3-22.

Wingard, John C. "Sin and Skepticism about the Trustworthiness of Our Cognitive Endowment." Philosophia Christi 6, no. 2 (2004): 249-264.

Other Sources

Allen, David L. "Claims, Clarity, Charity—Why the Traditional Baptist Statement on Soteriology Is Not and Cannot Be Semipelagian." David L. Allen. October 1, 2018. Accessed May 6, 2019, http://drdavidlallen.com/baptist/claims-clarity-charity-why-the-traditional-baptist-statement-on-soteriology-is-not-and-cannot-be-semipelagian/.

Anderson, David R. "Regeneration and the Ordo Salutis." Lecture at the Annual Conference of the Free Grace Alliance, Irving, TX, October 14, 2014.

Barrett, Matthew. "Reclaiming Monergism: The Case for Sovereign Grace in Effectual Calling and Regeneration." PhD diss., Southern Baptist Theological Seminary, 2011. Kindle.

Bing, Charles C. "Can an Unregenerate Person Believe the Gospel," Grace Notes. No. 46. n.d. Accessed April 15, 2017. http://gracelife.org/resources/gracenotes/?id=46.

_____. "Free Grace and Views of Election." Grace Notes. No. 72. n.d. Accessed April 15, 2017. http://gracelife.org/resources/gracenotes/?id=72.

_____. "How God Draws People to Salvation." Grace Notes. No. 75. n.d. Accessed April 15, 2017. http://gracelife.org/resources/gracenotes/?id=75

_____. "Lordship Salvation: A Biblical Evaluation and Response, GraceLife Edition." PhD diss., Dallas Theological Seminary, 1991.

Christiano, Donna. "A Baby's View of Birth." Parents. (January 2008) Accessed April 15, 2017. http://www.parents.com/pregnancy/giving-birth/labor-and-delivery/a-babys-view-of-birth/.

Correia, John. "Let's Meet in the Middle: Middle Knowledge Untie the Gordian Knot of Sovereignty and Free Will." Lecture at the Annual Conference of the Free Grace Alliance, Irving, TX, October 13-15, 2014.

Driscoll, Mark. "Real Conversations: Pastor Mark Driscoll, Part 2." The Debrief Show. June 4, 2019. Accessed July 18, 2019. https://www.youtube.com/watch?time_continue=3534&v=4OsQm6YU3OY.

_____. "What does the Bible say about Calvinism vs. Arminianism." Mark Driscoll Ministries. July 16, 2019. Accessed July 18, 2019, https://www.youtube.com/watch?v=KU0szpsemeU.

Flowers, Leighton. "Does Regeneration Precede Faith?" Soteriology 101. June 27, 2018. Accessed May 6, 2019. https://soteriology101.com/2018/06/27/does-regeneration-precede-faith-2/.

Geisler, Norman L. "God's Sovereignty in Election." Lecture at the Annual Conference of the Free Grace Alliance, Irving, TX, October 13-15, 2014.

Greear, J. D. "What about Calvinism?" Video from The Summit Church, "Ask Any Friday," November 5, 2010. Accessed July 21, 2015. https://vimeo.com/16506952.

Hansen, Colin. "Still Young, Restless, and Reformed? The New Calvinists at 10." 9Marks. February 5, 2019. Accessed May 6, 2019, https://www.9marks.org/article/still-young-restless-and-reformed-the-new-calvinists-at-10/.

Hodges, Zane C. "God's Role in Conversion." Grace in Focus. (Sep.-Oct. 1993) Accessed March 20, 2017. http://faithalone.org/magazine/y1993/93sep1.html.

Lazar, Shawn. "Election for Baptists: Why Biblical Election is to Service and Privilege, Not to Eternal Life." Grace in Focus, September & October 2014.

Lukaszewski, Albert L and Mark Dubis. The Lexham Syntactic Greek New Testament: Expansions and Annotations. Logos Bible Software, 2009.

Piatt, Christian. "Driscoll, Piper, Calvin and God's Gift of . . . Racism?" Huffington Post. January 10, 2013. Accessed July 19, 2017. http://www.huffingtonpost.com/christian-piatt/driscoll-piper-calvin-and-gods-gift-of-racism_b_2050070.html.

Schreiner, Thomas R. "Does Regeneration Necessarily Precede Conversion?" 9Marks, March 1, 2010. Accessed July 24, 2015. http://www.9marks.org/journal/does-regeneration-necessarily-precede-conversion.

Shepherd, Norman. "The Grace of Justification." Paper presented to the Board of Trustees of Westminster Theological Seminary, Philadelphia, PA, February 8, 1979. Accessed July 15, 2015. http://www.hornes.org/theologia/norman-shepherd/the-grace-of-justification.

Sproul, R. C. "The Father's Gift to the Son." Ligonier Ministries, May 13, 2011. Accessed July 12, 2017, http://www.ligonier.org/blog/fathers-gift-son/.

Wilkin, Robert N. "The Lord Opened Her Heart." Grace in Focus. (Sep.-Oct. 1995) Accessed March 15, 2017. http://faithalone.org/magazine/y1995/95E2.html.

Wilson, Ken. "How Does God 'Draw' a Person Unto Belief for Justification?" Lecture at the Annual Conference of the Free Grace Alliance, Irving, TX, October 13-15, 2014.

Witherington, Ben. "'Behavior Doesn't Interrupt Your Relationship with Christ': A Recipe for Disaster." Christianity Today, July 12, 2012. Accessed November 3, 2017, http://www.christianitytoday.com/ct/2012/julyweb-only/behavior-relationship-with-christ.html.

Witherington, Ben and Roger Olson. "Roger Olson's Arminian Theology—Part 7." Society of Evangelical Arminians, November 11, 2016. Accessed November 3, 2017, http://evangelicalarminians.org/ben-witherington-and-roger-olson-roger-olsons-arminian-theology-part-7/.

GRACE THEOLOGY PRESS

Timely **Resources.**
Timeless **Grace.**

Birthed from a desire to provide engaging and relevant theological resources, Grace Theology Press is the academic imprint of Grace School of Theology. In a world where many say "truth is relative," Grace Theology Press holds fast to the absolute truth of God's Word. We are passionate about engaging the next generation of ministry leaders with books and resources that are grounded in the principles of free grace, which offers a gift you cannot earn and a gift you can never lose.

gracetheology.org

Available Titles from Grace Theology Press

Bewitched
The Rise of Neo-Galatianism

By Dr. Dave Anderson

Companions With Christ
How to Walk with Jesus

By Jeremy Vance

God's Grace for Daughters of Eve
Lovers, Mothers and Others

By Sandra Abbott

Final Destiny
The Future Reign of the Servant Kings

By Dr. Jody Dillow

Maximum Joy
First John--Relationship or Fellowship?

By Dr. Dave Anderson

Going for the Gold
Bible Study Edition

By Dr. Joe Wall

Triumph Through Trials
The Epistle of James

By Dr. Dave Anderson

Free Grace Soteriology
Third Edition

By Dr. Dave Anderson

gracetheology.org

www.ingramcontent.com/pod-product-compliance
Lightning Source LLC
Chambersburg PA
CBHW062152080426
42734CB00010B/1660